I0793152

IMAGES
of America

NEW YORK PRESS PHOTOGRAPHERS

On the Cover: A group of still and newsreel photographers gathers at the Polo Grounds in 1917. The stadium in Upper Manhattan was home to the New York Yankees and other local sports teams until its demolition in 1963. The photographers are carrying a mixture of Graflex and Borsum cameras. (Courtesy of the New York Press Photographers Association.)

IMAGES
of America

NEW YORK PRESS PHOTOGRAPHERS

Marc A. Hermann and the
New York Press Photographers Association

ARCADIA
PUBLISHING

ISBN 978-1-4671-3361-6

Published by Arcadia Publishing
Charleston, South Carolina

Printed in the United States of America

Library of Congress Control Number: 2015930664

For all general information, please contact Arcadia Publishing:
Telephone 843-853-2070
Fax 843-853-0044
E-mail sales@arcadiapublishing.com
For customer service and orders:
Toll-Free 1-888-313-2665

Visit us on the Internet at www.arcadiapublishing.com

In honor of Jack MacMillan (1891–1969), first official historian of the NYPPA, in whose shadow it is an honor to stand

Contents

ACKNOWLEDGMENTS

Despite the resulting mountains of papers and photographs consuming each and every one of my work surfaces, I was thrilled to be named the historian of the New York Press Photographers Association (NYPPA), and my thanks are due to past president David Pokress. All my fellow board members, including current president Bruce Cotler, Susan Markisz, William Perlman, and Chip East, rendered their unwavering support.

Unless otherwise noted, the materials herein are from the NYPPA archives, and unlike many newspapers of the mid-20th century, efforts have been made to credit the original photographers. The *Daily News*, where I had the pleasure of working as a photographer and assignment editor for many years, was essential to this book's completion. Former managing editors of photography Alexander Hitchen and Gretchen Viehmann, Claus Guglberger, and Angela Troisi were as generous as ever in making sure the archives of "New York's Picture Newspaper" stay in the spotlight.

The support of Mary DiBiase Blaich and past president Susan Watts, both of whom provided additional photographs, is greatly appreciated. Patti Wendlinger Rosen provided images and memories of her father's days "on the job." Jackson Pokress was kind enough to provide photographs and encouragement alike. I am grateful for having had the chance to know the late Marty Lederhandler, Paul Rice, and Morris Warman, all of whom spoke fondly of the "good old days."

Past president Herb Schwartz, who started at the *Sun* and ended up at CBS, has always been willing to share his colorful experiences with me, and it is a real treat to hear a story from this veteran. Likewise, Jim Romano gives one an authentic glimpse of what the old breed of lensmen was like.

Many thanks to Sharon McAllister, former editor at Arcadia, and her successor, Henry Clougherty, who would be right at home on the assignment desk of a big-city daily.

Finally, this book would not have been possible without the personal guidance and support of NYPPA vice president Todd Maisel and former *News* director of photography Michael Lipack. If I have achieved any success as a photographer, it is because of Todd's mentorship in the streets and Mike's willingness to give me a shot in the big leagues. The rest, as they say, is history.

Introduction

There is history in everything, even in a business that is based solely on current events. It is amazing how quickly a story can become irrelevant and obsolete once something more urgent and, in the minds of editors, more important breaks. The phrase "What have you done *lately*?" may very well be the mantra of the news photographer. Thus, it is easy to forget that the people whose photographs illustrate our collective view of history have a history of their own.

Competition between publications is fierce, and photographers are front-line soldiers in the battle for circulation and, nowadays, the quest for Web hits. Nevertheless, a sense of camaraderie was instantly recognized by the men who once lugged their Graflex cameras and cases laden with glass plate holders around town. Whether they were hustling for the *Herald*, the *World*, the *Post*, or the *Tribune*, these photographers shared a common bond and endured the same hardships. Tenement fires in freezing weather, uncooperative criminals, or fast-moving ball games were seen on the photographer's ground glass viewfinder, and it was clear that working together, rather than against one another, was the best method. After all, no one was exempt from making a mistake, and if it was the other guy this time, it could be you the next time.

As early as 1913, there was talk in New York City of press photographers creating a fraternal organization. Fate would intercede, however, and it seemed that every attempt to gather together would be preempted by one breaking news story after another. However, on April 17, 1915, nearly 60 photographers got together for a dinner at Castle Cave, a restaurant formerly located at Seventh Avenue and West Twenty-sixth Street. They called themselves the News Photographers Association of New York and endeavored not only to advance the photographic trade but also to provide a system of support for its members in case of financial or personal hardship.

As the field of newspaper photography flourished, so too did the association. An increasing number of newsreel cameramen began joining, which caused a bit of disagreement within the ranks of the still photographers. Just who, exactly, was to be considered a "photographer"? Feeling ostracized, 61 newsreel cameramen left the organization in 1920, leaving only 78 members on the rolls.

While it was made clear at the outset that the association was not going to serve as a trade union, it advocated for many issues that photographers were facing, one of which was the issuance of press credentials. The New York City Police Department was the responsible agency, since press cards entitled their holders to cross through police lines at emergencies—a privilege afforded to news writers but not automatically granted to their camera-carrying counterparts. Before long, photographers were able to obtain these essential tools for themselves through the efforts of the association.

In 1928, a slight reorganization occurred, and the group rebranded itself as the Press Photographers Association of New York, under which name it incorporated 10 years later. Its officers now found themselves among the press representatives tasked by Mayor Fiorello La Guardia to vet and approve applications for press cards. When a major trial was to occur in the local courts, it would send a committee to meet with the district attorney to ensure adequate photographic coverage. No longer a secondary function of the fourth estate, photographers were being recognized for the historic images they were producing. Disasters such as the explosion of the dirigible *Hindenburg* were well documented, the Park Avenue elite were now accustomed to posing at their society functions, and the crack of the bat at Ebbets Field was echoed by the click of the shutter.

While it is difficult to fathom today, celebrities tended to appreciate the press photographers. The respect went both ways, and photographers did not seek to catch people in compromising or embarrassing positions. The very nature of the cameras themselves—one shot, with one flashbulb at a time—made the experience of being photographed much less jarring than it would become in the era of repeated strobe flashes and eight frames per second. Out of this cooperation, the rousingly successful Press Photographers' Annual Ball was born.

Held in such venues as the Waldorf-Astoria and Hotel Commodore, these soirees would often not get under way until 9:00 p.m. and go on well after midnight. Headliner celebrities such as Frank Sinatra, Cab Calloway, and Jimmy Durante were fixtures. Normally austere politicians could be counted on to attend and rub elbows with the photographers. Presidents Franklin D. Roosevelt and Harry S. Truman enjoyed exceptionally cordial relationships with them.

The advent of tabloid newspapers, which craved extensive use of photographs in their coverage of the day-to-day life in New York, meant that photographers had to know their way around crime scenes. Police headquarters on Centre Market Place in Lower Manhattan was a hive of activity, as photographers would wait for a police Teletype to provide information about a breaking story. Later, a building across the street would serve as a communal press center for the various publications concerned with crime news. In the 1930s, when the police department began using radios to dispatch its units, the press tuned in as well. The fire department remained on a hardwired bell telegraph system, however, so getting to the scene of an unfolding conflagration was hit or miss, dependent upon luck, proximity, and good sources in the field.

Arthur Fellig was among the headquarters crowd, having the right Speed Graphic camera but neither credentials nor assignments. What he lacked in accreditation, though, he made up for with determination. Regarded as the classic freelance news photographer, "Weegee," as he was known, was reportedly the first photographer permitted to install a police radio receiver in his car—a perk previously reserved for well-connected columnists like Walter Winchell. Fellig set up shop in an apartment next door to the press building, where he also managed to install his own extension of the fire department's bell system. Although synonymous with the concept of spot news photography, Fellig was hardly without peers. His flair for self-promotion, including writing several books, helped anchor him in legend. He focused on spot news for only a decade before moving on to celebrities and experimental portraiture. A bit aloof at times, he never joined the Press Photographers Association and eschewed the natty dress that had become the standard among his colleagues. As one contemporary remembered, "You could tell what he had for lunch by looking at his tie." His insistence on credit lines accompanying his pictures—"Weegee the Famous"—ensured that people would remember his name, even while others in the field, whose work was of equal quality and importance, would be generally forgotten.

While photographers worked their skills covering bloodbaths on the streets of New York, many of them were about to witness death on a grander scale. When the United States entered the Second World War, the armed forces sought news photographers to serve as official cameramen. Others, particularly those affiliated with wire services, such as the Associated Press, Acme, and International News Pictures, would take special assignments from their employers and become embedded with the troops, documenting the action. It was a dangerous job, and the complement of New York press photographers who went overseas between 1941 and 1945 did not come back unscathed. Though their coverage of the battlefield would fill the pages of their papers back home, there was still domestic news to be covered, along with a sudden shortage of personnel.

As in many trades during the war, women started going to work for the newspapers. Pioneers among them were Evelyn Straus of the *Daily News* and Adelaide Levy of Acme. It would take several years for Straus to be accepted into the membership of the Press Photographers Association;

by 1961, there were only three female members of the group. Their number would exponentially increase over the coming decades, but many would continue to face discrimination and hostile work environments. In 1997, *News* staffer Susan Watts, an intrepid photojournalist who would survive a harrowing kidnapping in Honduras the following year, was sworn in as the association's first female president.

In 1952, the group underwent one final name transposition and became the New York Press Photographers Association. Six years later, it became clear that the 43-year-old organization's plethora of materials pertaining to the trade was worth preserving and cataloging. Reams of pages of meeting minutes, newsletters, financial information, and other trappings of a predigital world were retained in binders and manila folders. In addition, members had submitted many photographs of them in action and donated old ephemera from the stories they covered, and these items, along with photo exhibition booklets, found their way into the association's files. In April 1958, veteran photographer Jack MacMillan was appointed the association's official historian. MacMillan began the process of organizing the association's holdings and grouping them into some semblance of order. Interspersed among these files are MacMillan's own longhand notes, drawing on his own memories, as well as those of his colleagues. As the years wore on, MacMillan fell on hard times and suffered health problems that forced him to retire from actively taking pictures. When he died in 1969, a widower with no close relatives, it was his old friends at the NYPPA who handled his affairs. In the final instructions he had written before his death, MacMillan stipulated that he be buried wearing his Life Membership pin. His writings indicated his wishes to publish a book about the history of the organization and trade to which he had dedicated his life—a wish that went unfulfilled. This volume does not presume to be a comprehensive history of a century of New York City photojournalists, but it fills a void that has remained empty for far too long. We have seen their work but have seldom seen them. The occasion of the centennial of the NYPPA provides us with an opportunity to rediscover the people behind the cameras during what was arguably the golden era of press photography in the media capital of the world.

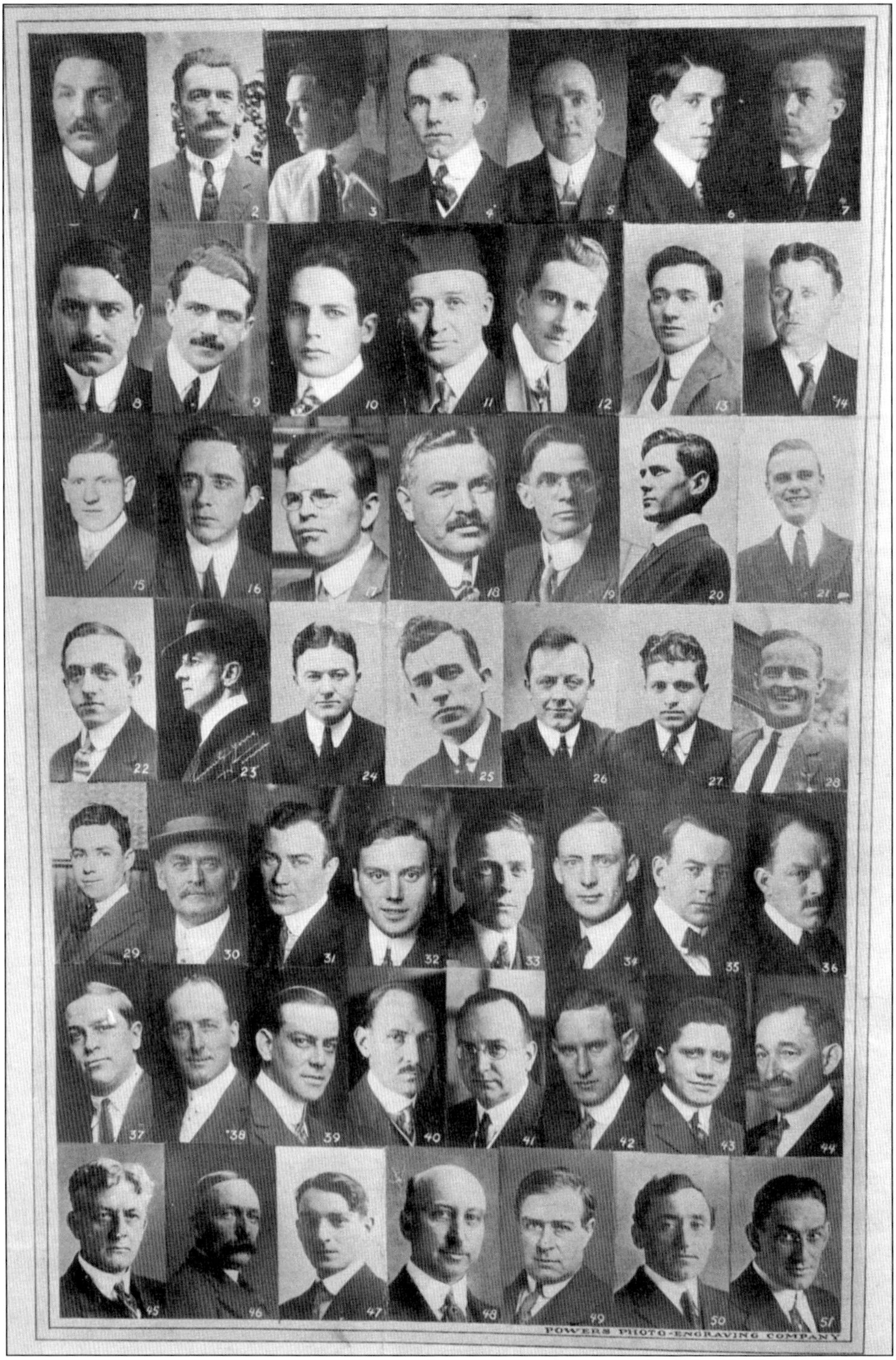

This 1915 montage features some of the founding members of the News Photographers Association of New York. These men were the nucleus of the organization that would become the New York Press Photographers Association. The group's first president, Frank Ryberg of the *New York World*, is pictured second from right in the bottom row.

One

ON ASSIGNMENT

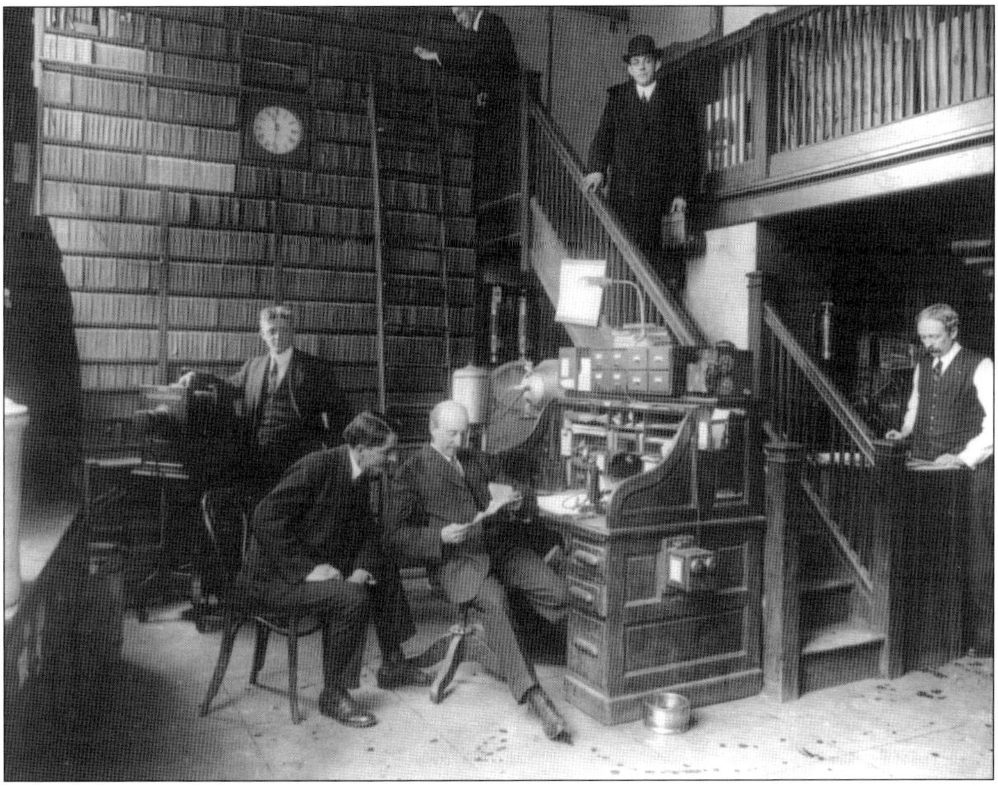

In this 1909 view of the photograph department of the *New York World*, the photographer on the stairs carries a portable Graflex camera, while another camera is equipped with a plate magazine atop the editor's desk. The plate magazine contained several glass plates and a lightproof leather bag, allowing a photographer to prepare for his next exposure as quickly as he could work the mechanism. (Courtesy of the Library of Congress.)

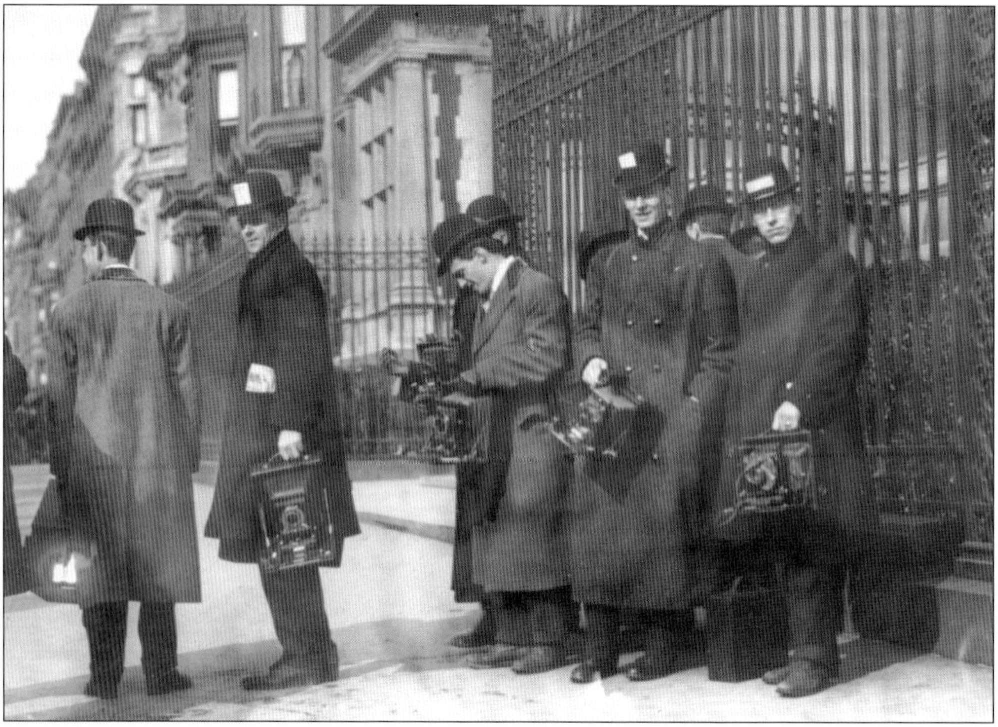

On January 27, 1908, photographers await a glimpse of Gladys Vanderbilt, the youngest daughter of railroad magnate Cornelius Vanderbilt, on the day of her wedding to Count László Széchenyi. They all carry large-format view cameras and wear an early press credential in their hats. (Courtesy of the Library of Congress.)

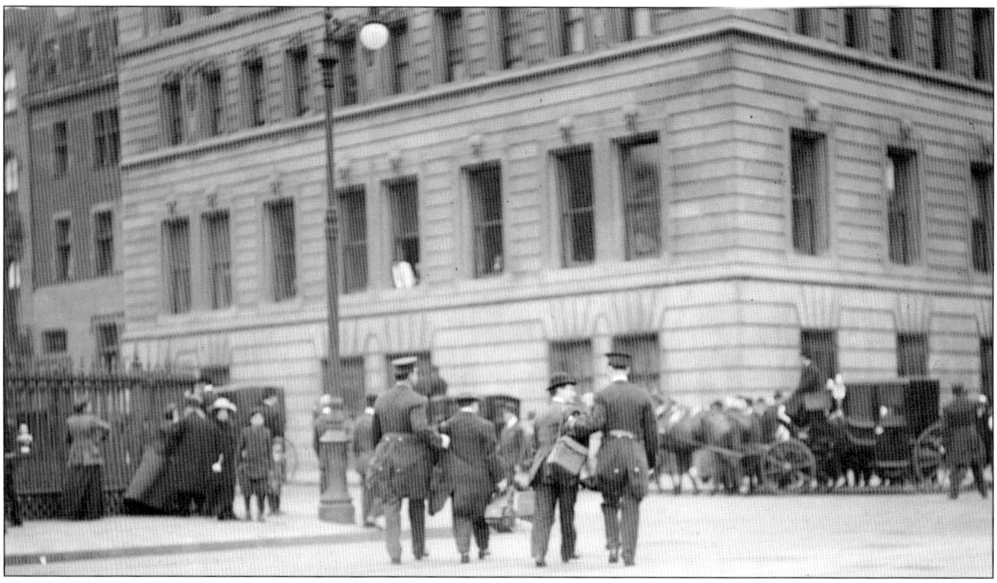

In a scene that might very well have pleased the deceased, police officers arrest a pair of press photographers at the funeral of financier J.P. Morgan on April 14, 1913. Morgan, who disliked being photographed, was mourned near Stuyvesant Square, and it is unclear what transgression the photographers made. (Courtesy of the Library of Congress.)

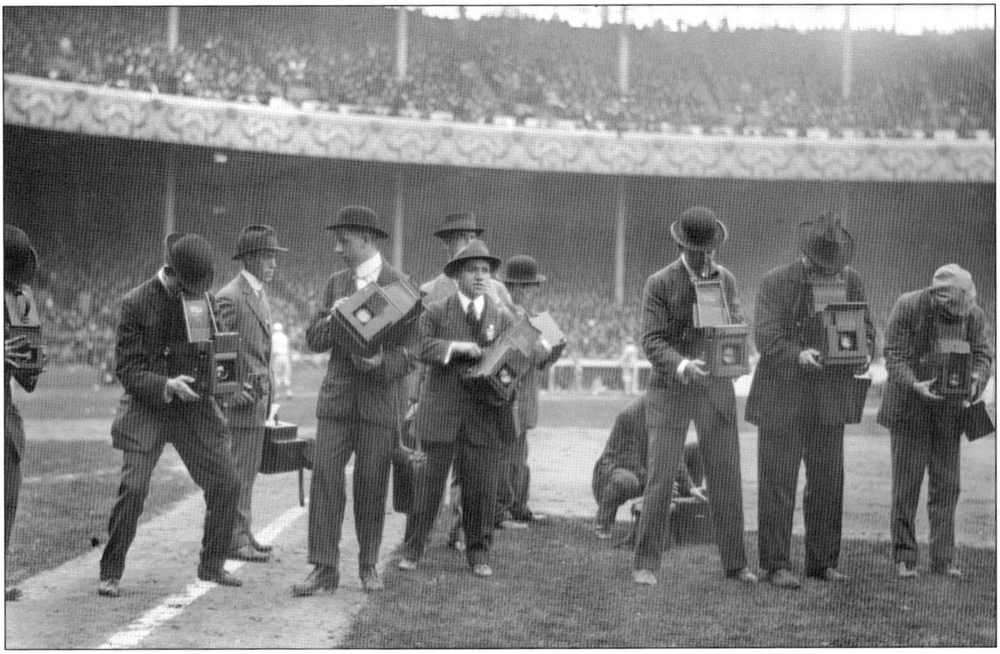

Photographers gather on the field at the Polo Grounds in 1914. These reflex cameras allowed the photographer to see an upside-down image of what his lens saw, thus allowing him to accurately focus before a lever would flip the internal mirror out of the way, and another would trip the shutter, a curtain with various-sized slits mounted on rollers. (Courtesy of the Library of Congress.)

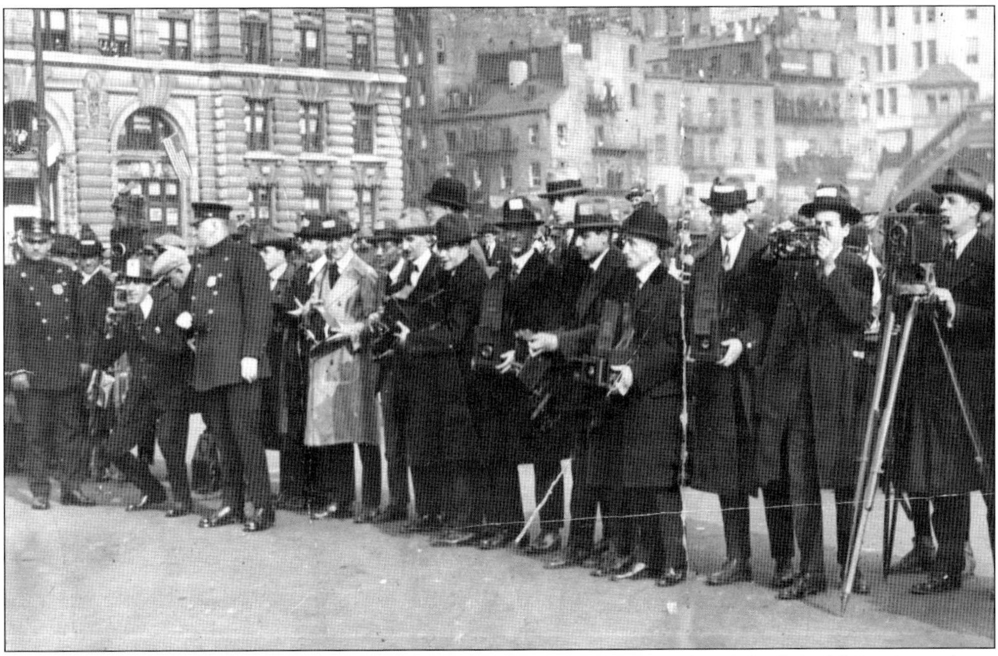

In 1919, a large crowd of photographers awaits the return of Gen. John "Black Jack" Pershing from Europe on Battery Place at the foot of Manhattan. The press covered many notables here, as well as those who were less than notable, as a police precinct occupied space in the pier, which was the backdrop of many prisoner perp walks.

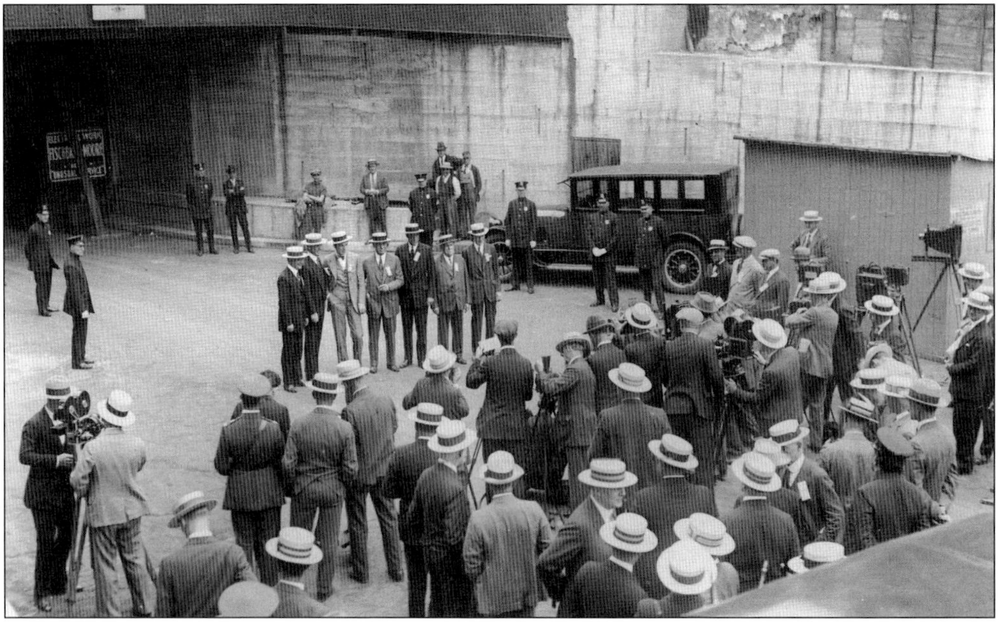

Still photographers and newsreel cameramen cover the opening of the Holland Tunnel, connecting New York and New Jersey under the Hudson River.

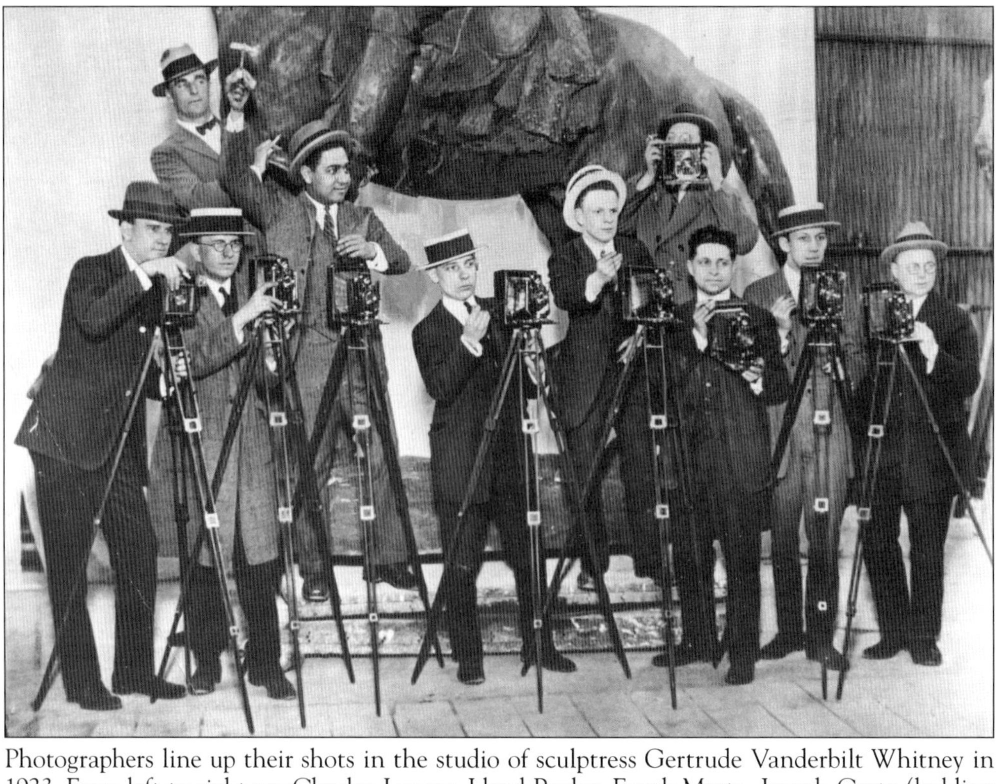

Photographers line up their shots in the studio of sculptress Gertrude Vanderbilt Whitney in 1923. From left to right are Charley Langer, Lloyd Pauley, Frank Merta, Joseph Costa (holding a flashgun), Bob Mortimer, Scotty MacGregor, George Bowers, Calvio Sileo, George Prangley, and Bill Bailey.

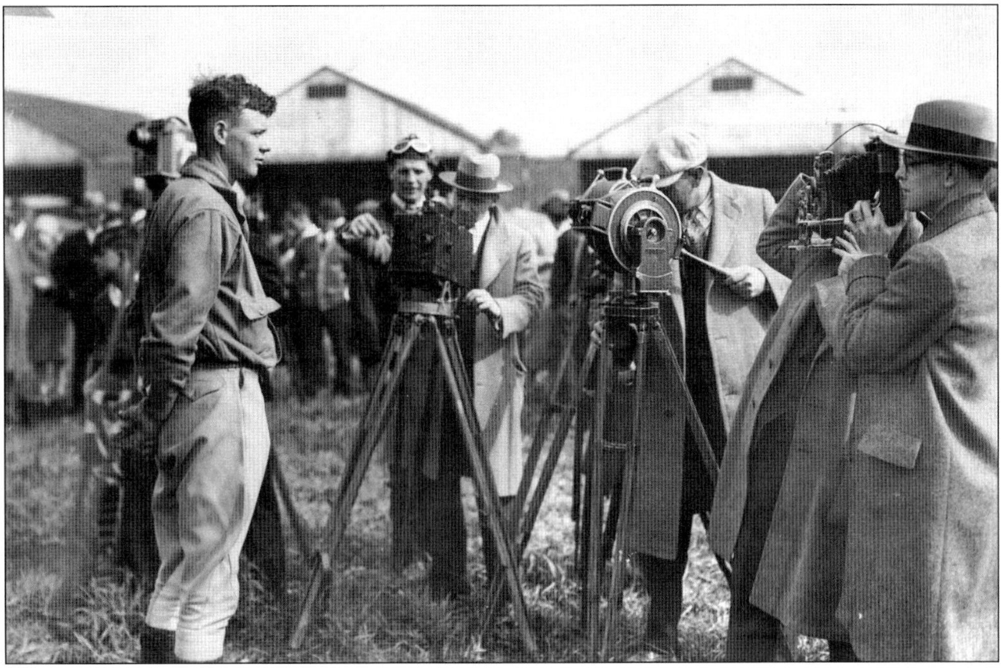

Charles Lindbergh faces the cameras at Roosevelt Field on Long Island in May 1927, prior to embarking on his transatlantic flight to Paris aboard the *Spirit of St. Louis*.

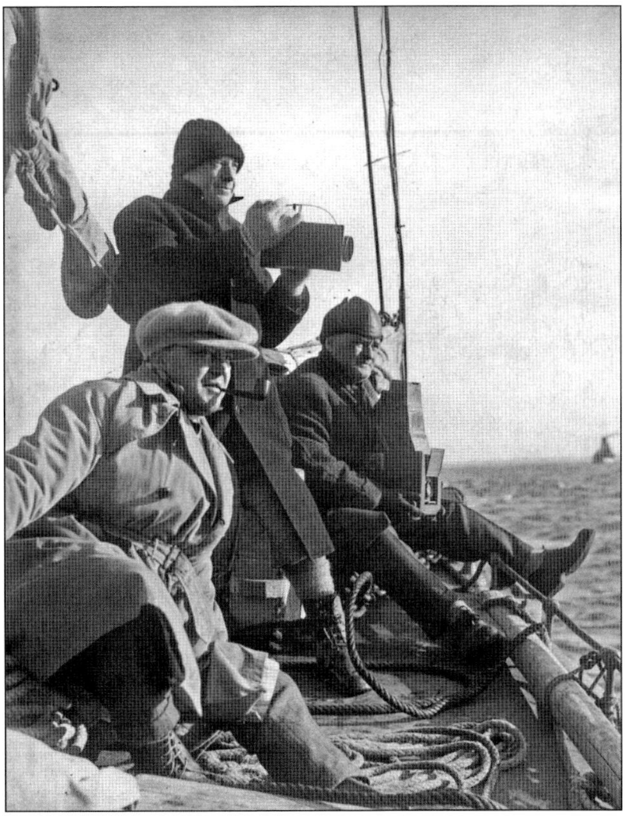

A tragic accident occurred in December 1927 when the USS *S-4* submarine sank after colliding with a Coast Guard destroyer off Cape Cod. All hands aboard the submarine perished. From left to right, photographers Harry Hardy, John Tresilian, and Eddie Jackson are seen documenting the recovery efforts.

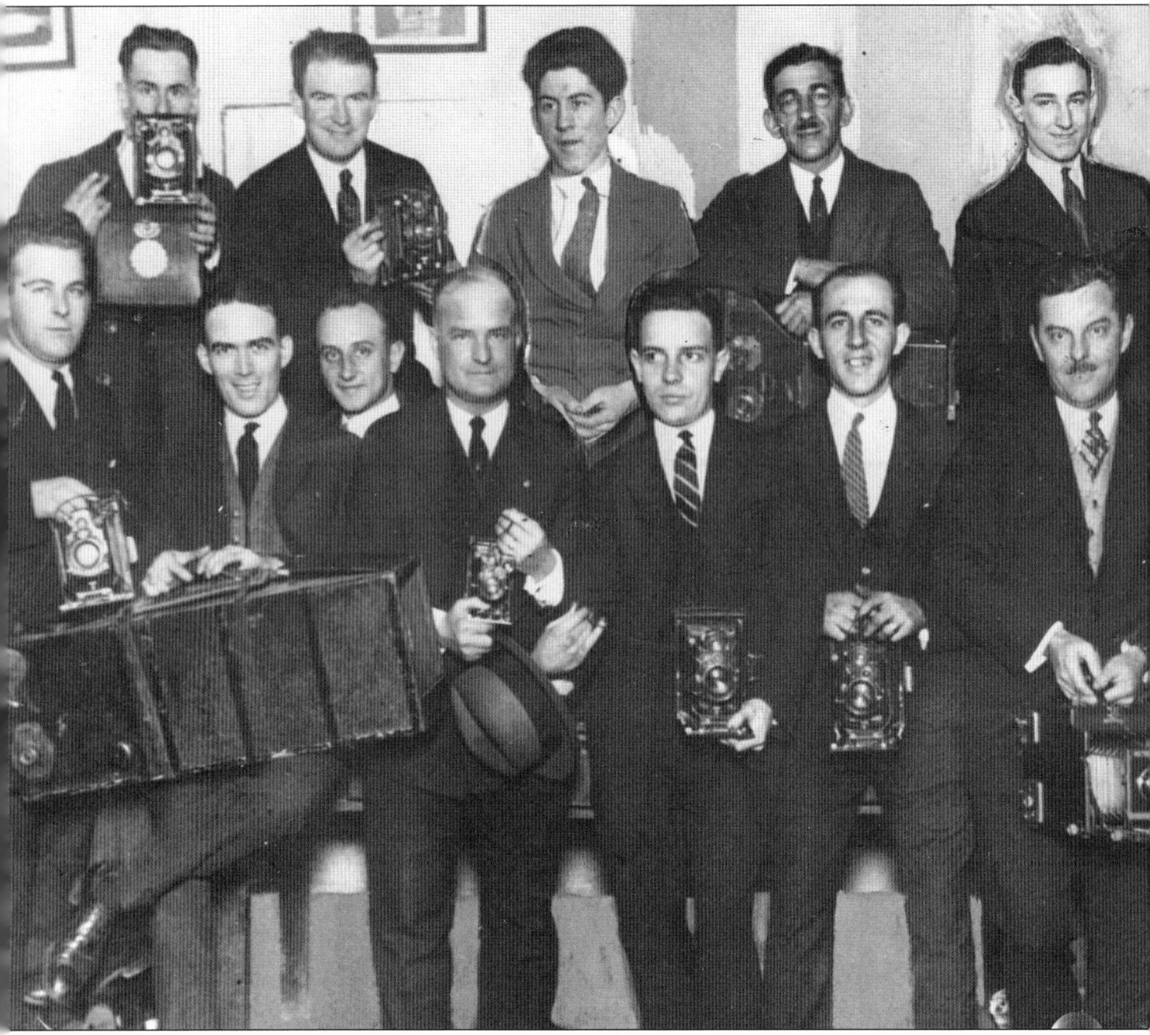

The photographic staff of the *Daily News* gathers for a group portrait in 1927. The variety of equipment in use at the time can be seen all at once, from what appears to be an aerial camera

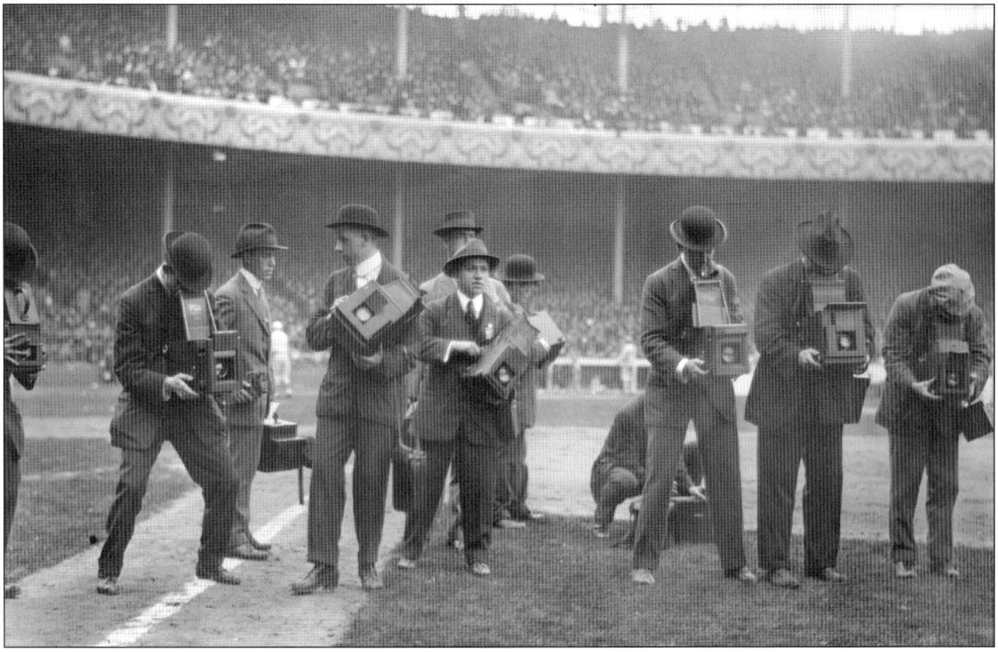

Photographers gather on the field at the Polo Grounds in 1914. These reflex cameras allowed the photographer to see an upside-down image of what his lens saw, thus allowing him to accurately focus before a lever would flip the internal mirror out of the way, and another would trip the shutter, a curtain with various-sized slits mounted on rollers. (Courtesy of the Library of Congress.)

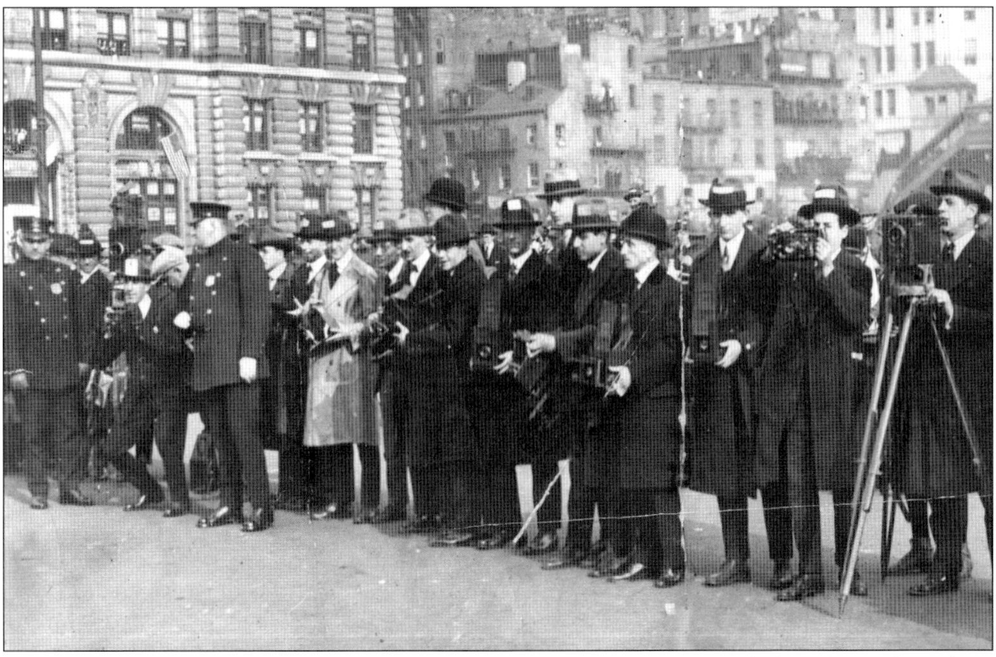

In 1919, a large crowd of photographers awaits the return of Gen. John "Black Jack" Pershing from Europe on Battery Place at the foot of Manhattan. The press covered many notables here, as well as those who were less than notable, as a police precinct occupied space in the pier, which was the backdrop of many prisoner perp walks.

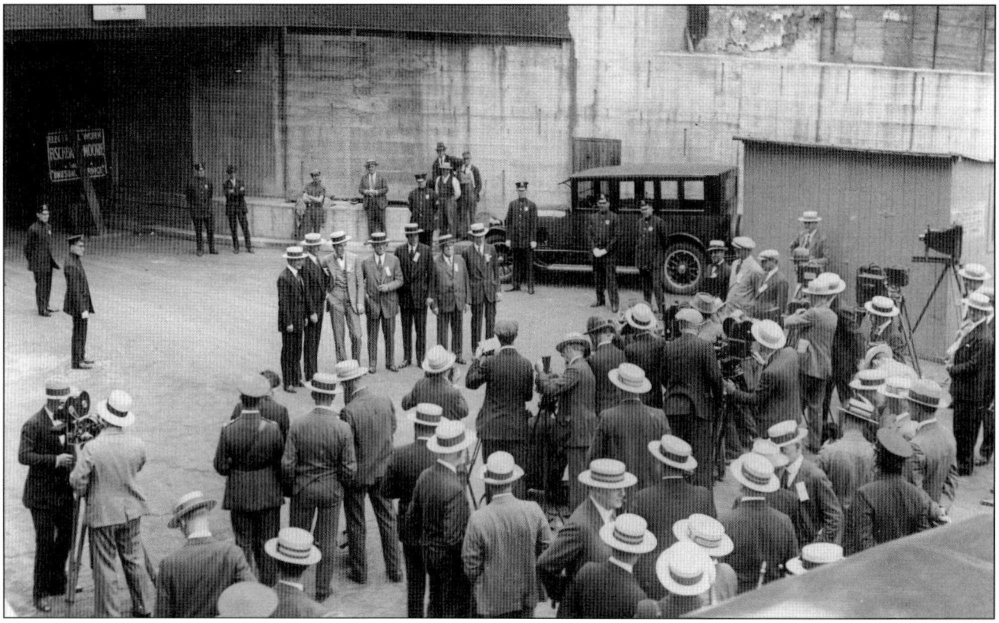

Still photographers and newsreel cameramen cover the opening of the Holland Tunnel, connecting New York and New Jersey under the Hudson River.

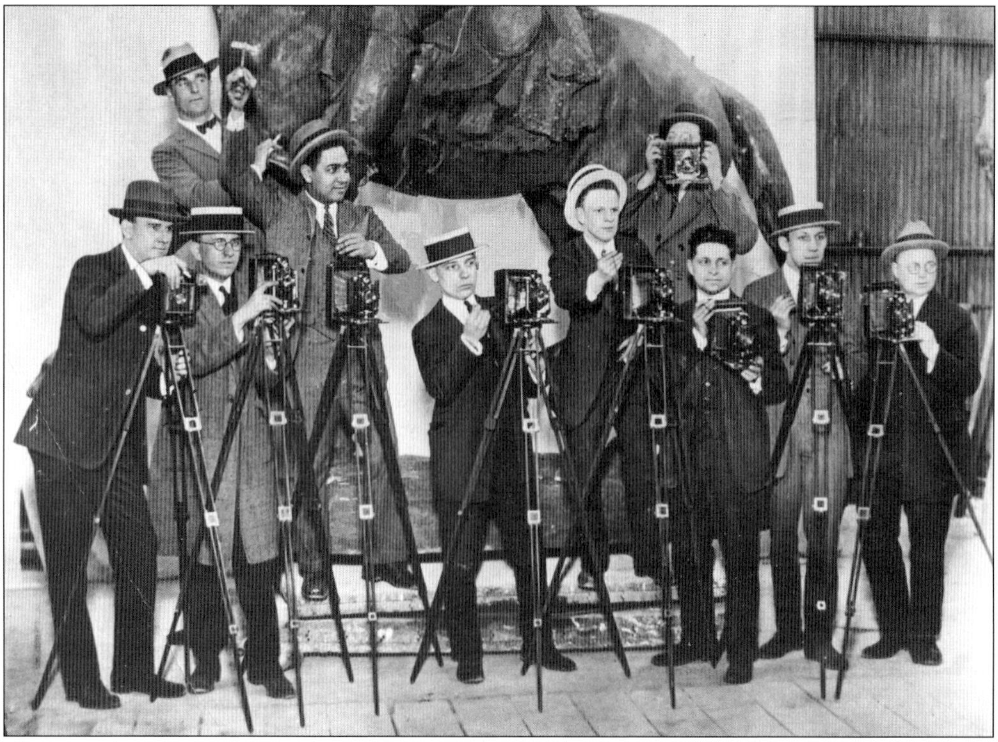

Photographers line up their shots in the studio of sculptress Gertrude Vanderbilt Whitney in 1923. From left to right are Charley Langer, Lloyd Pauley, Frank Merta, Joseph Costa (holding a flashgun), Bob Mortimer, Scotty MacGregor, George Bowers, Calvio Sileo, George Prangley, and Bill Bailey.

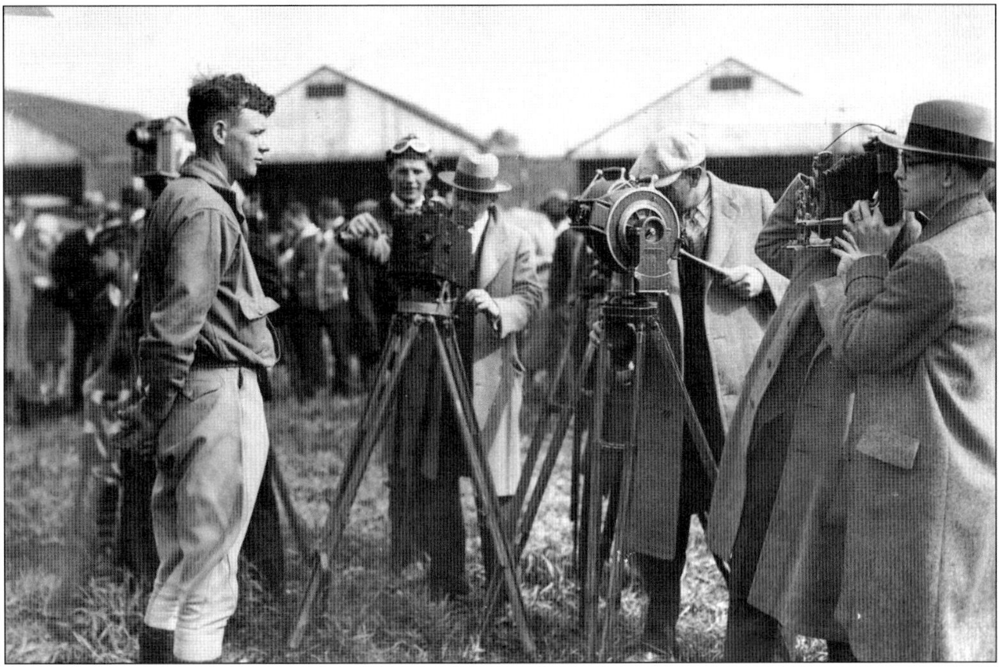

Charles Lindbergh faces the cameras at Roosevelt Field on Long Island in May 1927, prior to embarking on his transatlantic flight to Paris aboard the *Spirit of St. Louis*.

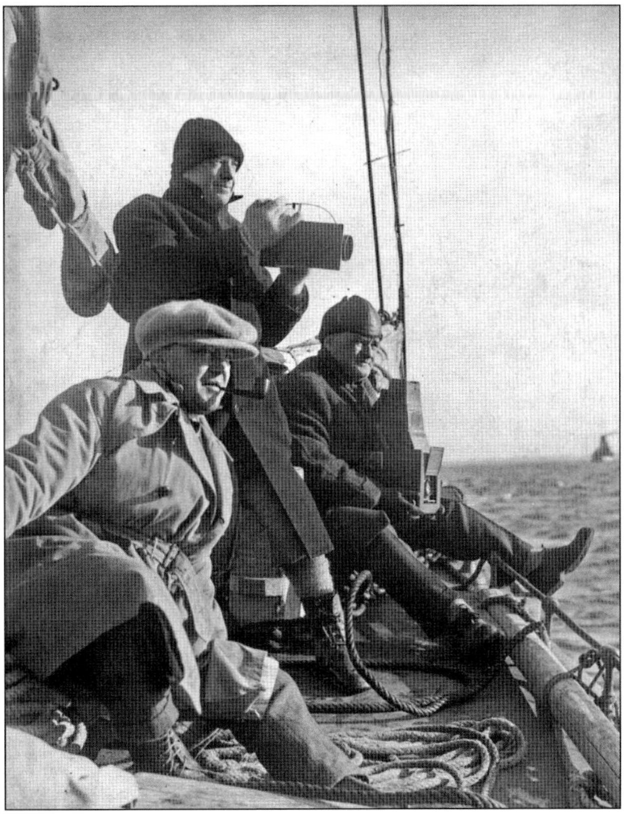

A tragic accident occurred in December 1927 when the USS *S-4* submarine sank after colliding with a Coast Guard destroyer off Cape Cod. All hands aboard the submarine perished. From left to right, photographers Harry Hardy, John Tresilian, and Eddie Jackson are seen documenting the recovery efforts.

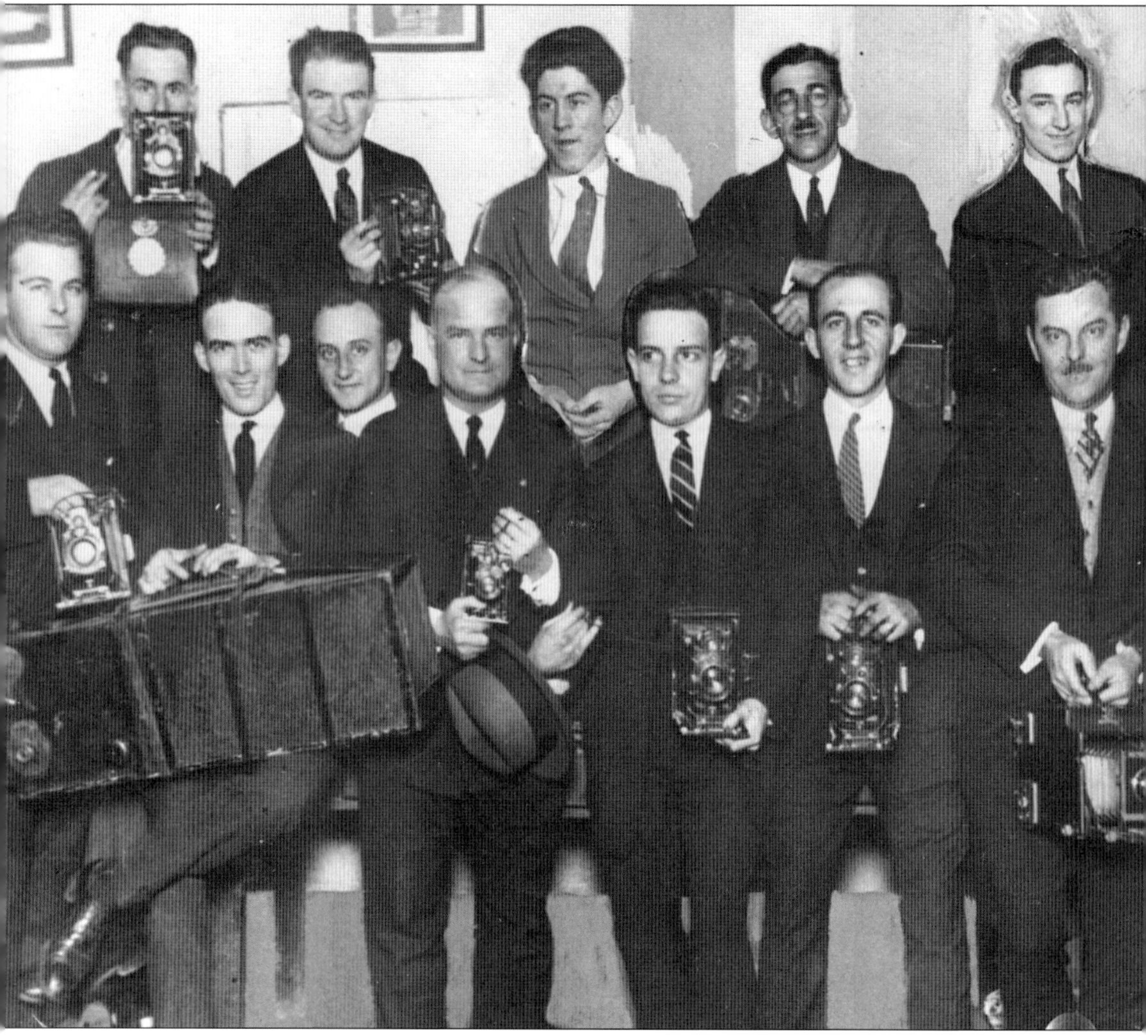

The photographic staff of the *Daily News* gathers for a group portrait in 1927. The variety of equipment in use at the time can be seen all at once, from what appears to be an aerial camera

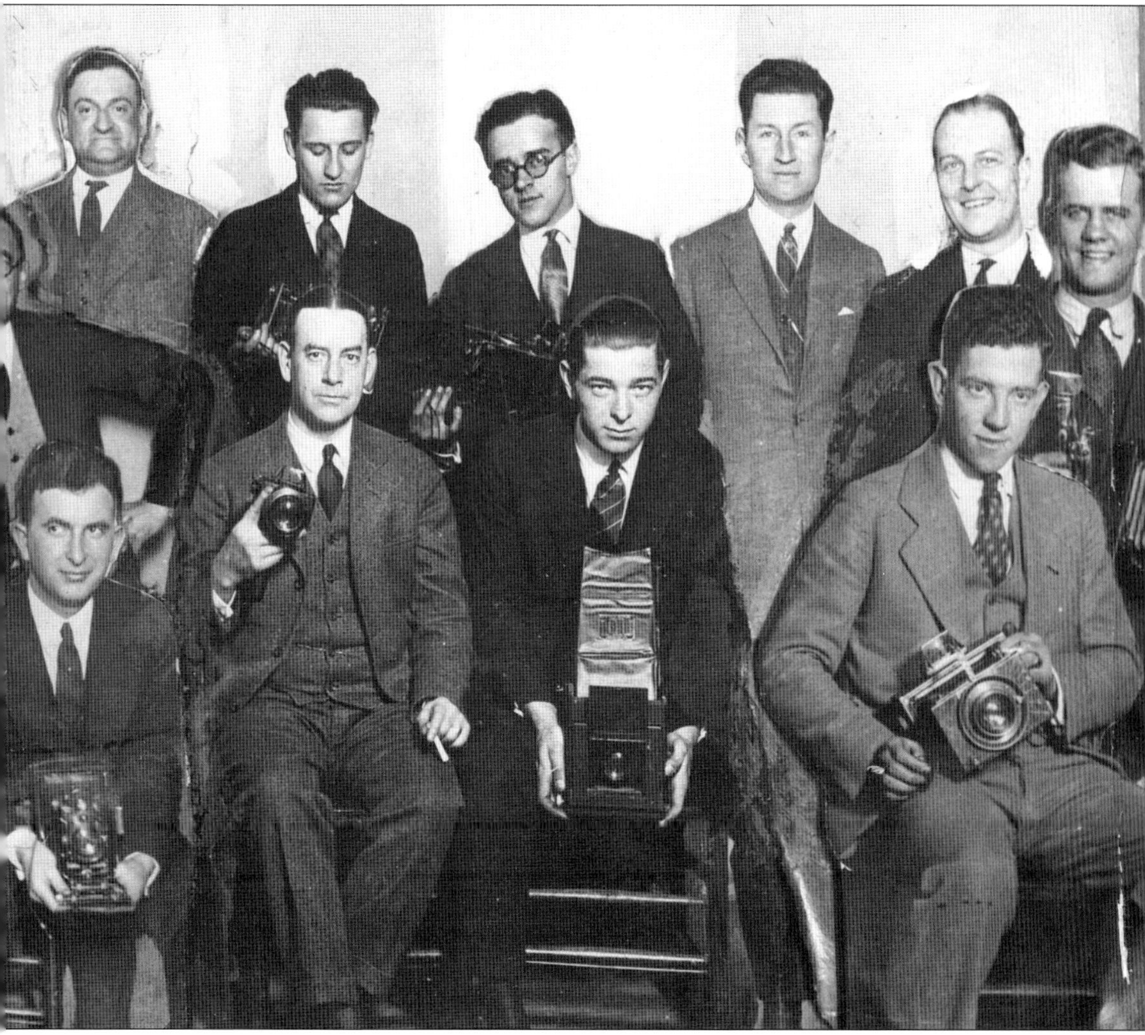

(first row, right) to a "Big Bertha" sports camera (first row, left) and everything in between. Many are carrying lightweight folding Ica plate cameras.

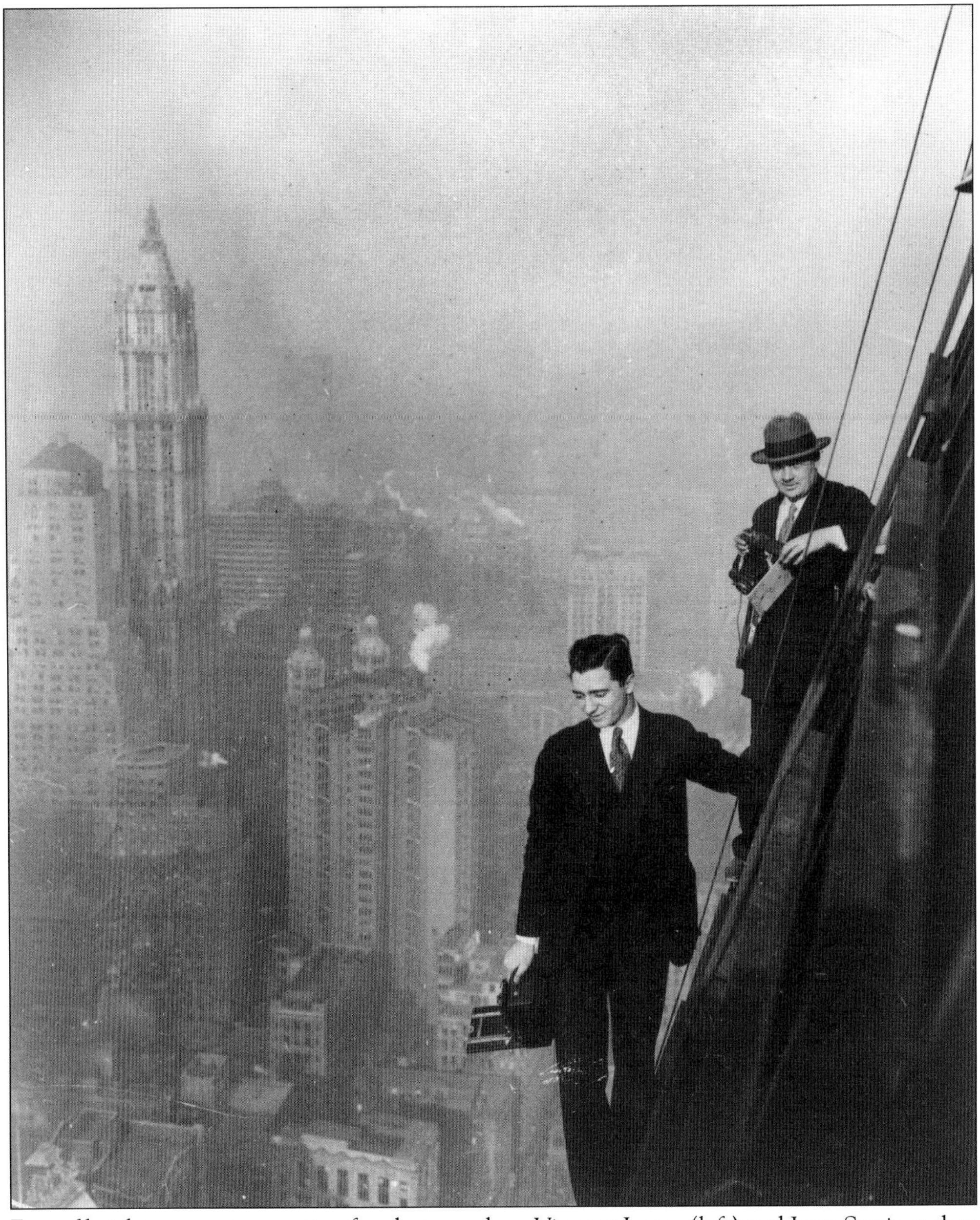

Fear of heights was not an option for photographers Vincent Lopez (left) and Jesse Strait as they reach the top of the new Bank of Manhattan Trust Building at 40 Wall Street in 1929. The skyscraper surpassed the Woolworth Building (seen in the background) as the tallest building in the world but lost the distinction upon the completion of the Chrysler Building.

It was a dirty job, but, from left to right, Bob Wands (*New York Times*), Seymour Zolotorofe (*Journal-American*), Barney Stein (*New York Post*), and Jerry Frankel (*Journal-American*) were up to the challenge of covering a Brooklyn sewage disposal plant in the 1930s.

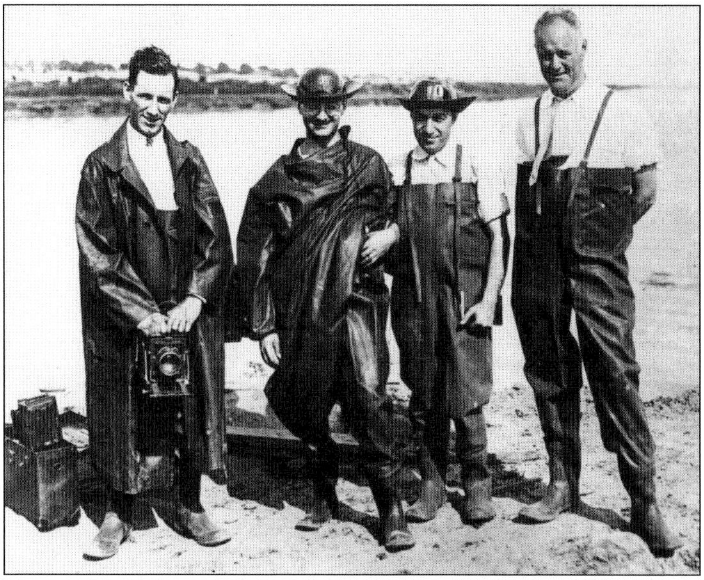

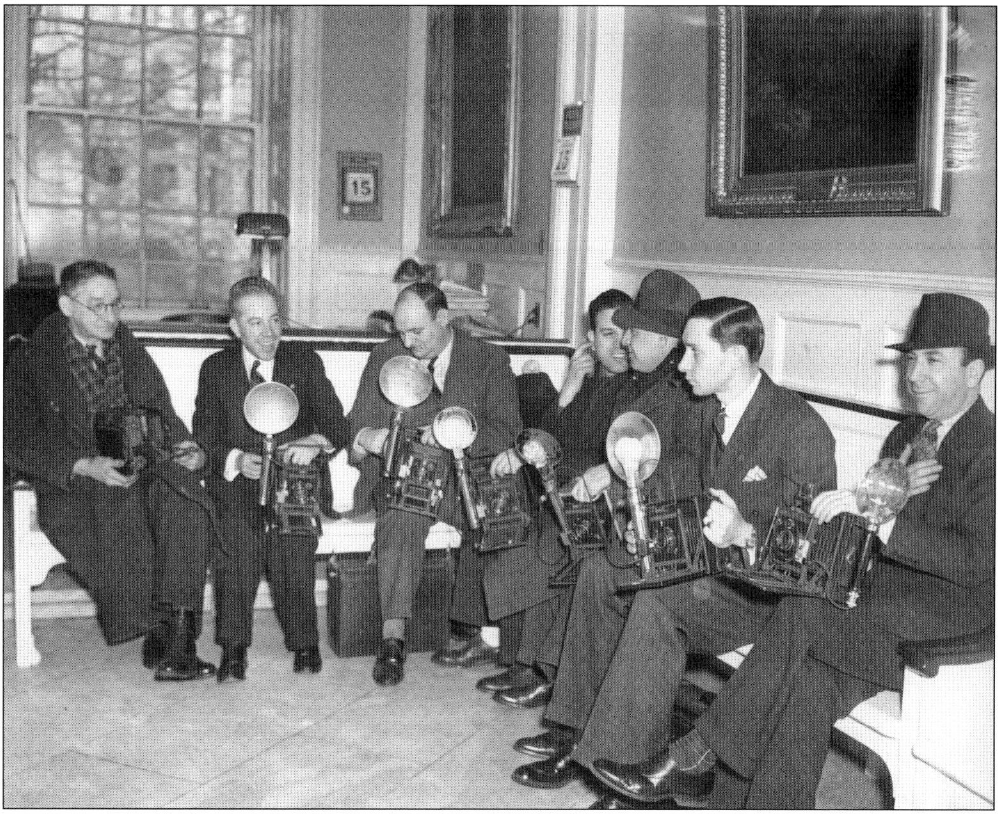

In the mid-1930s, a group of photographers waits outside the mayor's office in city hall. From left to right are William Warnecke, Anthony Quintieri, unidentified, Arthur Aidala, Tom Watson, Walter Albertin, and Jules Geller. They are all equipped with four-by-five-inch Pre-Anniversary Speed Graphic cameras and new battery-powered flashbulbs. Hazardous and smoky flash powder was a thing of the past.

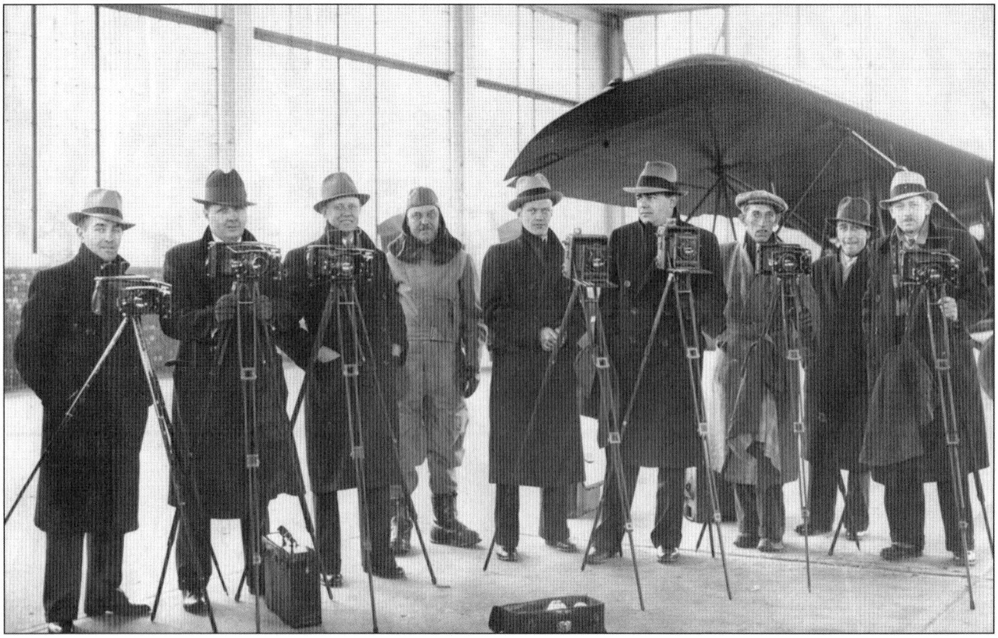

On January 4, 1934, aviators Capt. George Pond and Cesare Sabelli received word that authorities in Washington had grounded their flight to Rome, as the single propeller of their Bellanca J-5 was deemed unsafe. Photographers who had gathered for the occasion instead were content to be snapped by *Brooklyn Eagle* photographer Mike Helkin.

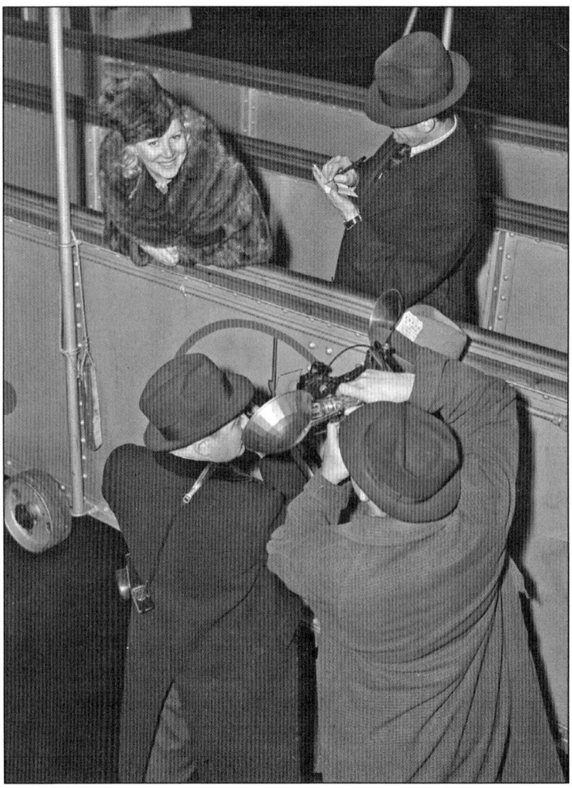

Comings and goings were always newsworthy for photographers. Here, on December 29, 1936, three lensmen jockey for a view of actress Barbara Blair. Visible in one of the men's hatbands is the badge-shaped card stock press pass that had been designed two years before. (Author's collection.)

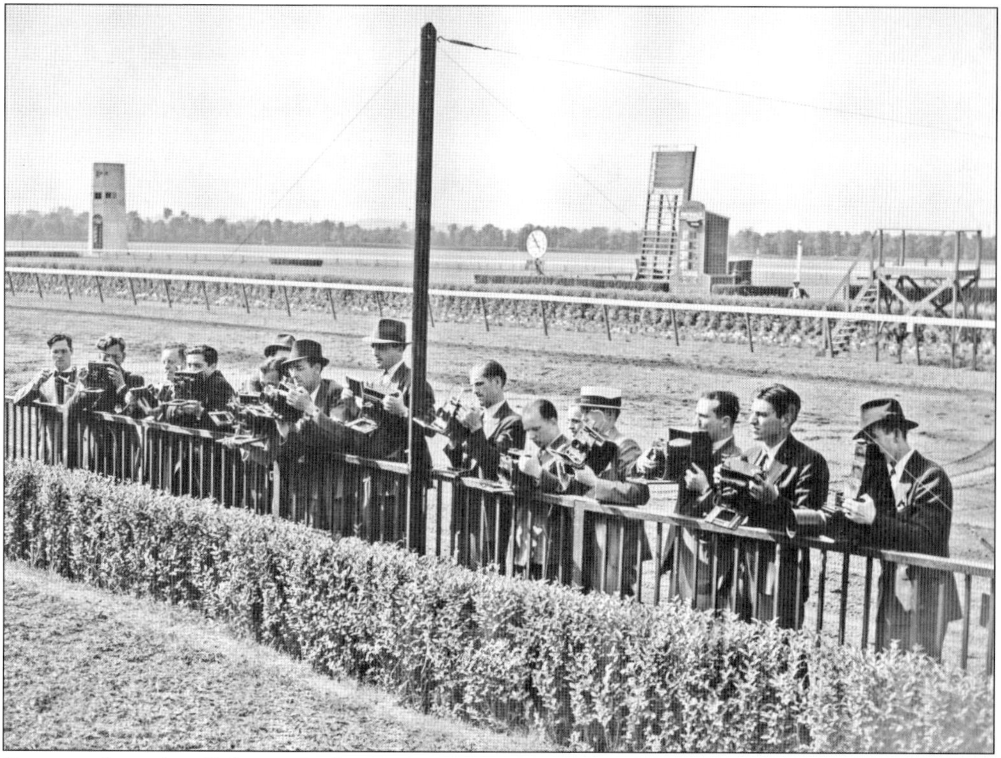

Seen on the rail at Belmont Park, photographers stake their positions adjacent to the winner's circle after the Belmont Stakes on June 7, 1937. (Author's collection.)

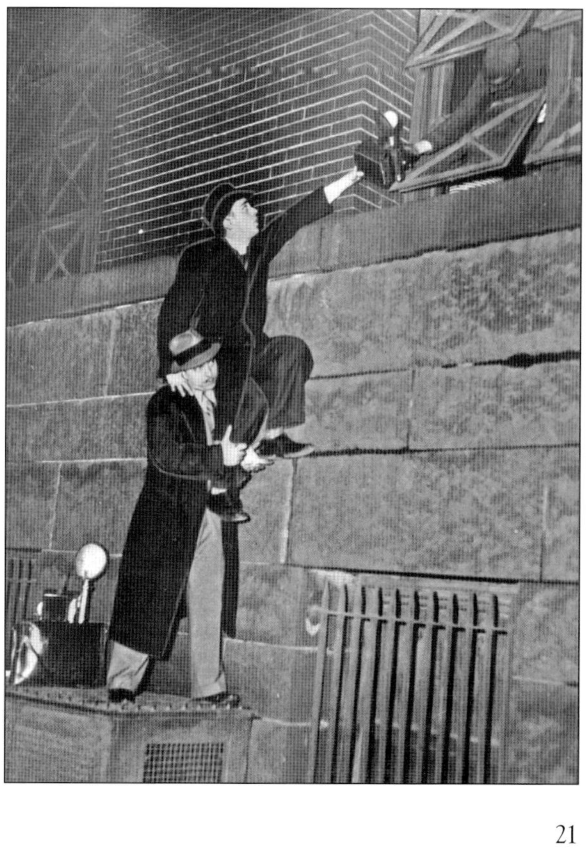

Resourcefulness is, and always has been, the key to being a good photographer—even if it means not getting the shot. Here, on January 25, 1937, an Acme photographer hands his camera through a window to a worker inside a power plant during a subway strike. Photographers were not allowed access to the site, but Acme got the shot anyway. (Author's collection.)

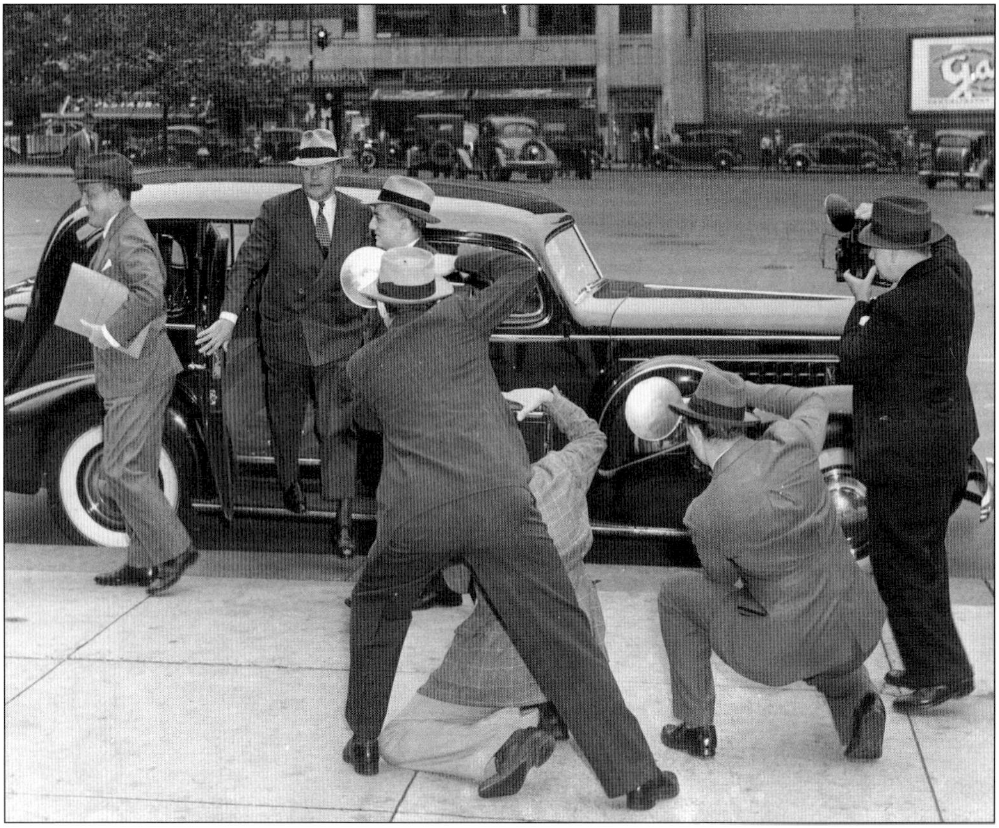

Tammany Hall boss Jimmy Hines, on trial for his involvement with the mob, arrives at the courthouse in Manhattan in 1938. A mistrial ensued, but he was convicted the following year. The photographers seen here have prefocused their cameras on the point where they knew Hines would emerge from the car, so there was no need to jostle or shove into position when he arrived.

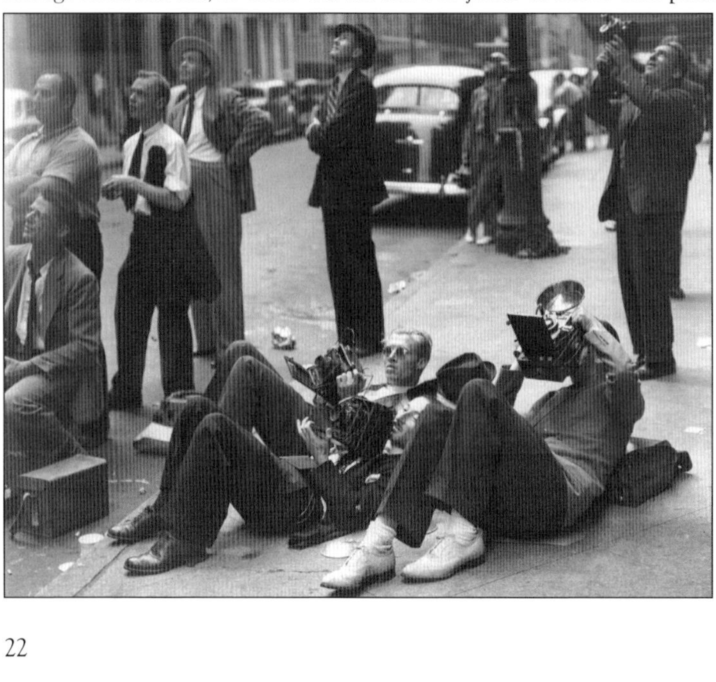

These photographers remained steadfast at the Hotel Gotham on Fifty-fifth Street while John William Warde precariously stood on the ledge of the 17th floor. After an 11-hour standoff, Warde jumped to his death that night, July 26, 1938. The incident, complete with photographers lying on their backs to catch the shot, was dramatized in the 1951 film *Fourteen Hours*.

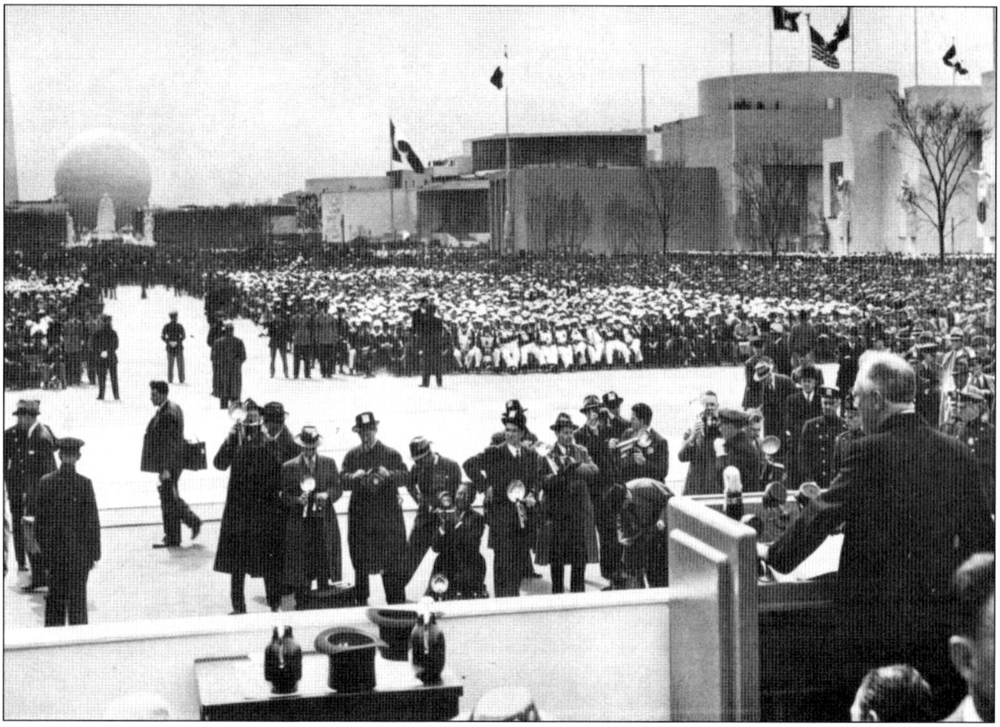

Pres. Franklin D. Roosevelt speaks at the opening of the 1939 World's Fair in Flushing, Queens. The fair was a focal point of media coverage, and photographers were issued special credentials to cover it. Roosevelt, a former New York governor, was a familiar face to local photographers, and he often supported their social events.

An enthusiastic fire buff, Mayor Fiorello H. La Guardia (left) visits the scene of a fire on Cherry Street in 1939. La Guardia's administration worked closely with the Press Photographers Association, impaneling a Mayor's Advisory Committee on Press Cards. "Photographers are the one group of newspaper men I can get along with," he said. "The people can get more information—and more accurate information—from newspaper pictures than from any editorial." (Courtesy of the *Daily News*.)

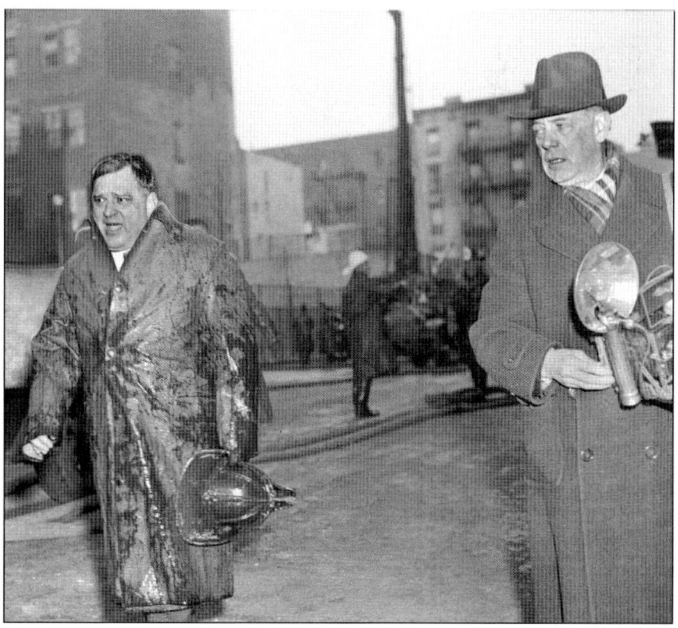

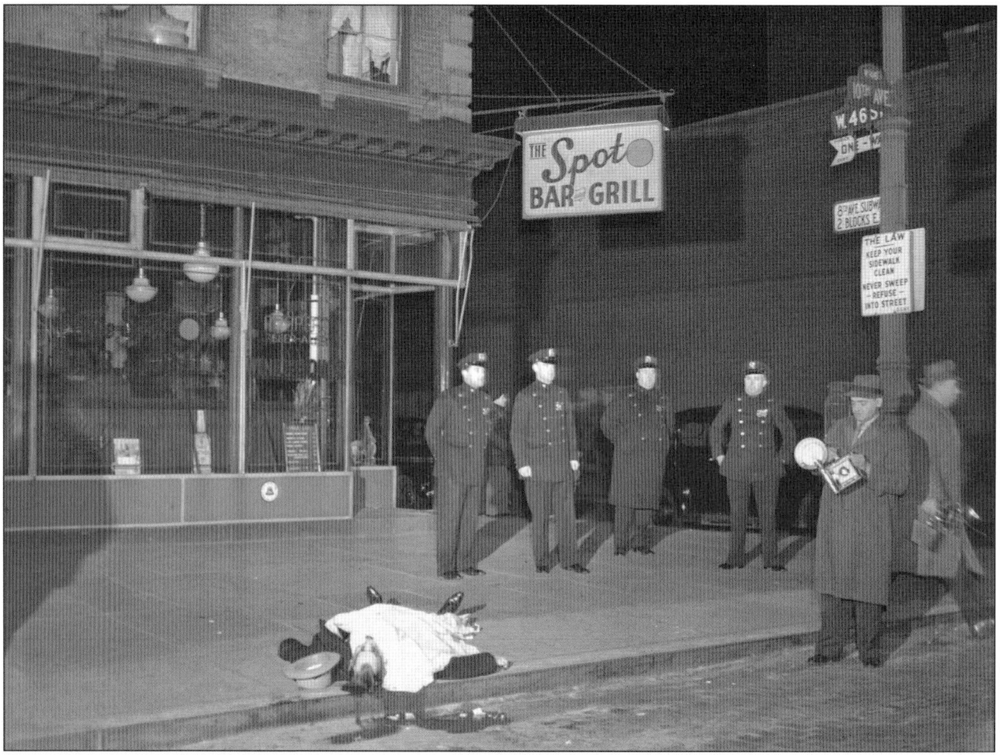

David "The Beetle" Beadle, a longshoreman, stopped in a bar on Tenth Avenue and West Forty-sixth Street at 1:00 a.m. on December 9, 1939. The 32-year-old, who was once believed to have shot three men just to prove his mettle, suffered from a heart condition and needed a glass of water to wash down a pill. As he exited the bar, two men emerged from a taxi. They pumped several bullets into his head before jumping back into the cab and taking off. Believed to be the end result of a dock dispute, the murder was never solved, but it was well documented. Arthur "Weegee" Fellig is seen at right; his nearly identical frame of this scene is one of his iconic New York crime shots. (Courtesy of the Associated Press.)

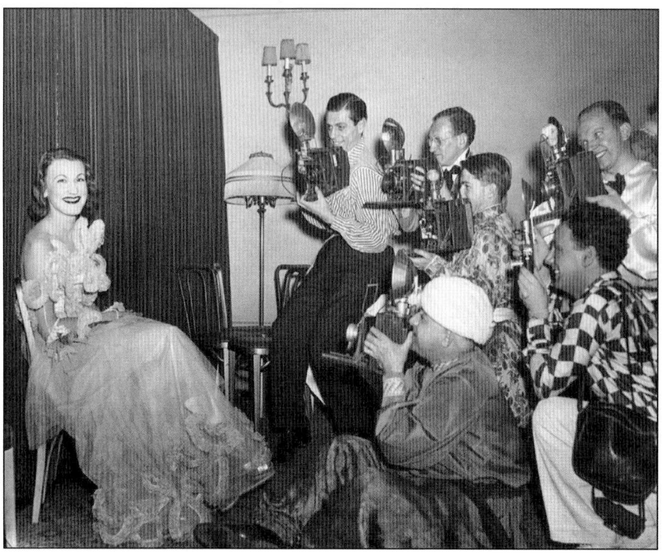

Definitely not wearing their usual work clothes, photographers train their lenses on Sylvia Kissel during the Beaux Arts Diamond Ball at the Ritz-Carlton Hotel on January 26, 1940. From left to right are (first row) Bert Morgan and Max Haas; (second row) Richard Sarno, Samuel Falk, unidentified, and Thomas Watson. (Photograph by the Morgan Brothers.)

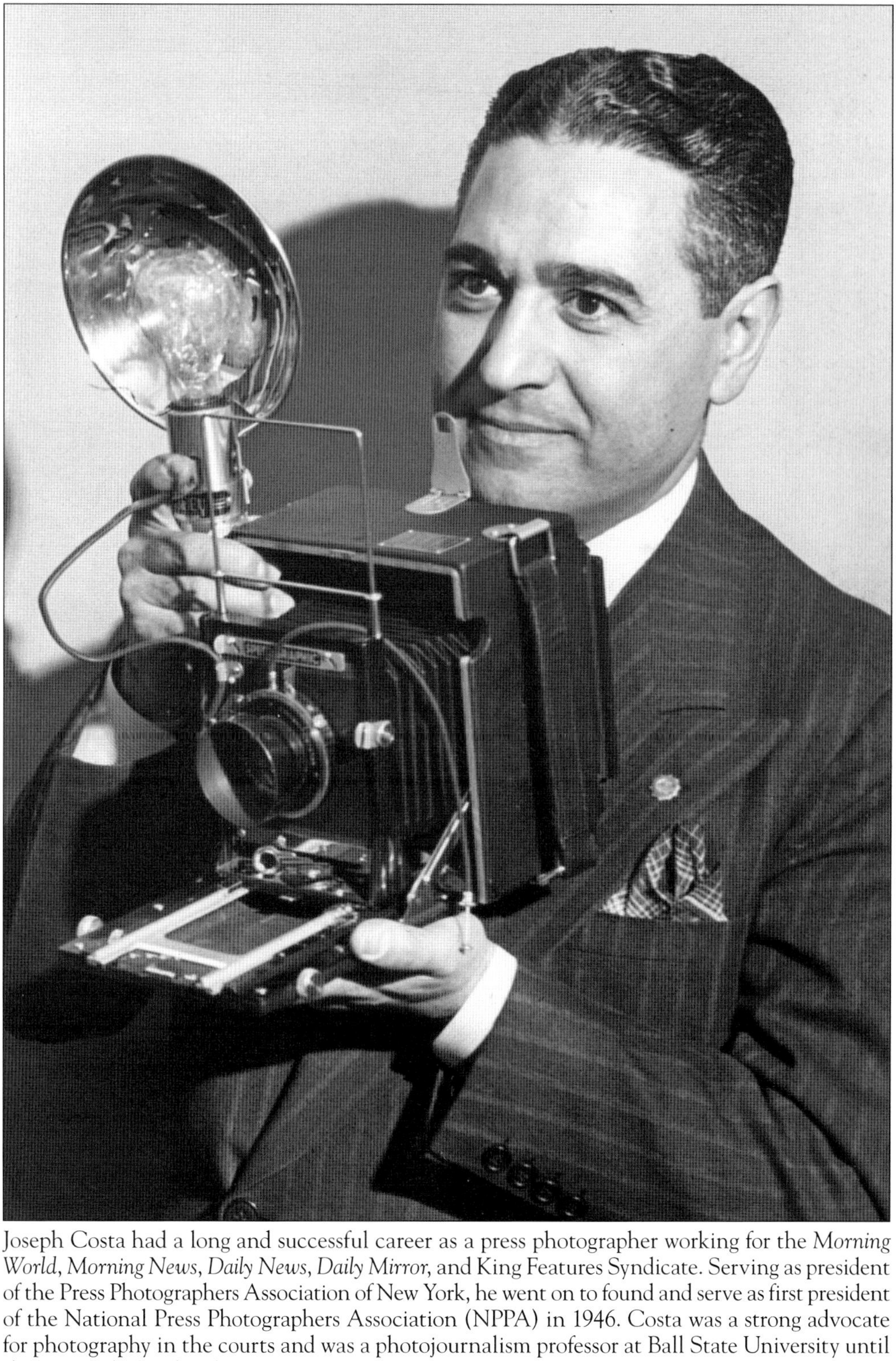

Joseph Costa had a long and successful career as a press photographer working for the *Morning World*, *Morning News*, *Daily News*, *Daily Mirror*, and King Features Syndicate. Serving as president of the Press Photographers Association of New York, he went on to found and serve as first president of the National Press Photographers Association (NPPA) in 1946. Costa was a strong advocate for photography in the courts and was a photojournalism professor at Ball State University until three years before his death at age 84 in 1988. (Author's collection.)

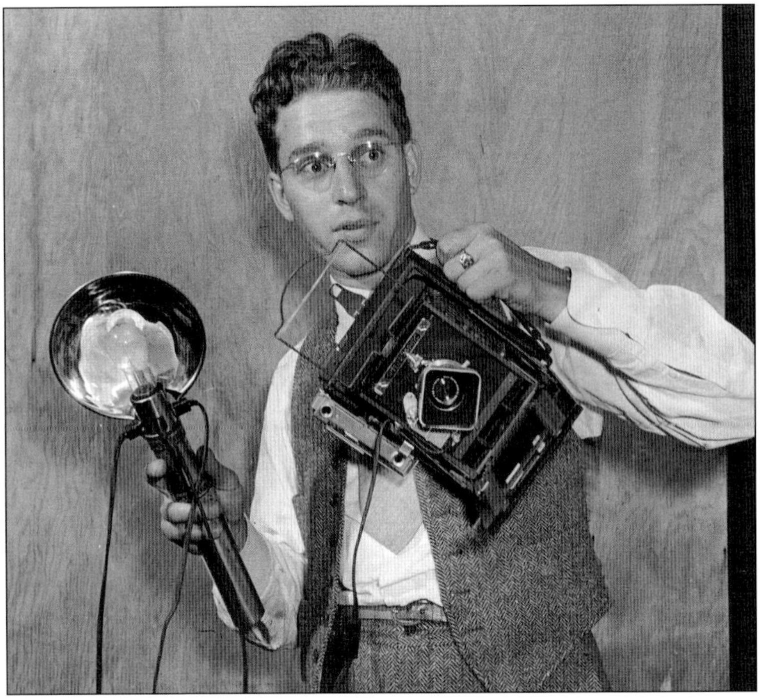

Alan Fisher of the *World-Telegram* prepares to take a shot in a studio setting. His Abbey flashgun is being held off camera; one cord connects to the shutter-tripping solenoid on the camera, while others are presumably linked to additional flashes. (Photograph by Leo Lieb, author's collection.)

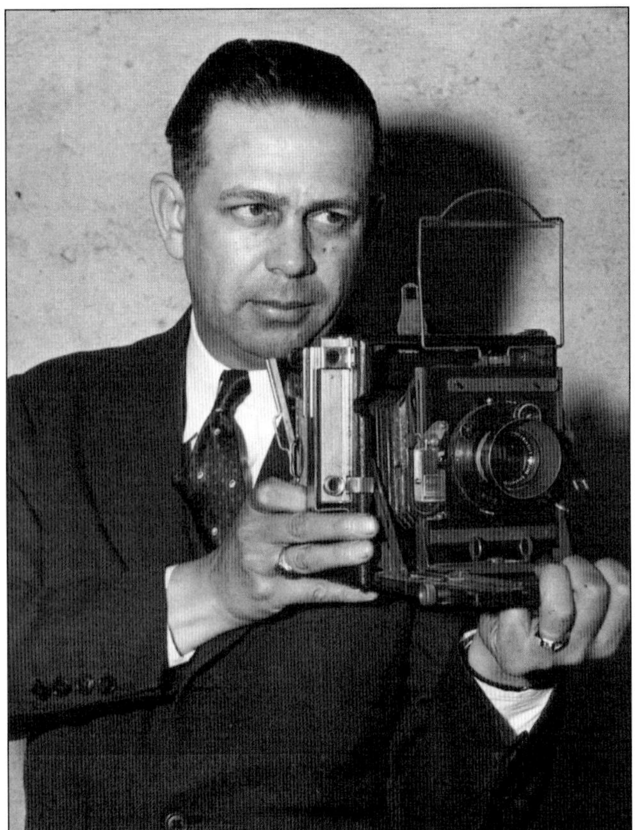

William C. Greene was a photographer for the *World-Telegram* and served as president of the Press Photographers Association. An accomplished sports photographer, Greene's photograph of Jackie Robinson entering the Brooklyn Dodgers' clubhouse is part of the National Baseball Hall of Fame collection. (Author's collection.)

Carl Nesensohn of the *New York Times* appears in this dramatically lit portrait. Nesensohn was no stranger to drama. In 1934, when the burning SS *Morro Castle* ran aground at Asbury Park, New Jersey, Nesensohn attempted to climb a rope to board the still-smoldering vessel, but a Coast Guardsman ordered him to "get down, or be shot down!" He complied but promptly filed a complaint, whereby he was grudgingly allowed to photograph aboard the wreck. (Author's collection.)

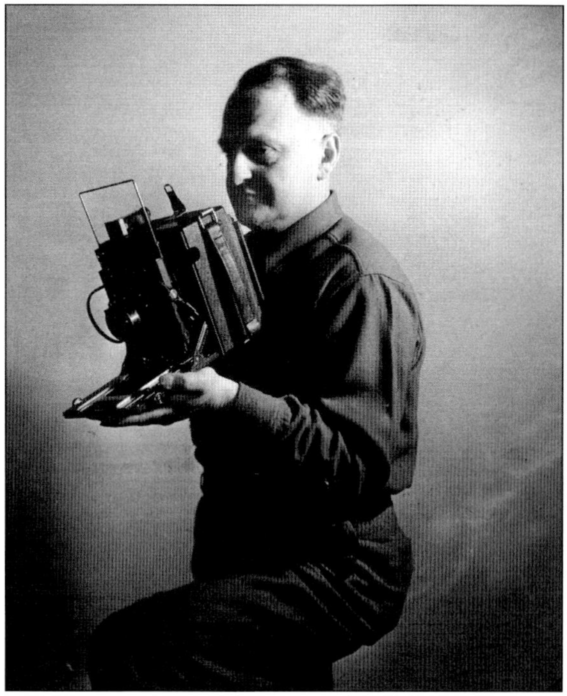

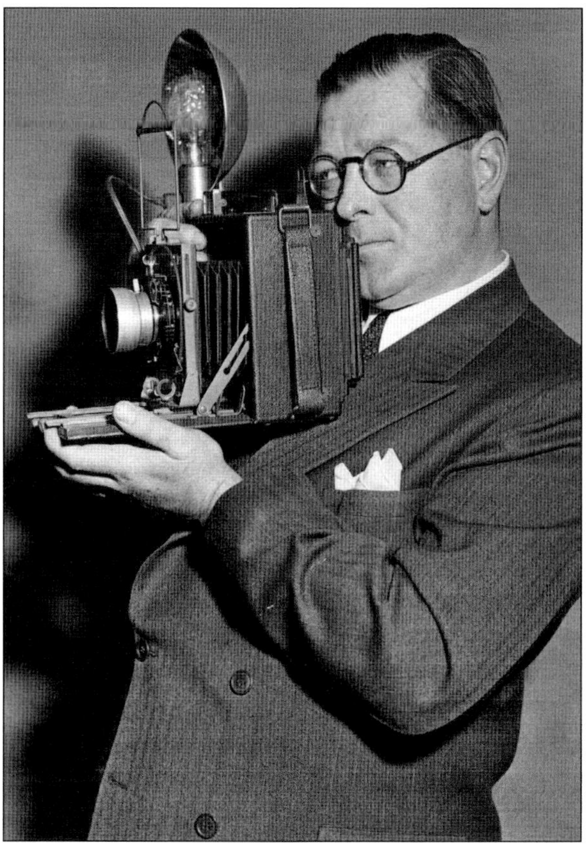

Larry Froeber of the *Daily News* was also at Asbury Park to cover the *Morro Castle*. Not to be outdone by the competition, Froeber also managed to make it aboard. After a while, however, he seemed to have disappeared. A rescue party found him unconscious from poisonous fumes, with his hands burned. He was tethered to a life ring and, with a makeshift zip line, returned to shore. The remainder of his career was spent safely covering sports. (Author's collection.)

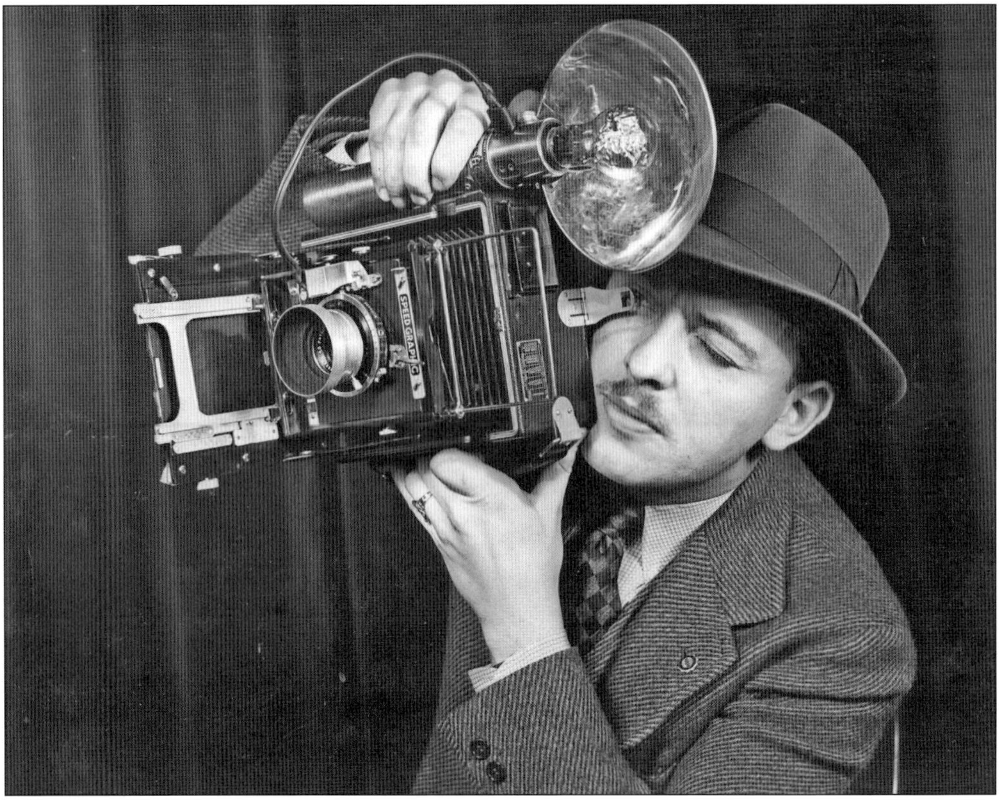

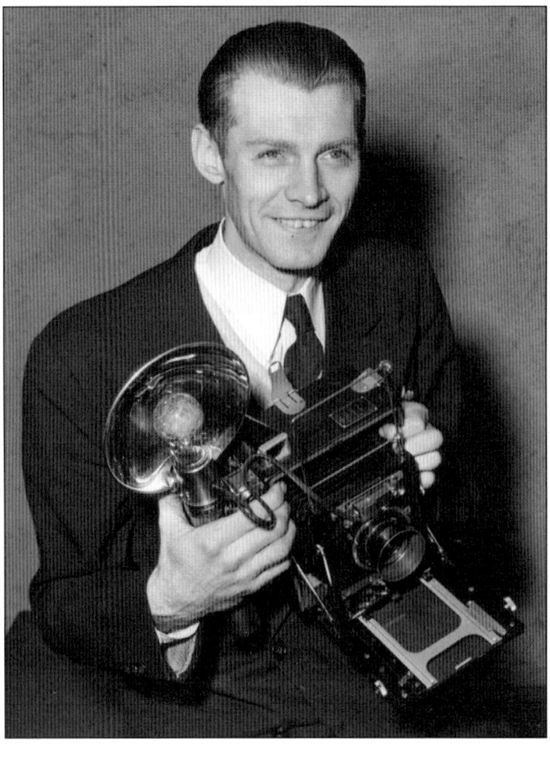

Charles Corte, seen here squinting through the sports viewfinder of his four-by-five-inch Graflex Anniversary Speed Graphic, was a staff photographer for Acme Newspictures. His flashbulb contains thin crumpled-up sheets of magnesium foil, which would ignite and burn relatively slowly; this design would be mostly replaced by faster-burning aluminum wire. In 1961, Corte and his wife were killed in an auto accident that also seriously injured their teenage daughter. (Author's collection.)

Albert Aumuller served as president of the Press Photographers Association and worked for the *World-Telegram*. Garnering many awards during his career, he taught photojournalism and authored a textbook on the subject. He was on hand when Albert Einstein received his US citizenship in 1940. (Author's collection.)

Fred Palumbo, a longtime member and trustee of the Press Photographers Association, proudly sports his membership lapel pin as he stands in the studio of the *World-Telegram*. Many of Palumbo's environmental portraits of prominent figures are part of the Library of Congress collection. (Author's collection.)

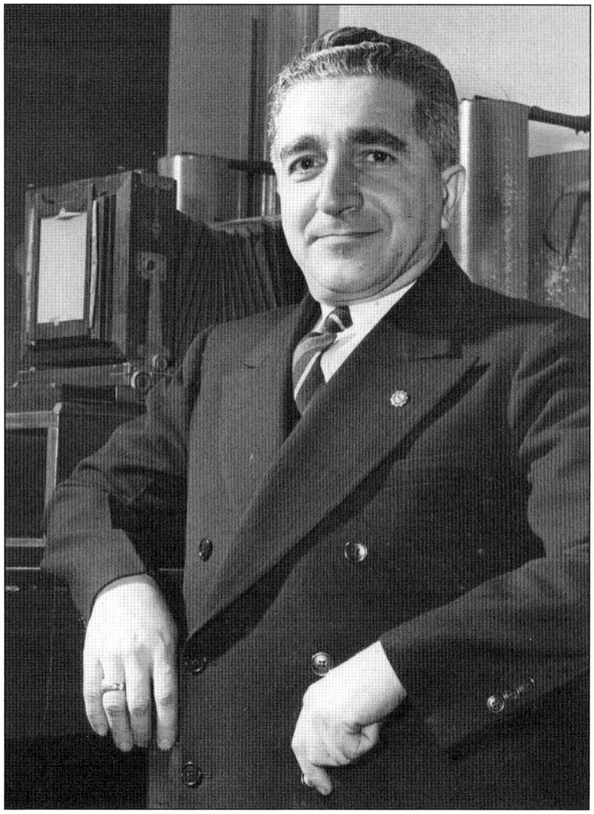

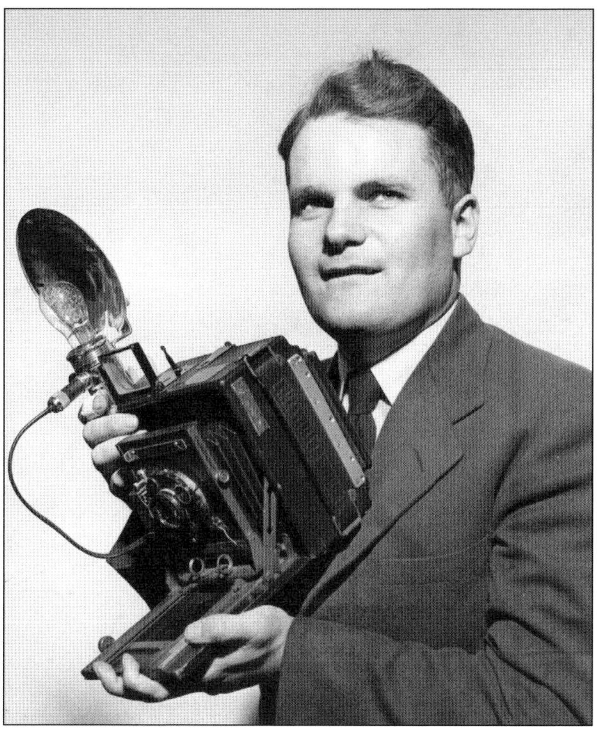

Harry Harris worked as a photographer for the Associated Press for nearly half a century, starting out in the Wall Street bureau, where he collected commodity prices. He started as a sports photographer in 1934 on a trial basis—one that lasted until his retirement in 1978. Harris died in 2002. (Author's collection.)

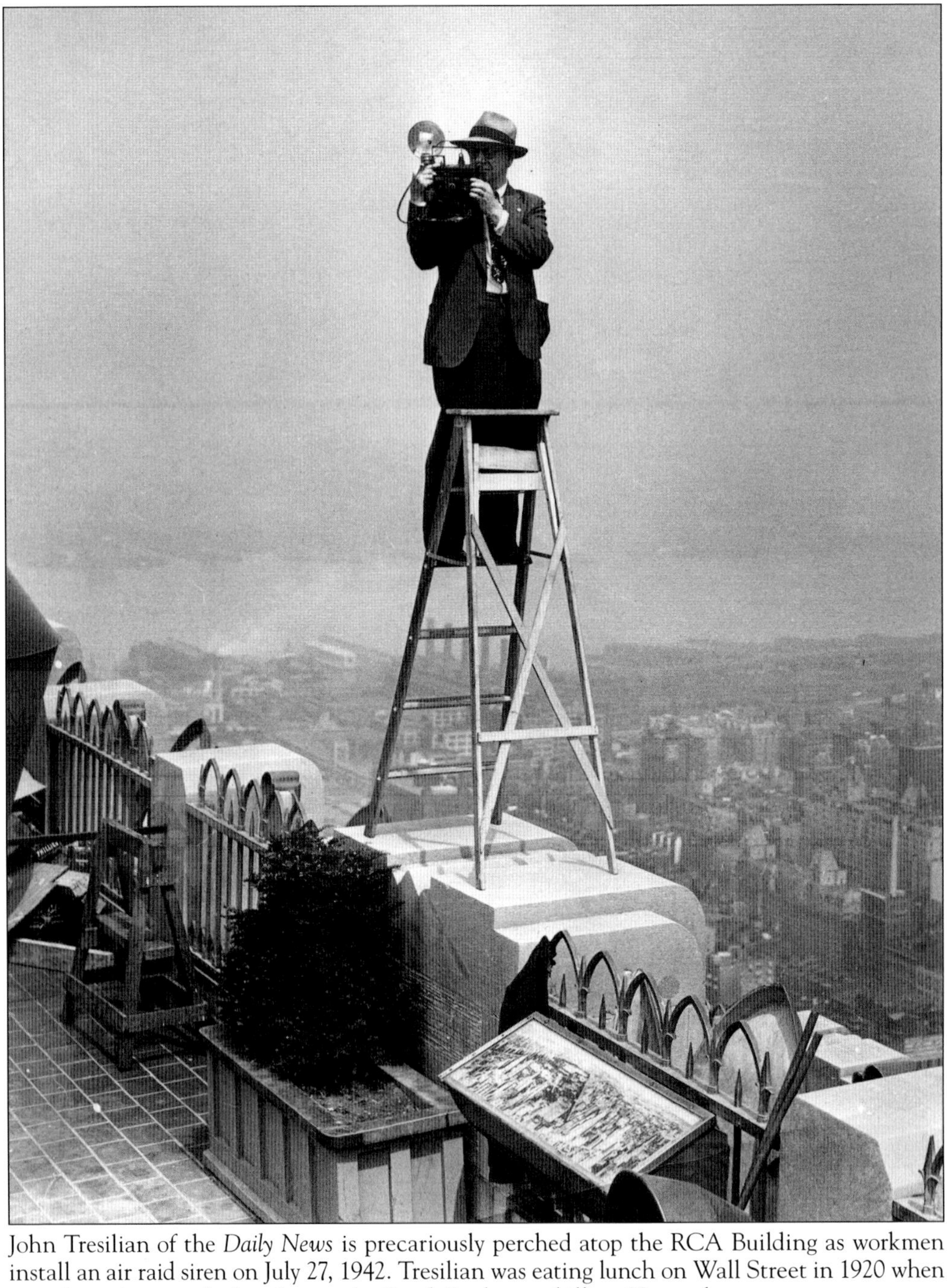

John Tresilian of the *Daily News* is precariously perched atop the RCA Building as workmen install an air raid siren on July 27, 1942. Tresilian was eating lunch on Wall Street in 1920 when anarchists detonated a bomb near the Stock Exchange, killing 39 people.

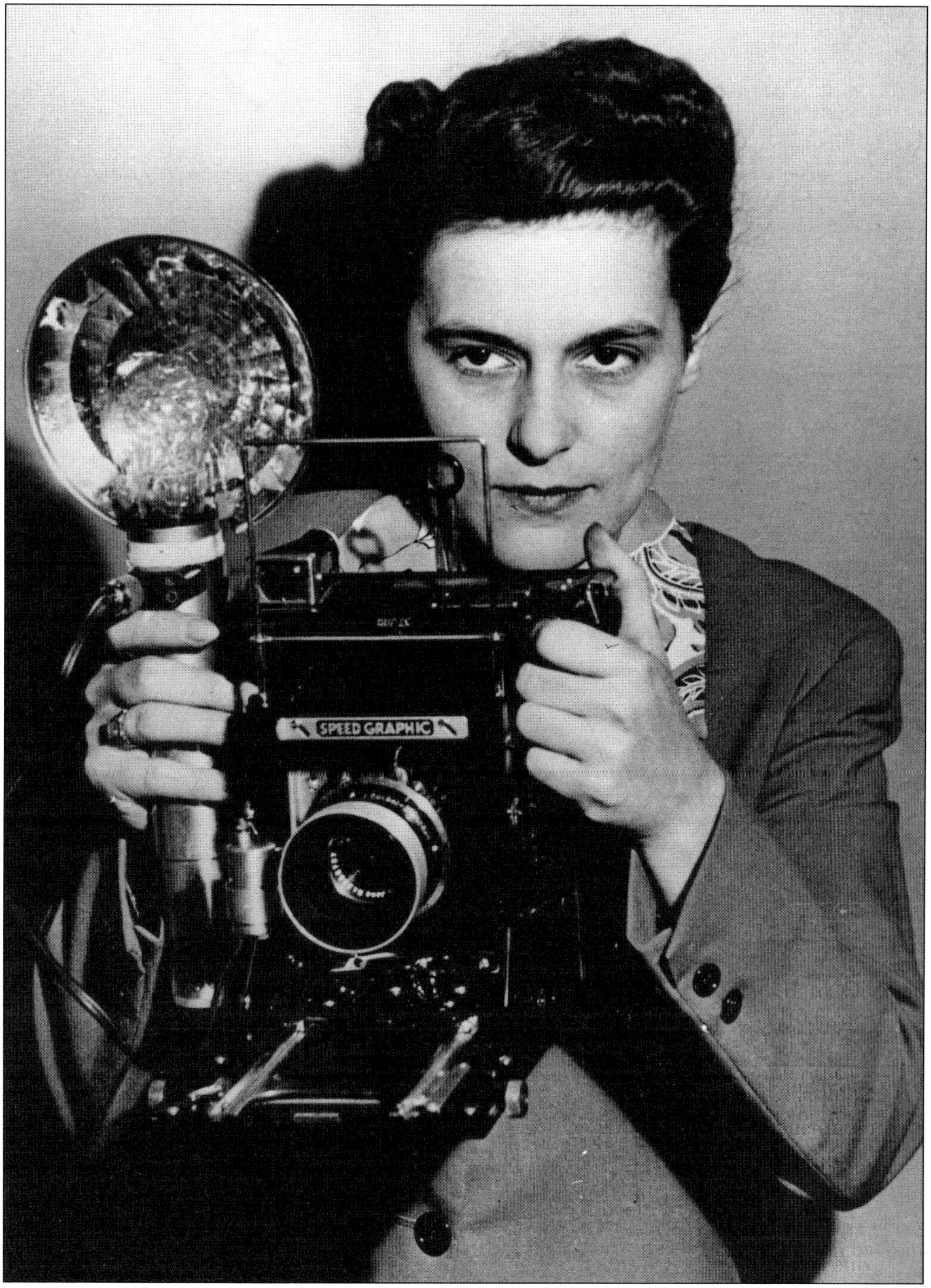

Evelyn Straus was one of the few women who made the foray into the male-dominated world of press photography in the 1940s. With the staff rosters depleted by World War II, she grabbed the chance to make a name for herself. Before long, Straus was regarded as one of most reliable staffers of the *Daily News*. She was known to wear tailor-made suits with special pockets to carry her four-by-five-inch film holders and flashbulbs.

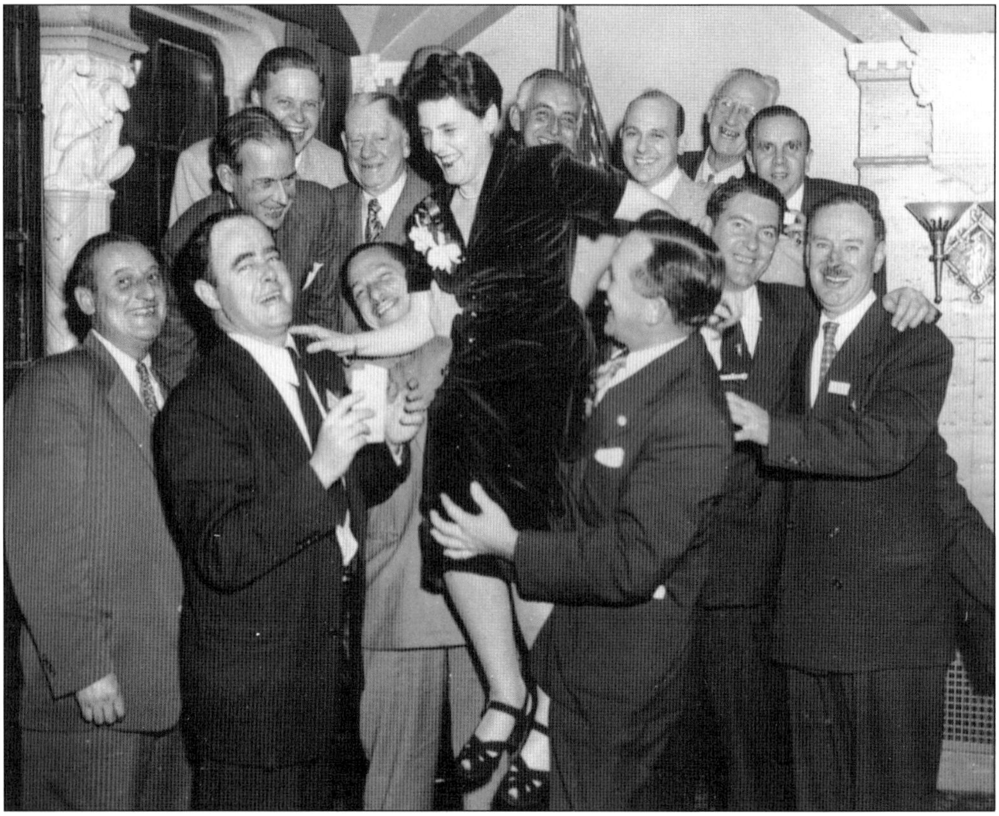

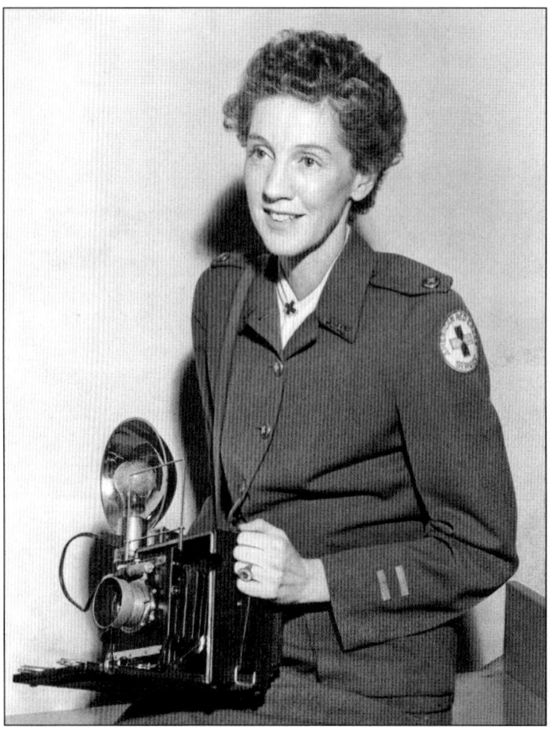

Although her daily work proved she could handle anything the boys could, it took a few years for Evelyn Straus to be accepted into the ranks of the Press Photographers Association. Despite mutterings of opposition from the old guard, she was finally welcomed with open arms, becoming its first female member by 1950.

Accomplished on the fashion circuit, Antoinette Frissell wanted more excitement. "I became so frustrated with fashions that I wanted to prove to myself that I could do a real reporting job," she said in 1941. Frissell got her wish when she was sent to Europe in 1942 to photograph wartime activities of the Red Cross. She returned to documentary portraiture, becoming the first female staff photographer for *Sports Illustrated* in 1953. (Author's collection.)

Adelaide Leavy started out taking pictures for the American Women's Voluntary Services in 1941 and, shortly thereafter, was placed in charge of darkroom operations. By 1943, she was covering general assignment for Acme Newspictures. Here, in 1943, she runs into a problem at Belmont Park when a track official denies her entry to the clubhouse—only the men were allowed to wear pants, he said. (Author's collection.)

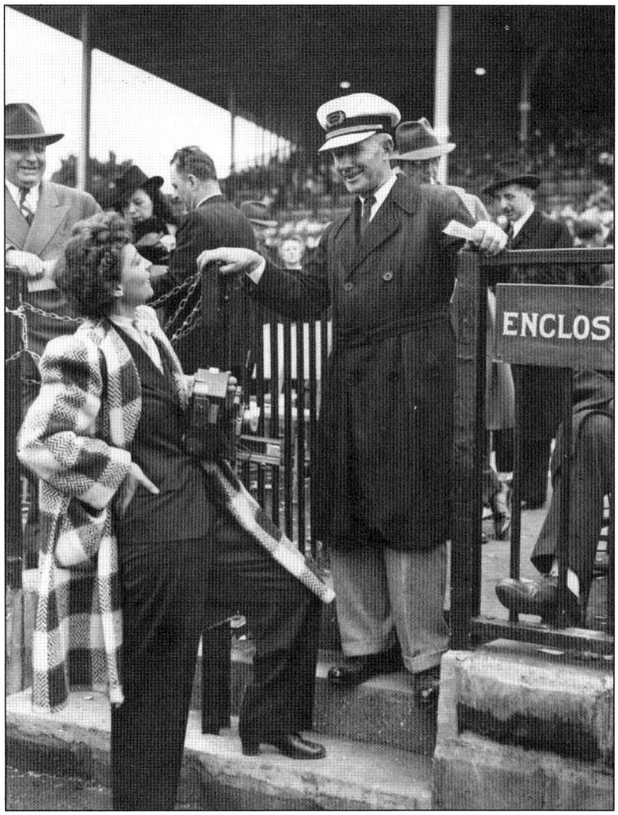

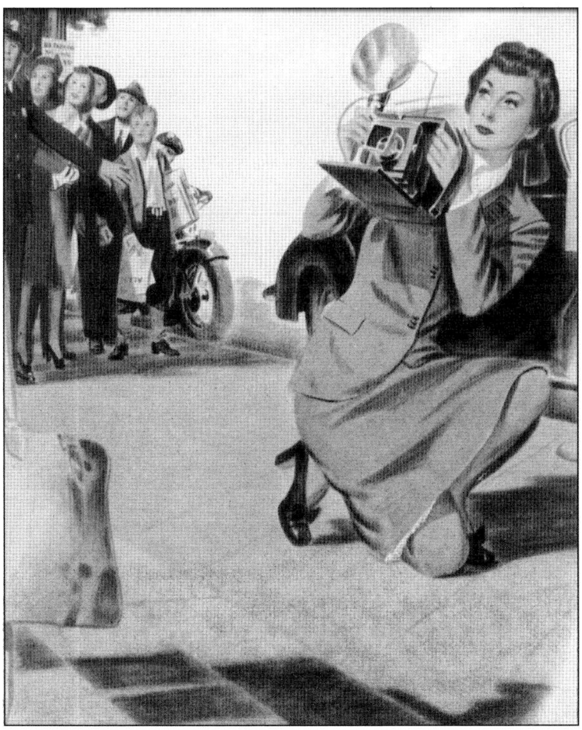

In 1944, Adelaide Leavy had the distinction of appearing, in illustration form, in a *Life* magazine advertisement for DuBarry cosmetics, part of a series depicting women in wartime jobs. "It's a busy, breath- and time-taking job. But regularly, every night, Miss Leavy finds the minutes for her DuBarry Beauty Preparations," the ad states. (Author's collection.)

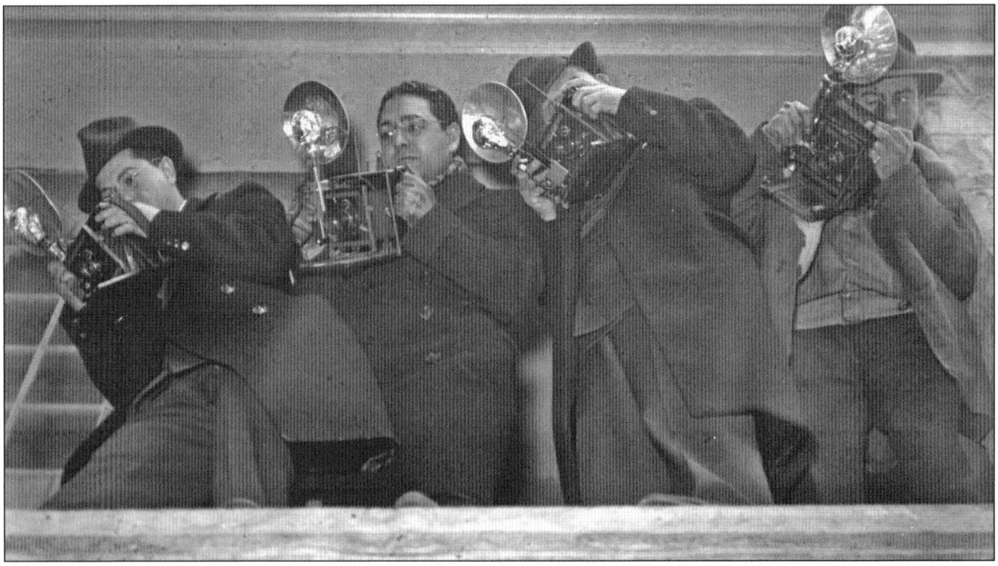

A quartet of photographers perches outside the Hunterdon County Jail in Flemington, New Jersey, awaiting a shot of Bruno Hauptmann during his 1935 trial for the infamous kidnapping of Charles Lindbergh Jr. Over 130 photographers were on hand to cover the trial, but only four were allowed in the courtroom at a time, serving as a "press pool" for all of the competing publications. The judge's strict prohibition of pictures while court was actually in session was not entirely complied with, but the photographers insisted that their presence never once disrupted the tumultuous proceedings. (Courtesy of the *Daily News*.)

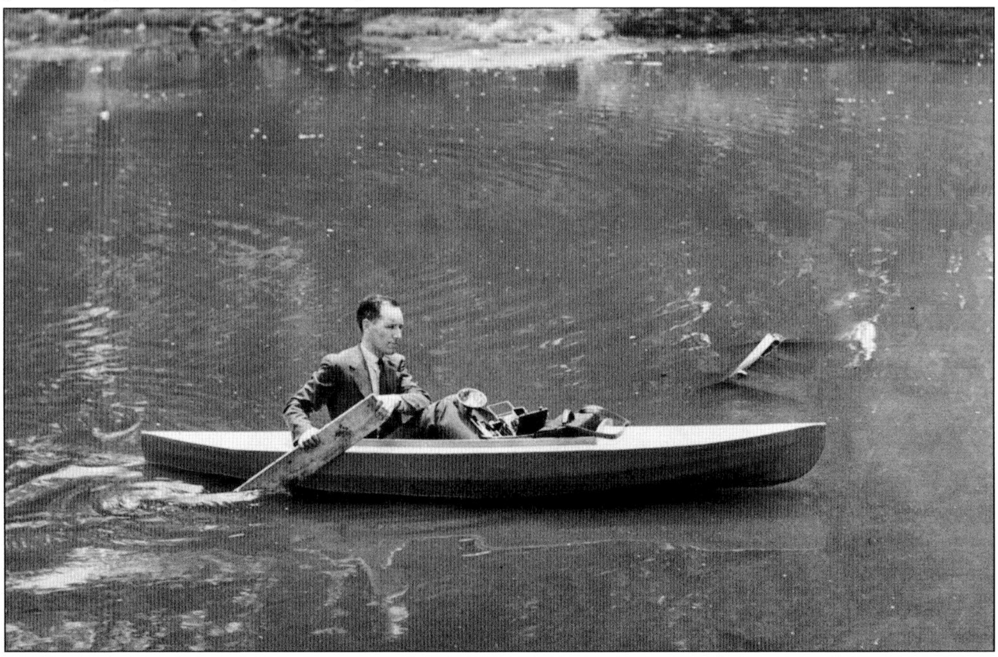

Robert Wands beats traffic as he paddles up the Bronx River toward the Bronx Zoo on September 4, 1943. His Speed Graphic camera is at the ready, with the accompanying brown leather case nearby. Often, photographers on assignment would store their cases in a central location so as not to be encumbered by extra gear.

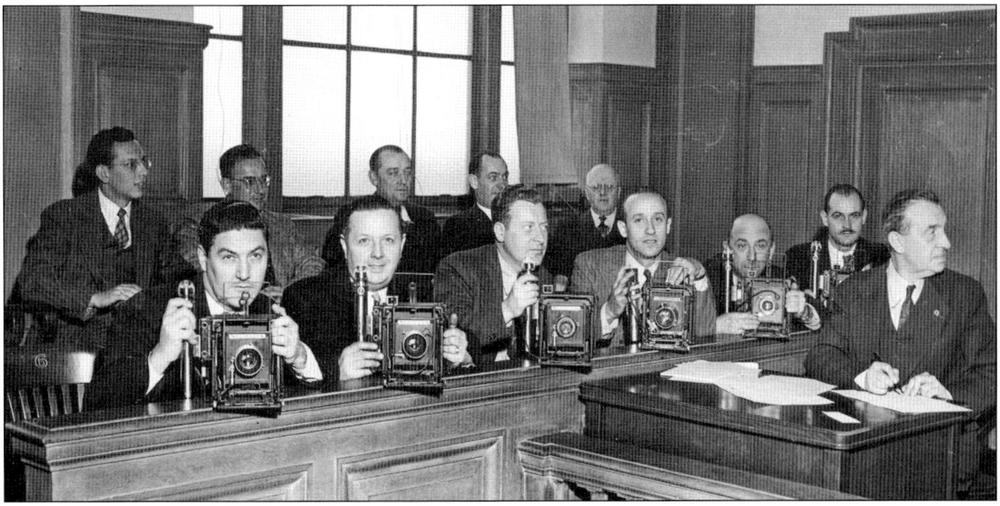

In the first row of the jury box at Kings County (Brooklyn) Criminal Court are, from left to right, Walter Kelleher, Jesse Strait, Red Gaston, Marty Black, Jules Geller, and Leroy Jakob. The men are using the battery cases of their flashguns, sans bulb, to trigger their cameras. Photography in courtrooms became a rarity after this instance in 1943, with only a few exceptions over the years. The movement in favor of allowing photography in New York's courtrooms finally made some progress in the mid-2000s. (Photograph by Irving Haberman.)

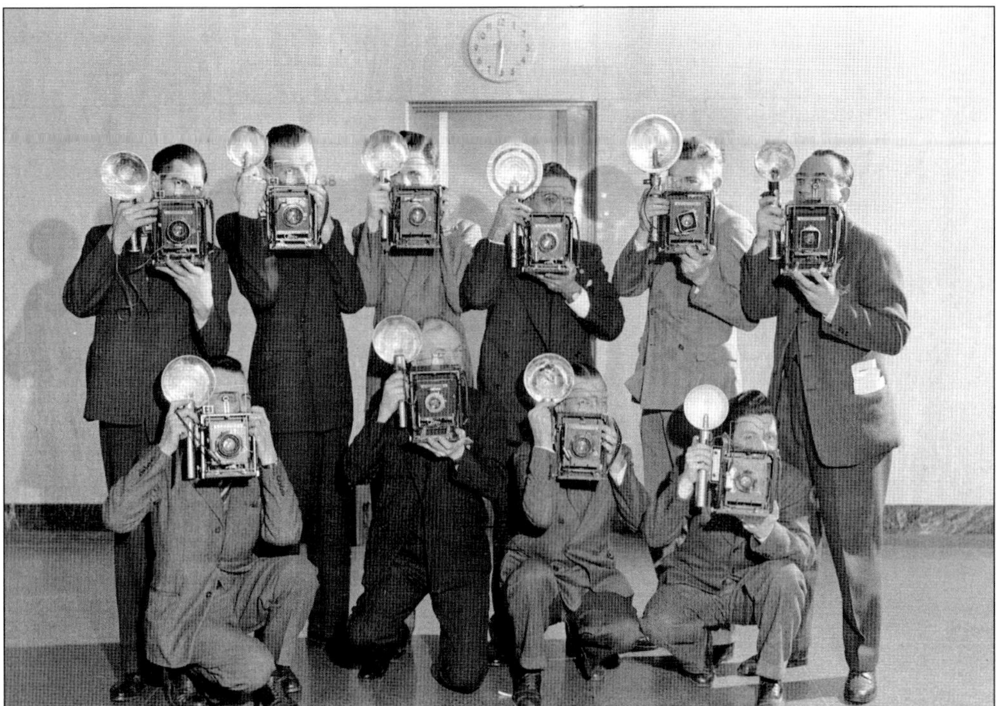

Photographers cover the Wayne Lonergan trial at the Manhattan Courts building, located at 100 Centre Street, in March 1944, but they are confined to the hallway of the 13th floor. News photographers still operate in this corridor; the clock above the doorway remains, although it is no longer functional. (Courtesy of the *Daily News*.)

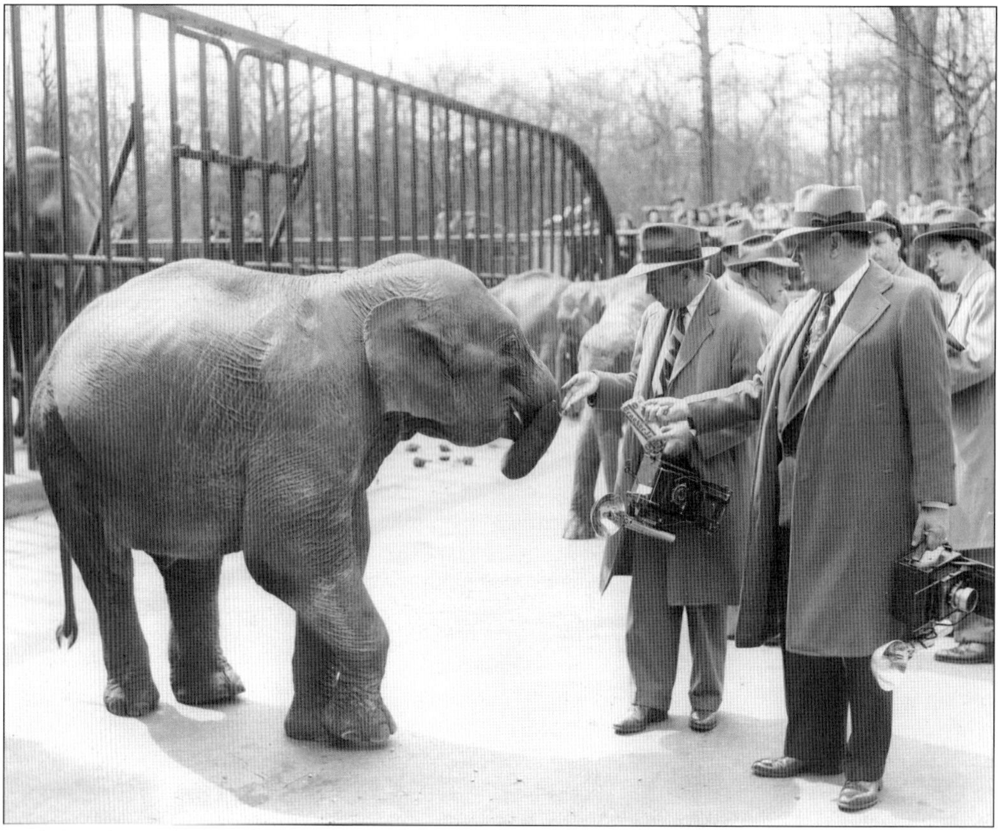

At left, Jules Geller of the *Brooklyn Eagle* and Jesse Strait of the *Daily Mirror* feed Cracker Jack to a baby elephant at the Prospect Park Zoo in 1946. Their Graflex flashguns are equipped with adapters that took new, smaller-size flashbulbs, better suited for situations where less harsh fill light was needed. *Star Wars* fans may recognize the flashguns as the basis of the infamous light saber.

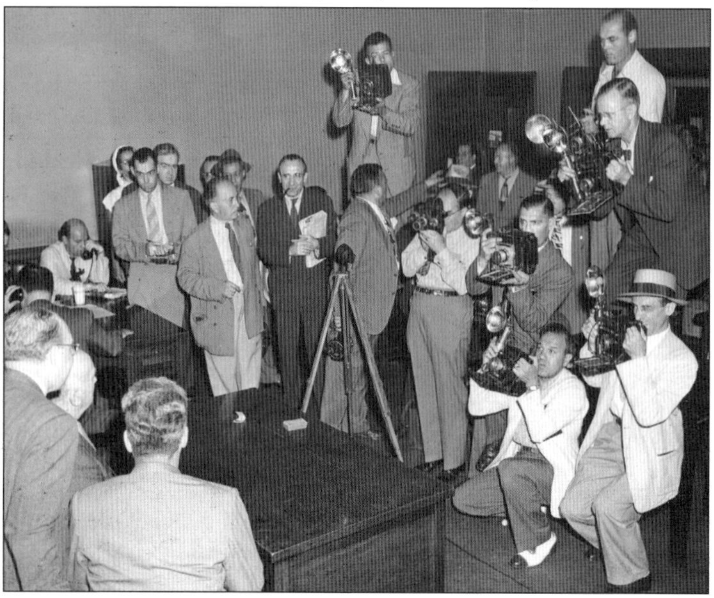

Believed to be taken around 1947 at an unspecified investigative committee hearing, this image shows, from left to right, Neal Boenzi, Frank Jurkoski, and Ed Pickwoad standing atop a desk. The photographers below them are, from left to right, unidentified, Eddie Jerry, Arthur Aidala, and Tony Lanza.

Acme Newspictures photographer William Wasilevich is on assignment in 1946. The following year, Wasilevich was able to get a smile out of the normally stone-faced Soviet diplomat Andrey Vyshinsky at a United Nations event—he told him to "hold it!" in Russian.

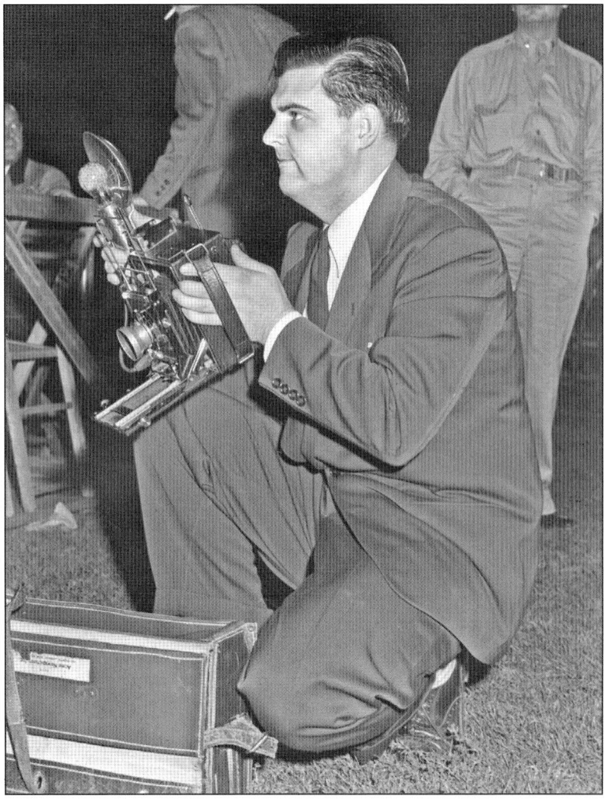

Edward McKevitt of the *Journal-American* receives an assignment from his editor via the two-way radio in his vehicle in 1947. Soon all the New York newspapers had fleets of "radio cars" on the street, with designated response areas within the city. Difficulties ensued with shared frequencies, however, and desk editors had to identify their station when transmitting to avoid confusion.

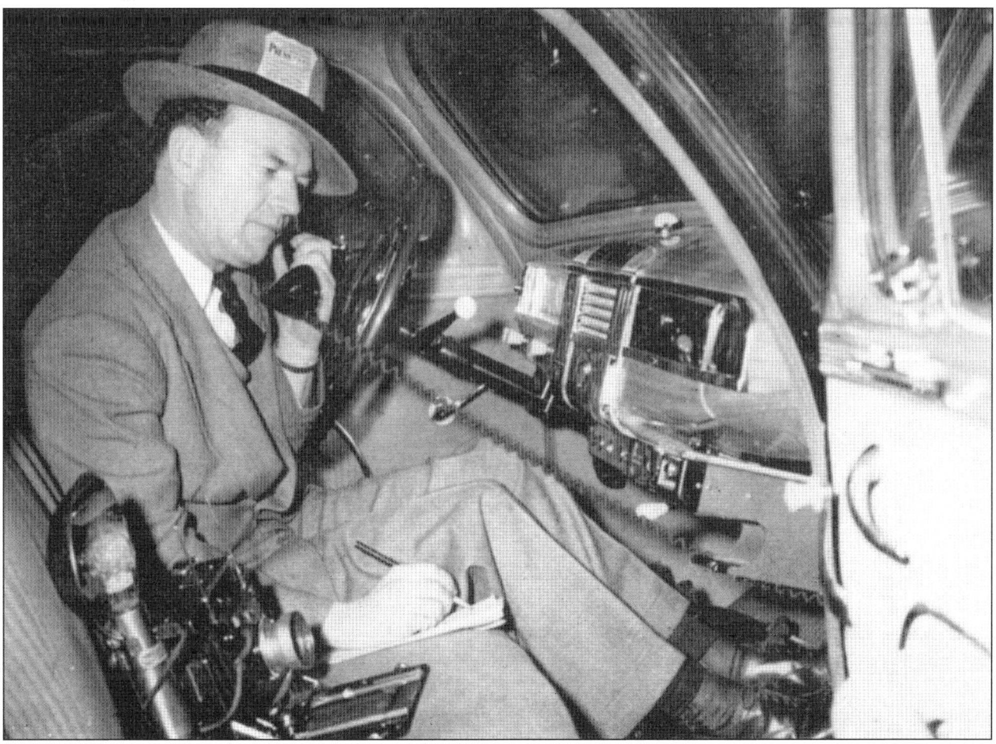

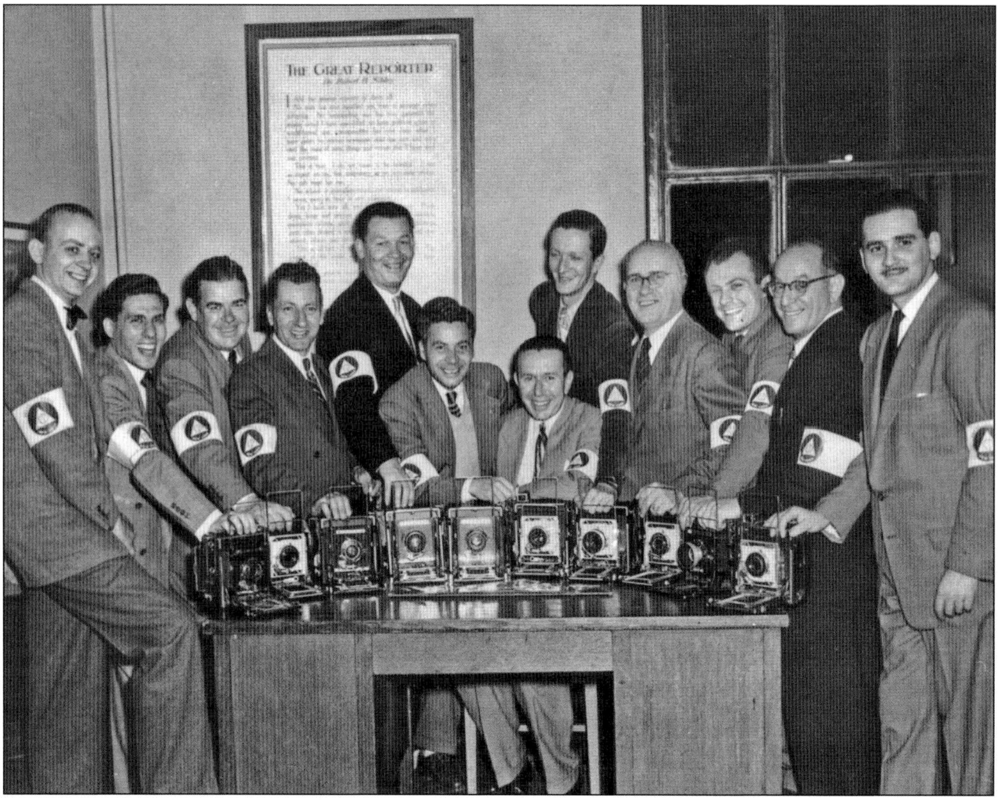

In 1948, *New York Times* photographers show off their Civil Defense press armbands. From left to right are Carl T. Gossett Jr., Larry Morris, George Alexanderson, Ernie Sisto, Patrick Burns, Arthur Brower, John Dugan, Fred Sass, Bill Eckenberg, Neal Boenzi, Mike Liebowitz, and Eddie Hausner.

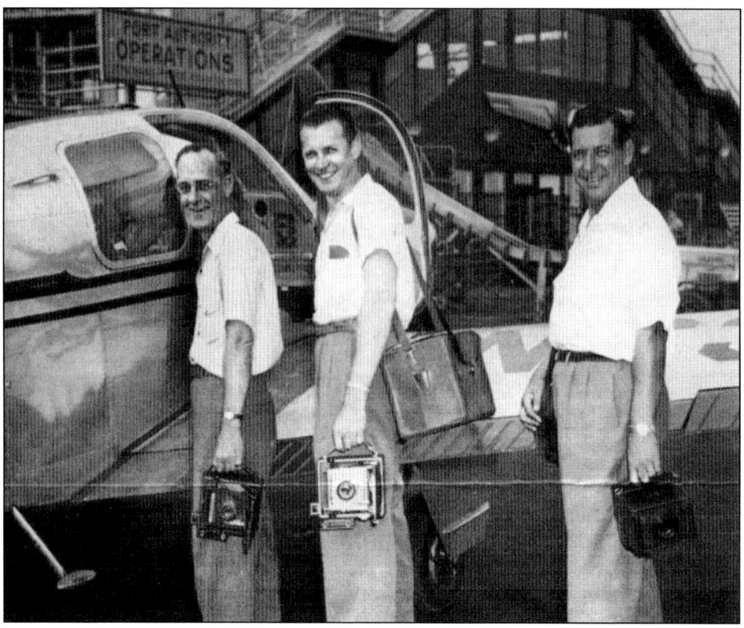

Covering the sea from the air are, from left to right, Joe Lyon of the *Sun*, Al Aumuller of the *World-Telegram*, and Frank Rino of the *Journal-American*. The trio is about to take off from La Guardia Field to photograph the arrival of the luxury French Line ship *Ile de France* in New York Harbor.

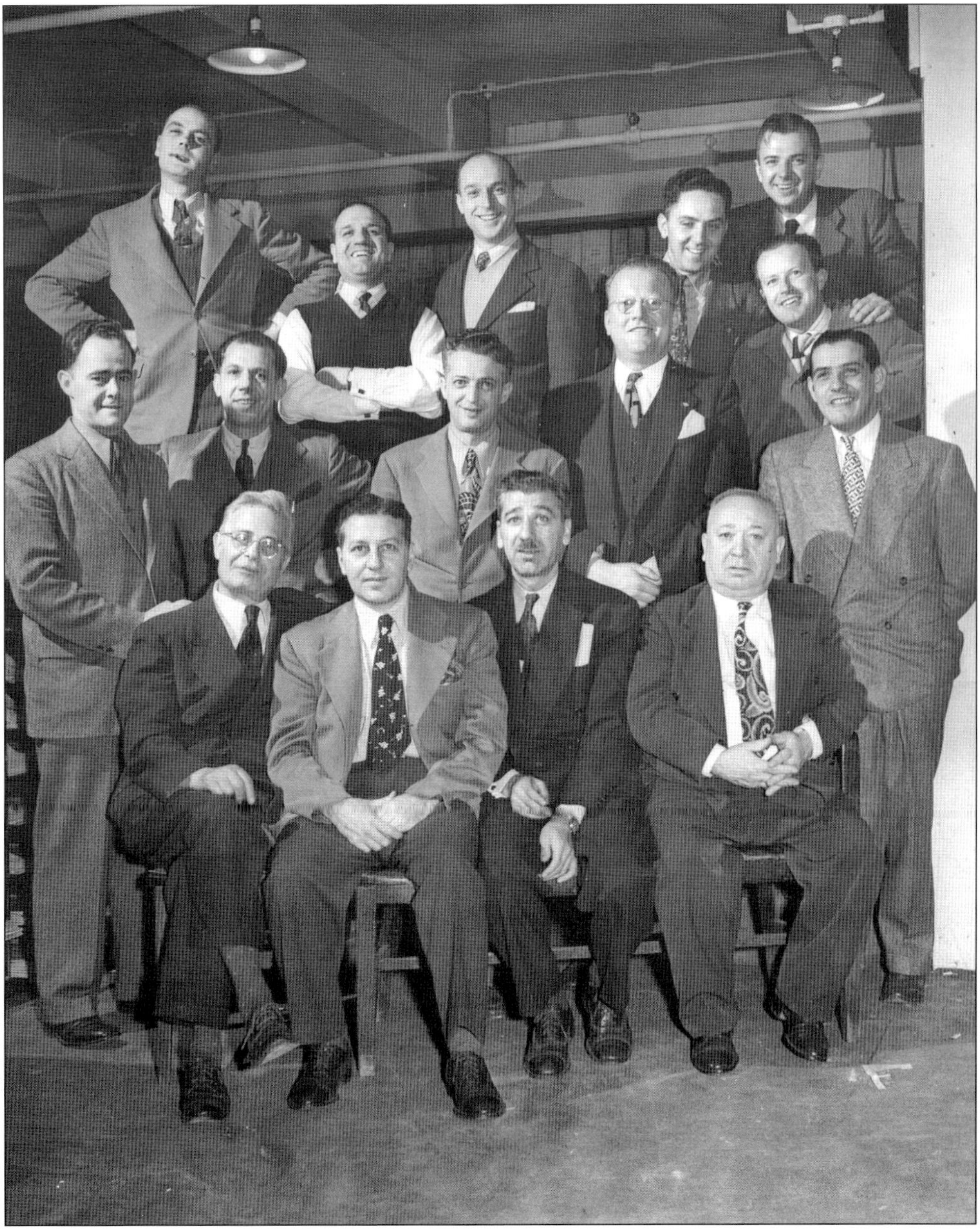

The photograph staff of the *Daily Mirror*, including darkroom technicians and assignment editors, gathers for a portrait in 1949. From left to right are (first row) Steve Funghini, Tom Governale, Manny Elkins, and Izzy Kaplan; (second row) Jack Downey, Fred Klein, Art Abfier, John Reidy, and Harry Hirsch; (third row) Bruce Hopkins, Arthur Aidala, Leon Hoffman, Tony Bernato, Eric Hedlund, and Barney Coons.

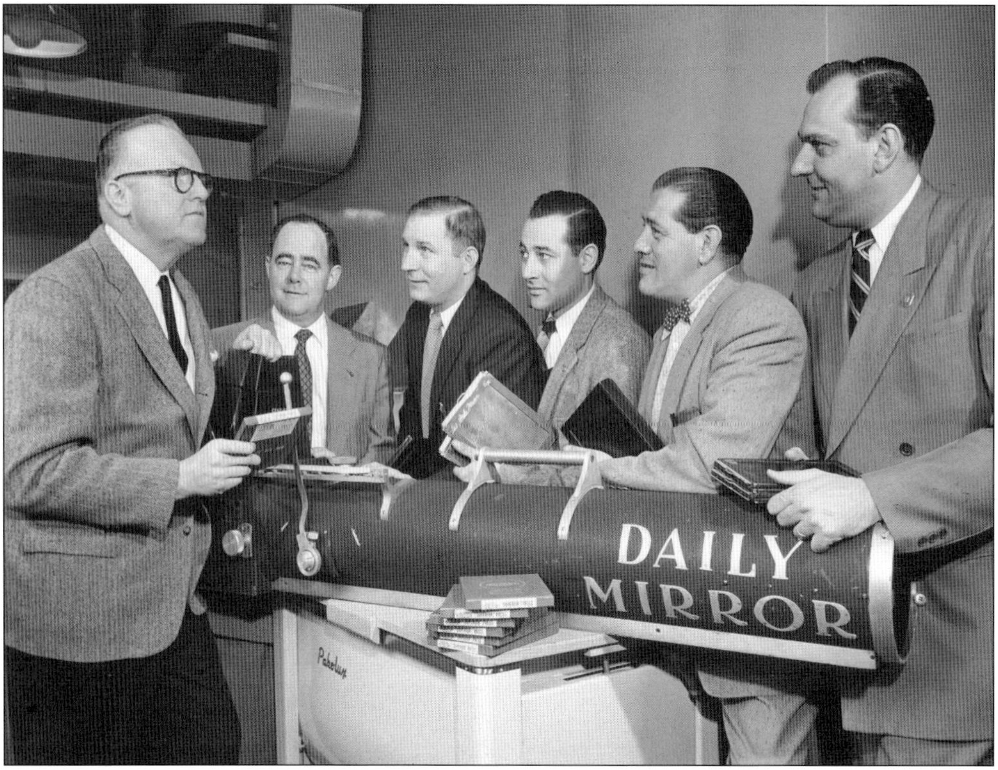

The *Daily Mirror* staff familiarizes itself with "Big Bertha," a five-by-seven-inch Graflex camera with a custom 40-inch telephoto lens mount. Deployed at baseball games, the lens had preset focusing positions, one for each key point on the field where a play was likely to be made. From left to right are chief photographer John Reidy, Jack Downey, Arthur Foote, Stanley Hall, Harry Hirsch, and Art Sarno.

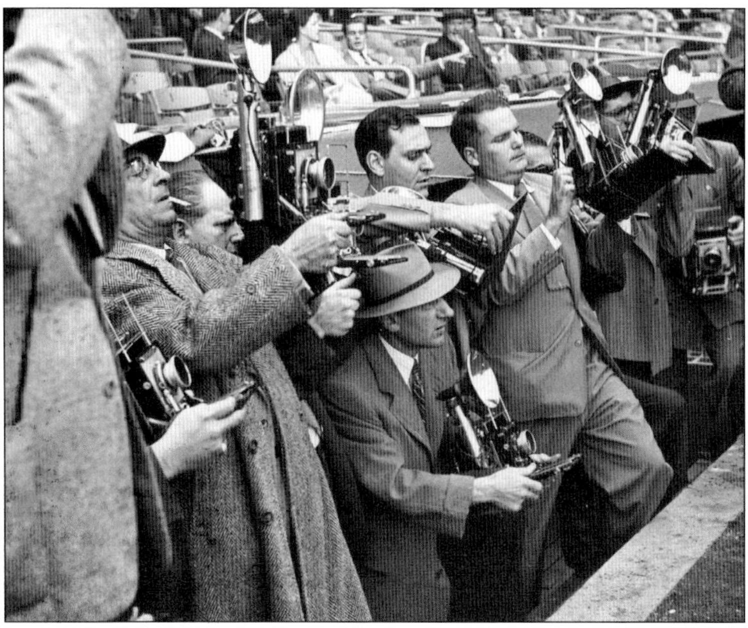

Close-range photography at the ball game was still accomplished with standard four-by-five-inch Speed Graphics. Here, from left to right, Hank Olen, Ernie Sisto, Art Sarno, Harry Harris, and William Jacobellis stand in the dugout at Yankee Stadium.

Al Aumuller works the picture assignment desk at the *World-Telegram* in 1951. The nerve center of the photographic department, the picture assignment editor received tips from the city desk as well as the police radio and was responsible for moving photographers around town efficiently. If all the staffers were occupied, they would call upon "stringers," or freelancers. (Photograph by Fred Palumbo.)

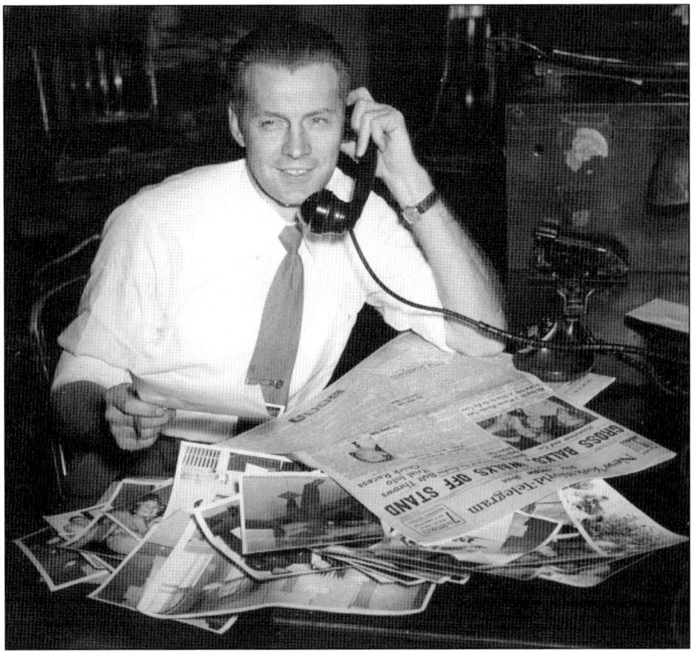

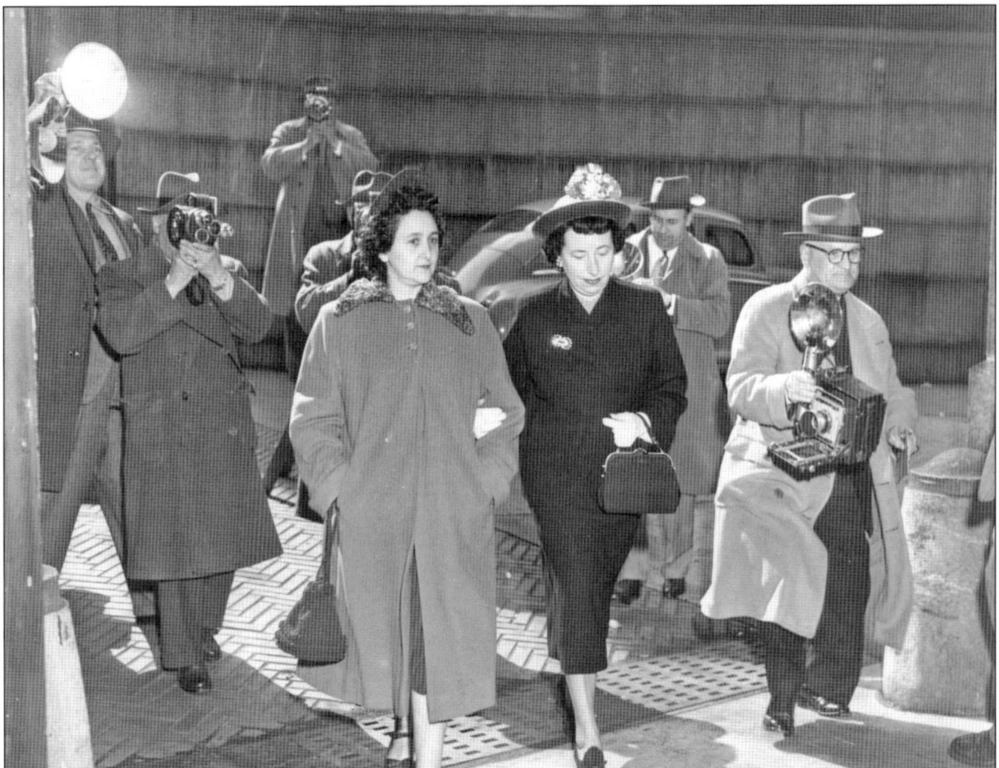

With photographers in tow, accused spy Ethel Rosenberg (left) makes her way past federal court in 1951. Eddie Jackson is at far right, trailed by Frank Hurley. The newsreel men are identified as, from left to right, Charles Schlesser, Urban Santone, and Harry Hardy. (Photograph by Jules Geller.)

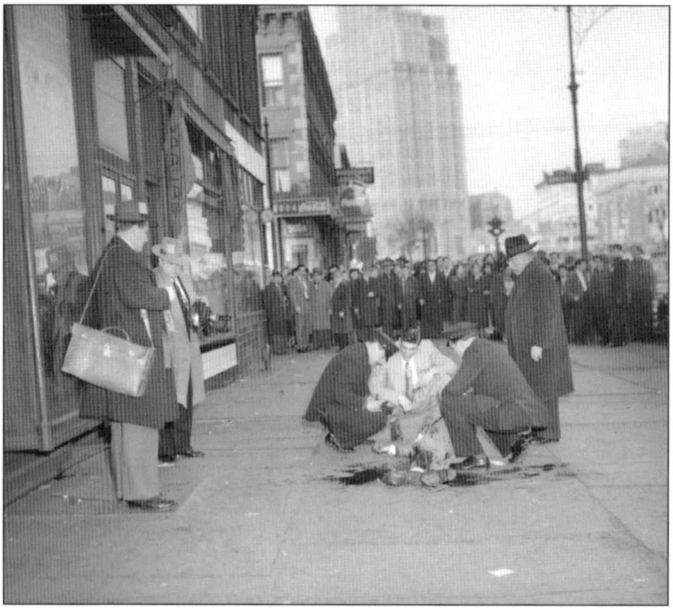

In a photograph indicative of the better access to crime scenes once afforded to the press, two photographers, with police press cards prominently displayed in their hats, get a close-up look at the aftermath of a 1951 shoot-out on Fourth Avenue in Brooklyn. The crowd of onlookers is kept at bay. (Courtesy of the New York City Municipal Archives.)

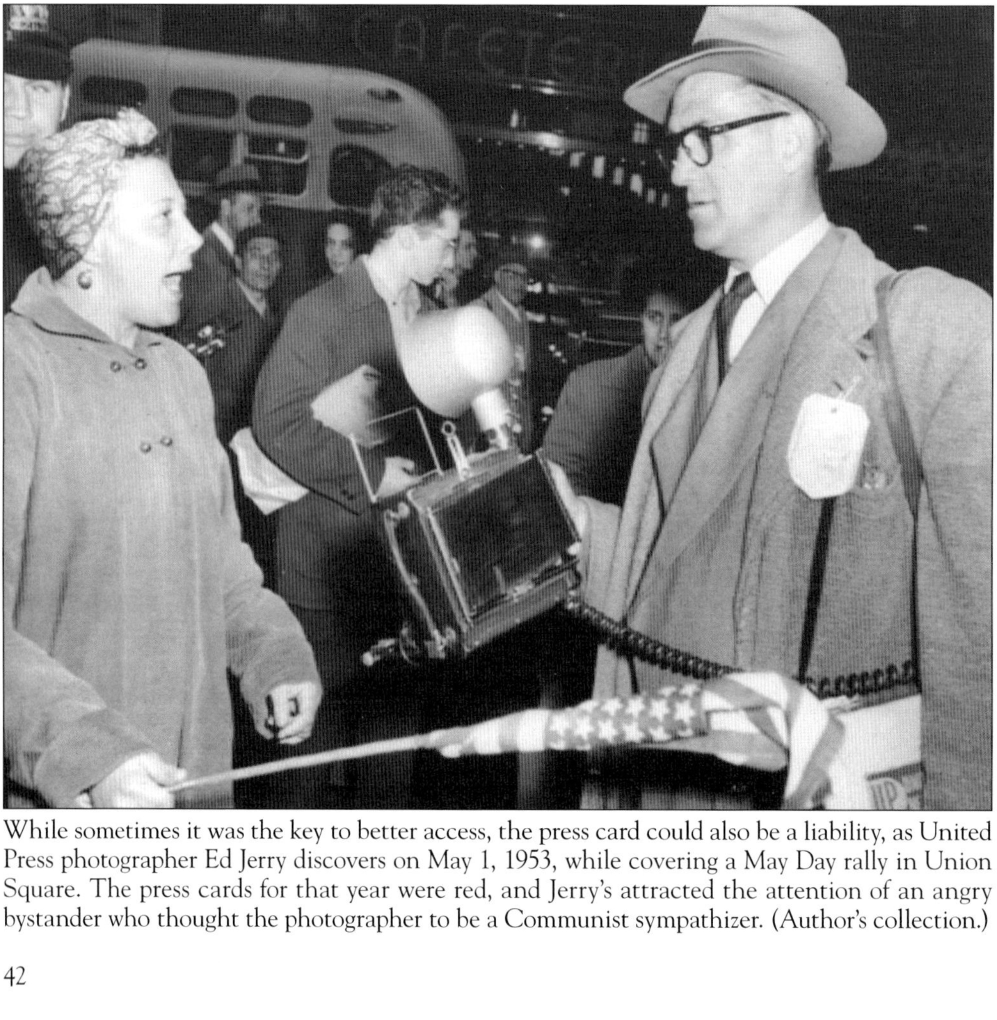

While sometimes it was the key to better access, the press card could also be a liability, as United Press photographer Ed Jerry discovers on May 1, 1953, while covering a May Day rally in Union Square. The press cards for that year were red, and Jerry's attracted the attention of an angry bystander who thought the photographer to be a Communist sympathizer. (Author's collection.)

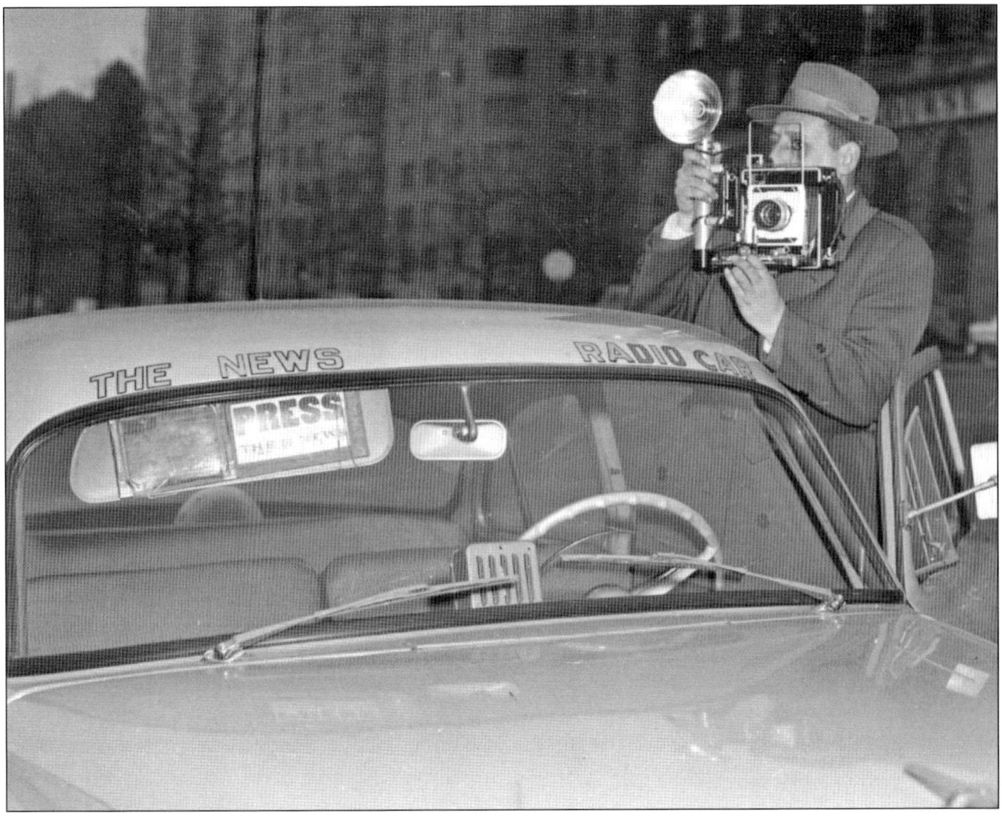

Daily News photographer Ossie Leviness is pictured with one of the vehicles from the radio car fleet in 1954. This Dodge Meadowbrook was emblazoned with the *News* logo on all sides. A police-issue press photographer vehicle card, as well as the placard of the *News*, is affixed to the passenger-side sun visor. (Courtesy of the *Daily News*.)

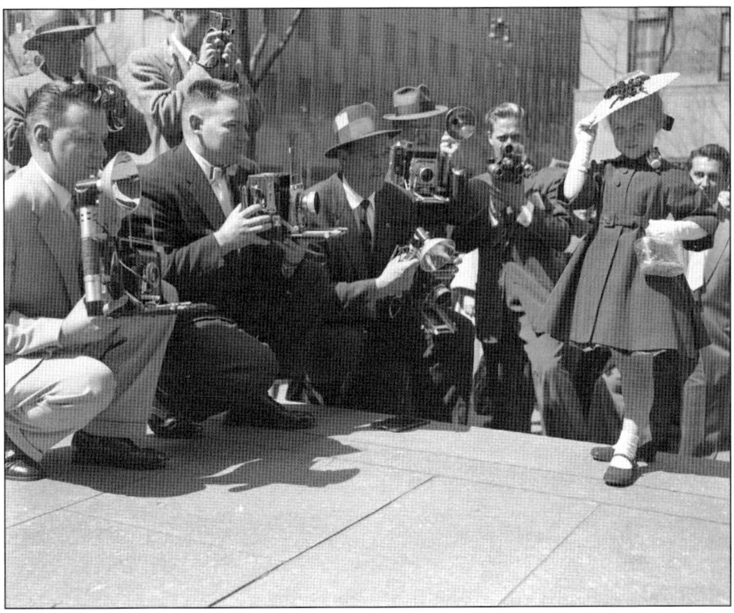

Seen on the steps of St. Patrick's Cathedral, four-year-old Sherry Brazz of Newark steals the spotlight during the annual Easter parade down Fifth Avenue on April 11, 1955. (Photograph by Ed Clarity; courtesy of the *Daily News*.)

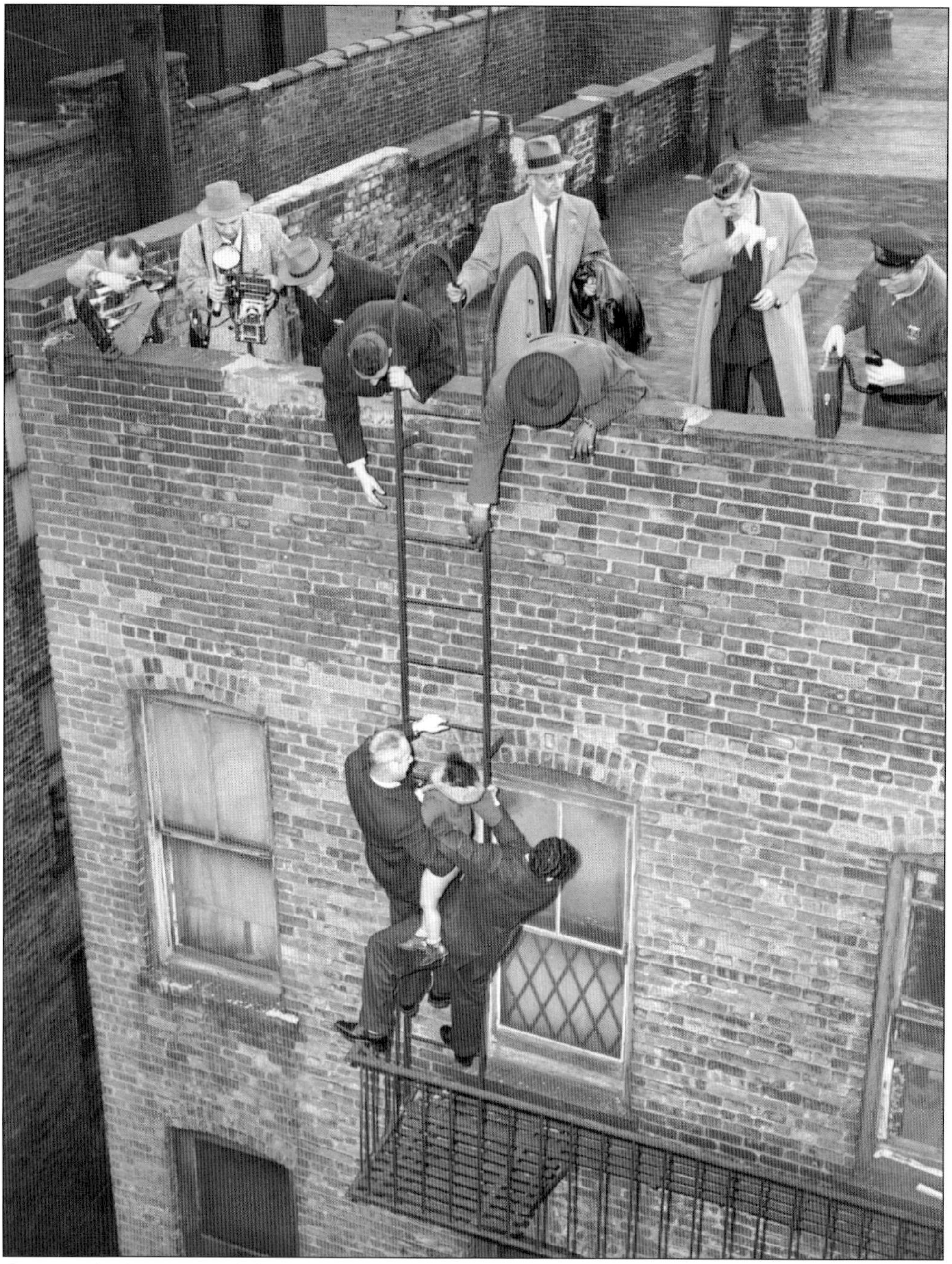

Getting the best view of the action, photographers stand shoulder to shoulder with cops as Det. James Fleming carries two-year-old Antonia Archeval up the fire escape of an East 112th Street building during a shoot-out on February 21, 1955. (Photograph by Charles Payne; courtesy of the *Daily News*.)

Photographers await Ann Woodward's departure from the Doctors Hospital on November 21, 1955. Woodward was believed to have killed her husband, though she was never indicted. From left to right are (first row) Bob Wendlinger and Fred Morgan; (second row) Tony Camerano, Carl Gossett Jr., Art Abfier, Frank Wurzel, and Ed Clarity. (Photograph by Dave McLane.)

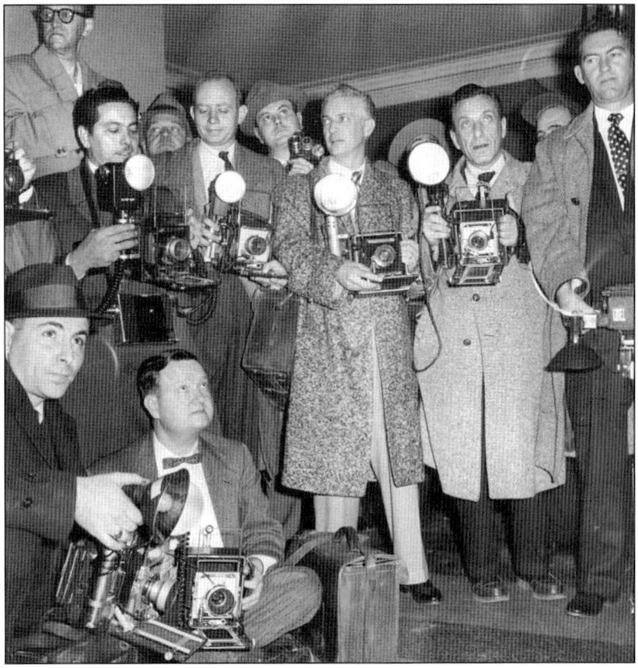

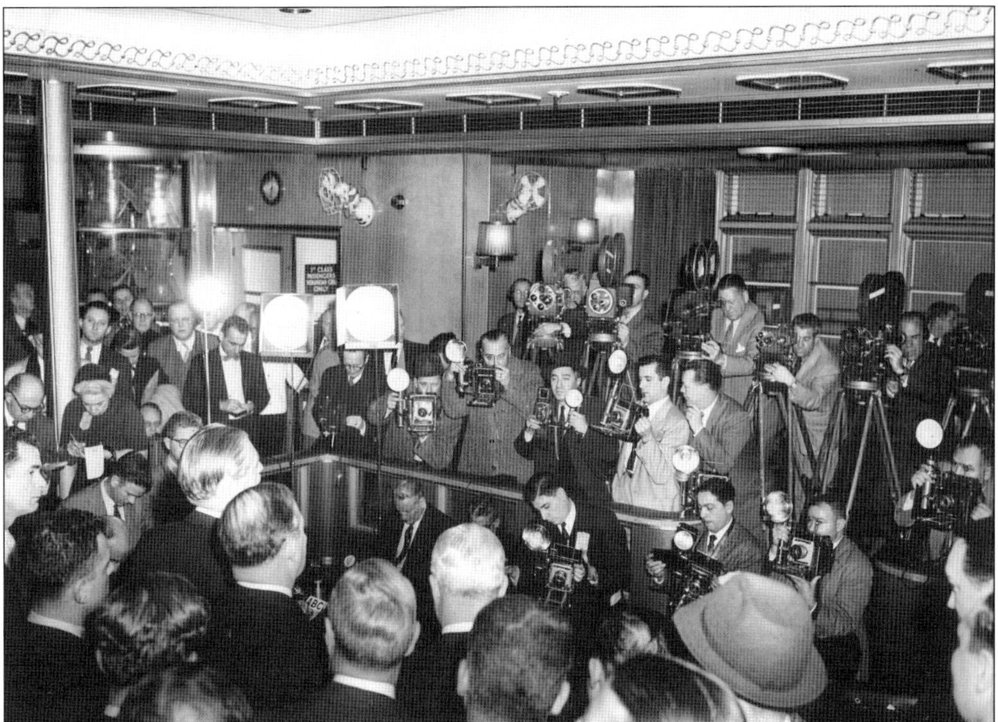

Photographers crowd aboard the *Queen Elizabeth* in 1956 to document the arrival of British prime minister Anthony Eden. Note that not all photographers are following the custom of doffing their hats while in an enclosed space. In addition, by the mid-1950s, the trend was to wear the press card upon the lapel, though some older photographers continued to wear it in their hats.

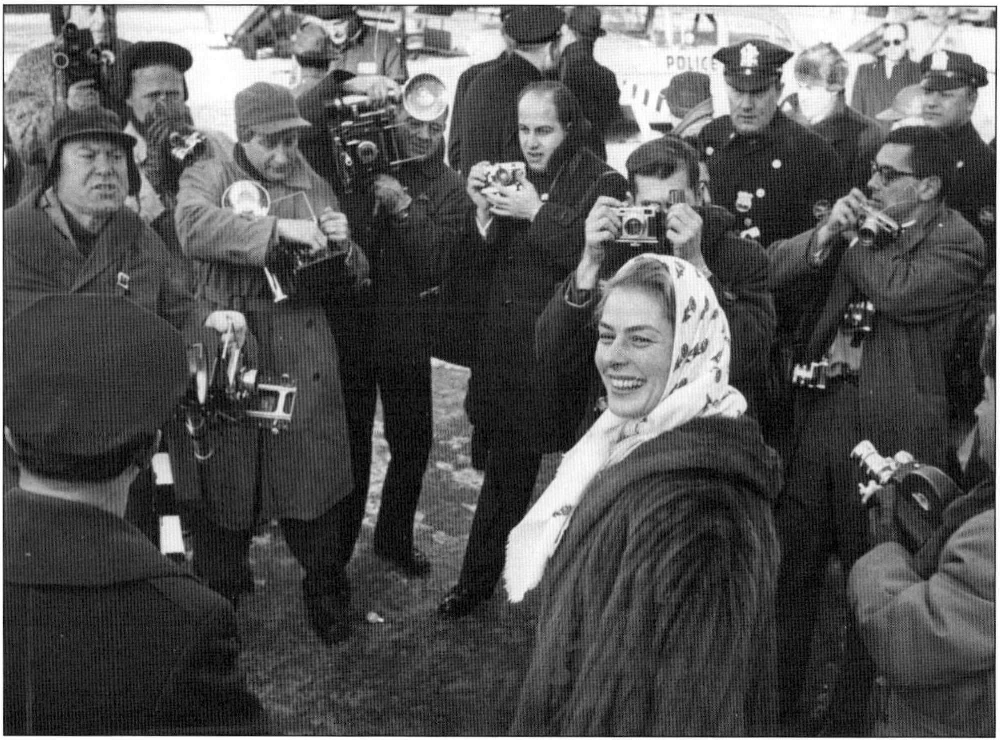

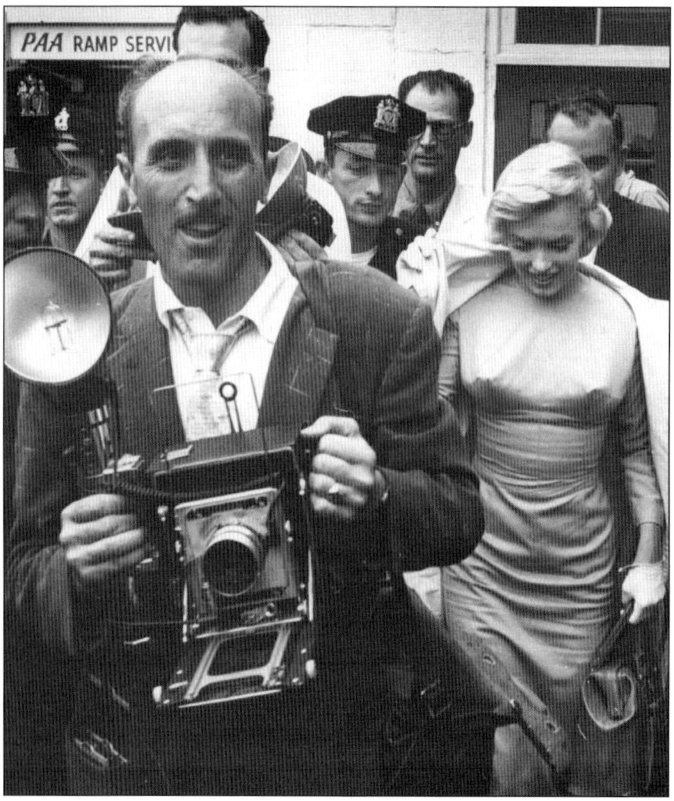

Ingrid Bergman beams as photographers surround her in 1956. Three photographers are still using their large-format four-by-five-inch Speed Graphics, while three others have opted for smaller, lighter 35-millimeter cameras.

Tony Sande of the United Press clearly has no objection to his assignment for the day—photographing Marilyn Monroe at Idlewild Airport. He is equipped with the Pacemaker version of the Speed Graphic camera, introduced in 1947, along with an electronic strobe flash. This eliminated the need to carry single-use flashbulbs but required a heavy battery pack, usually slung over the shoulder.

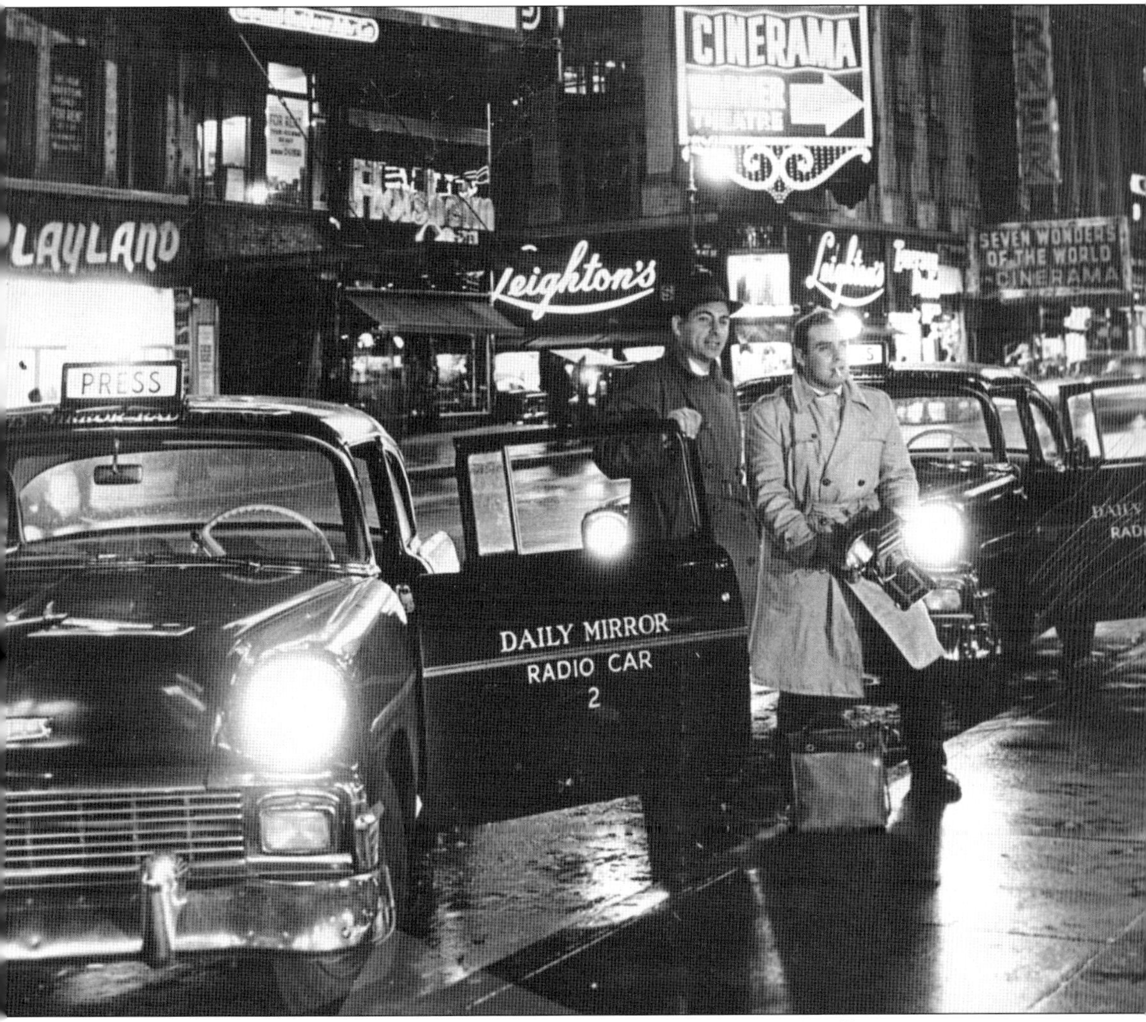

Daily Mirror photographer Bob Wendlinger (let) and an unidentified colleague convene in a rain-slicked Times Square in 1956. Wendlinger was assigned Radio Car No. 2, replete with an illuminated PRESS sign on the roof. A flick of a switch would set the sign blinking when responding to a story. A single parent, Wendlinger often brought his children with him to work. (Courtesy of Patti Wendlinger Rosen.)

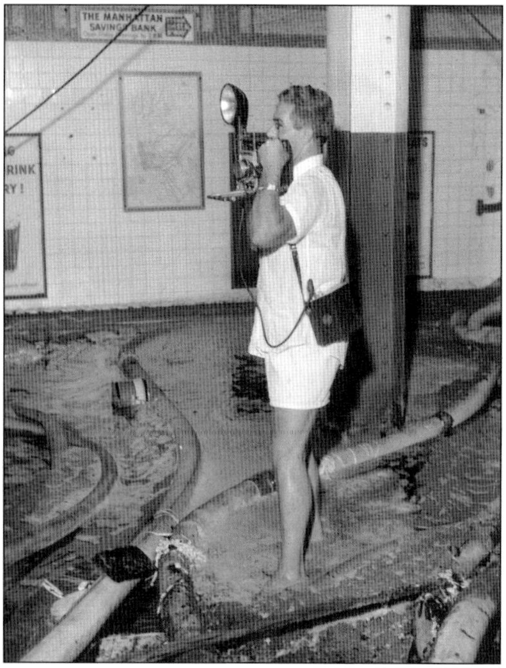

United Press photographer Andrew Lopez has divested himself of shoes, socks, and trousers to wade through the flooded subway station at Eighth Street and Broadway as flames engulf the Wanamaker's department store above. (Author's collection.)

On September 26, 1957, a tragic accident occurred on an elevated section of the Seventh Avenue subway line at 230th Street in the Bronx. An empty train rammed into the rear of another, killing the motorman. A photographer has made it to the roof of the wreckage for a clear vantage point of the rescue efforts. (Courtesy of the *Daily News.*)

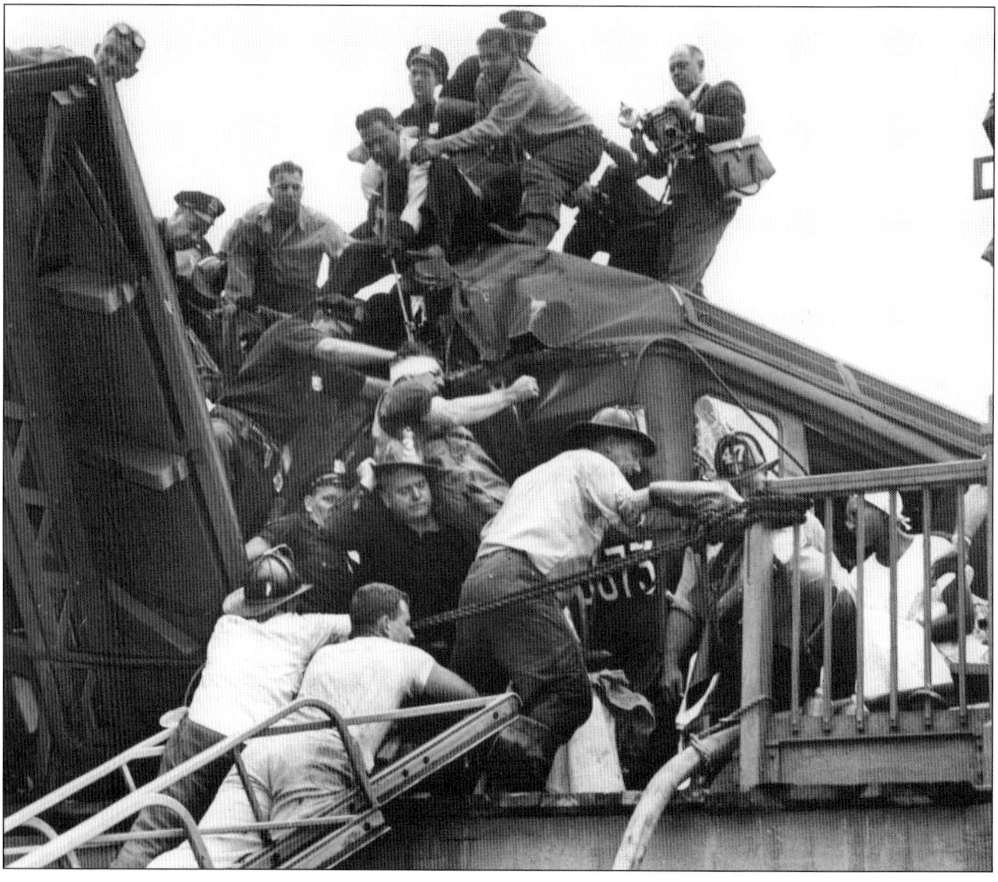

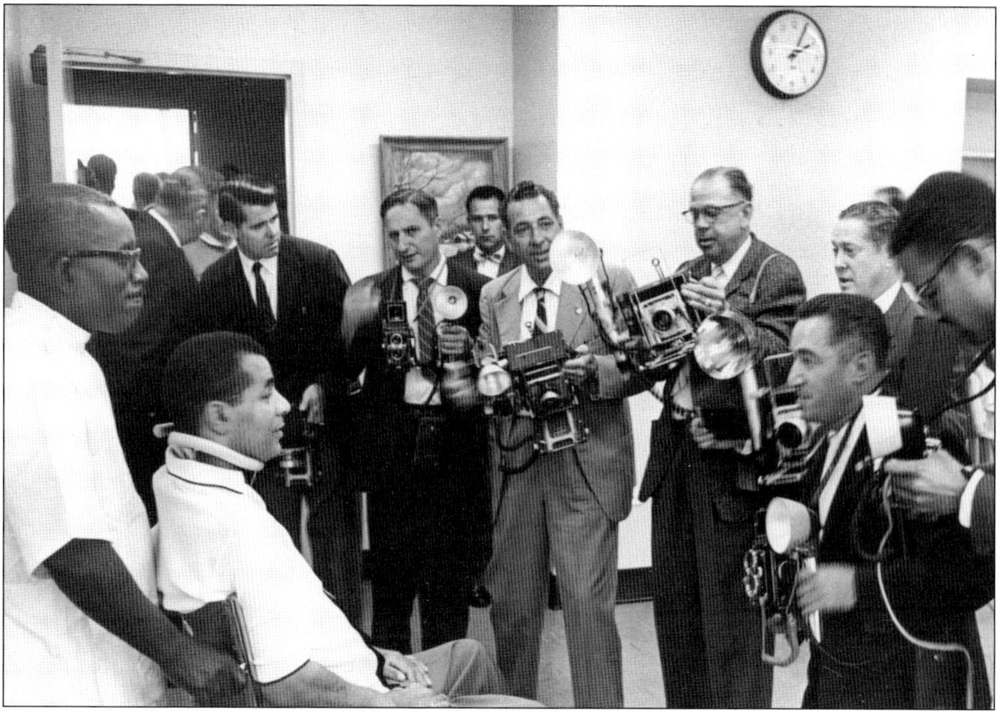

After a long, grueling rehabilitation following a 1958 automobile accident that left him mostly paralyzed, Brooklyn Dodgers catcher Roy Campanella is photographed at the hospital. (Photograph by Nat Fein.)

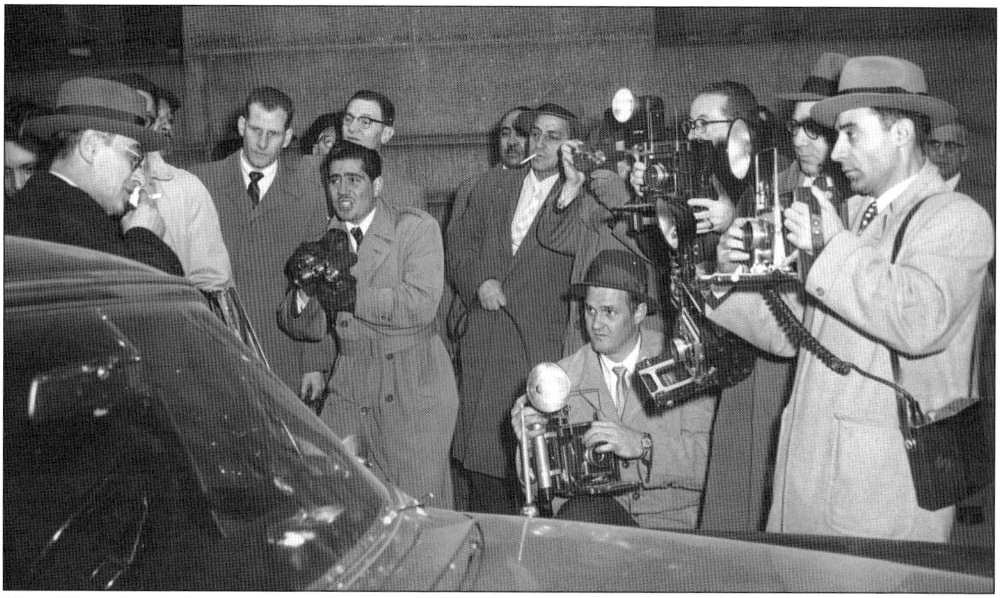

Vito "Don Vito" Genovese (far left) appears at Manhattan federal court in 1960. Known as "the Boss of All Bosses," Genovese is photographed turning himself in to begin a 15-year sentence. *New York Post* photographer Lou Liotta is seen at far right. Herb Schwartz, a former *Sun* photographer and future association president, had become a newsreel cameraman for CBS and appears in a trench coat to the right of Genovese.

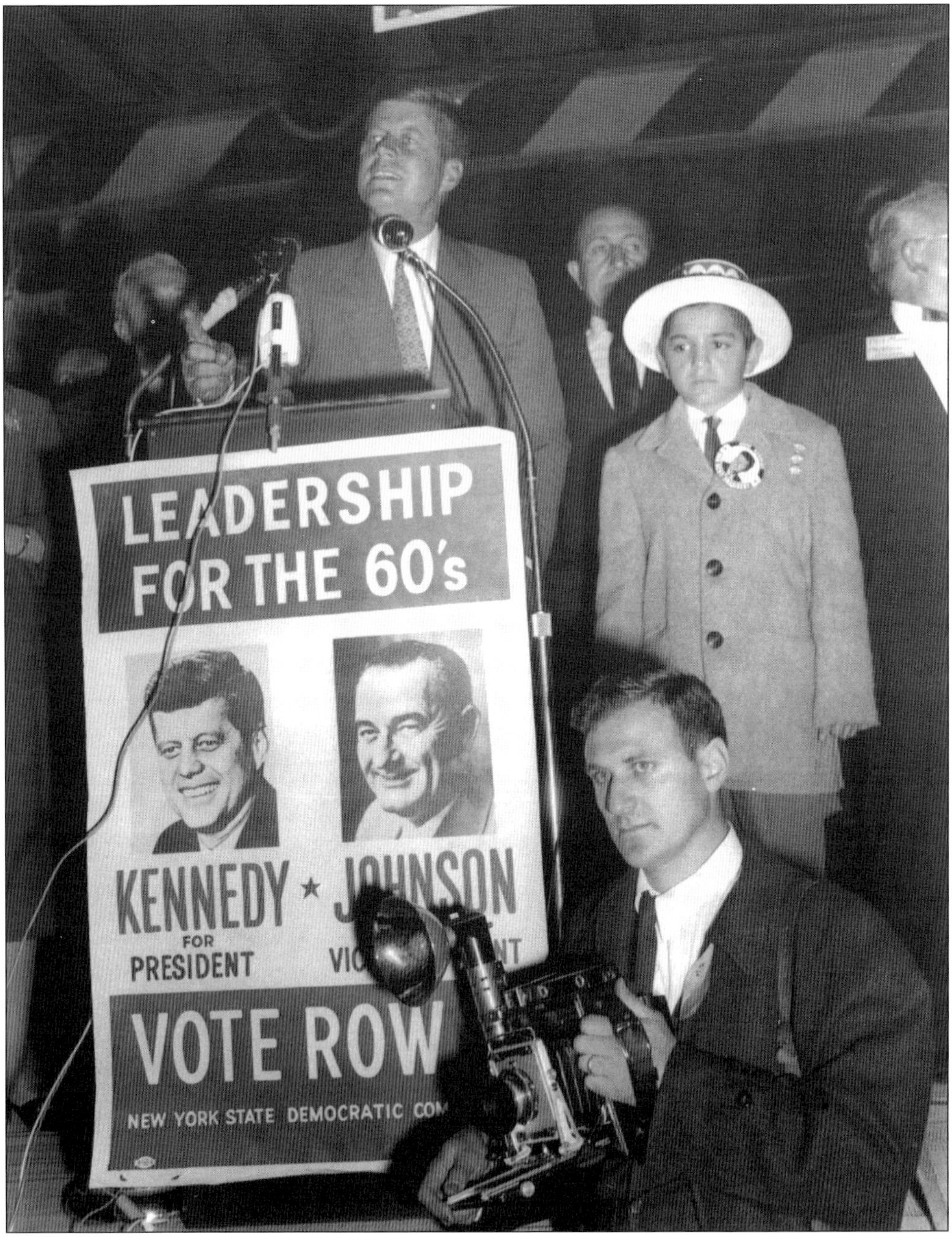

Staten Islander Jim Romano covers Sen. John F. Kennedy during the 1960 presidential campaign. The good-natured Romano once told Kennedy he considered him "a leader of men . . . and a follower of women." (Courtesy of Jim Romano.)

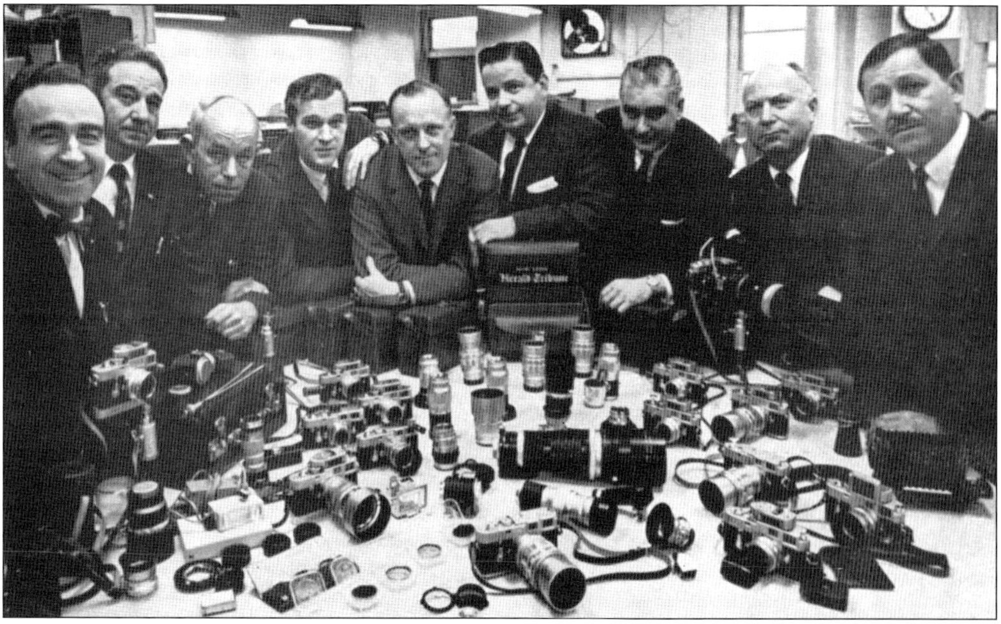

The staff of the *Journal-American* displays its latest complement of Leica cameras in 1962. From left to right are Morris Warman, Nat Fein, Don Rice, Terence McCarten, Joe Engels, James Kavallines, Robert Noble, Ted Kell, and Ira Rosenberg. According to editor Ben Price, "The boys on the staff tell me they couldn't be happier with the equipment."

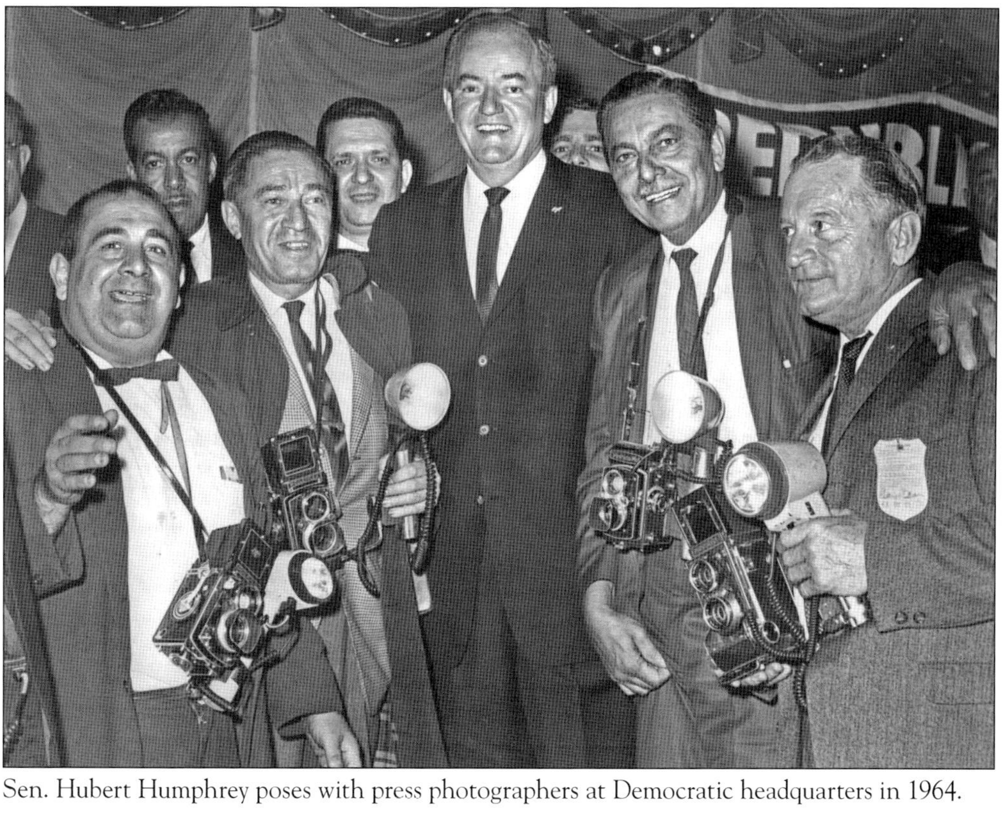

Sen. Hubert Humphrey poses with press photographers at Democratic headquarters in 1964.

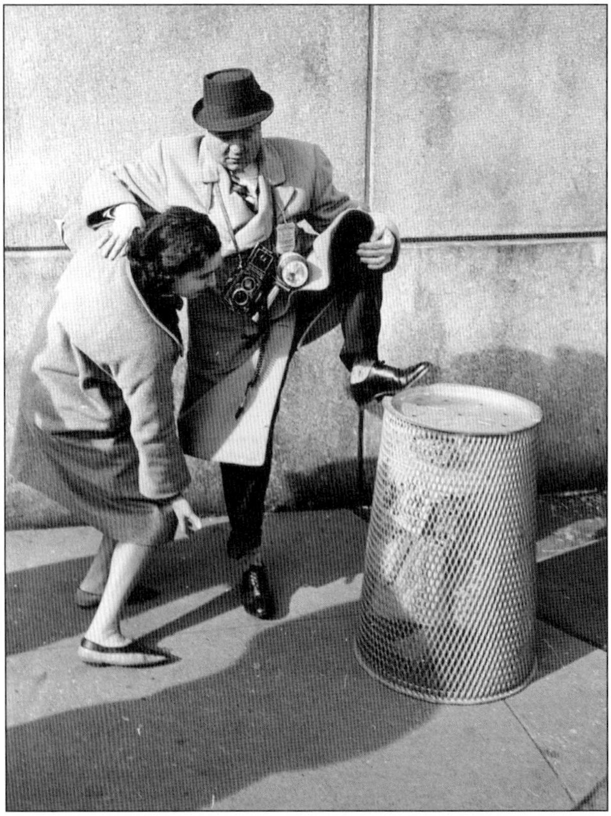

A photographer gets a boost atop an overturned trash can to gain some height on a story. His Rolleiflex twin-lens reflex camera, Strobonar electronic flash, and press card hanging from the lapel were the standard uniform of the photojournalist in the mid-1960s.

Seen outside the Madison Avenue Presbyterian Church, photographers cover the funeral of Susan Edwards Wagner, wife of Mayor Robert F. Wagner, on March 5, 1964. At the corner of the barricade is Paul Rice (far left) of the *Journal-American*. (Author's collection.)

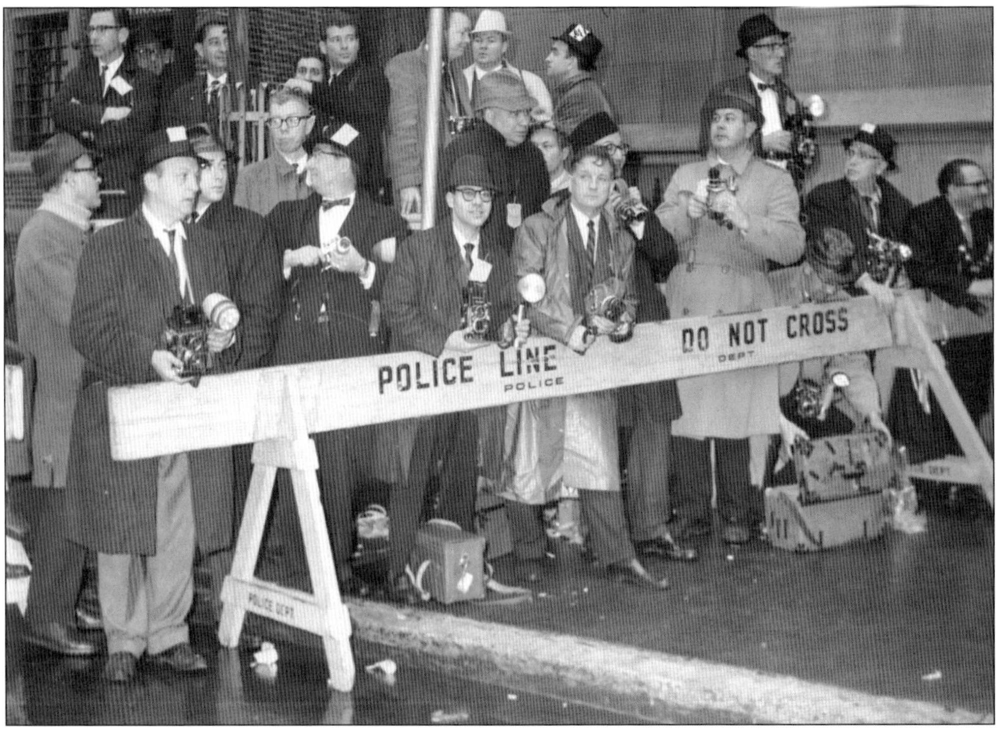

A ticker tape parade moves up Broadway's Canyon of Heroes around 1964. Photographers had the option of walking alongside the vehicle carrying the day's honoree, staking out positions in windows along the route, or riding on large trucks that preceded the celebrity. These folks have chosen the latter.

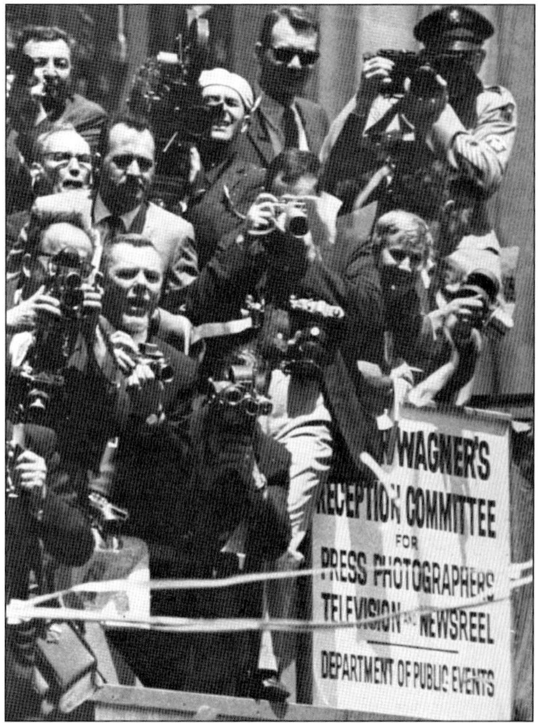

Calling in to the home office was almost as important as getting the picture. In an era before cellular phones and pagers, photographers would often make a mad dash to the nearest telephone booth to update their editors and receive further instructions. From left to right are William Jacobellis, Emil Herman, Harry Harris, and Joe Petrella. (Photograph by Ed Sisto.)

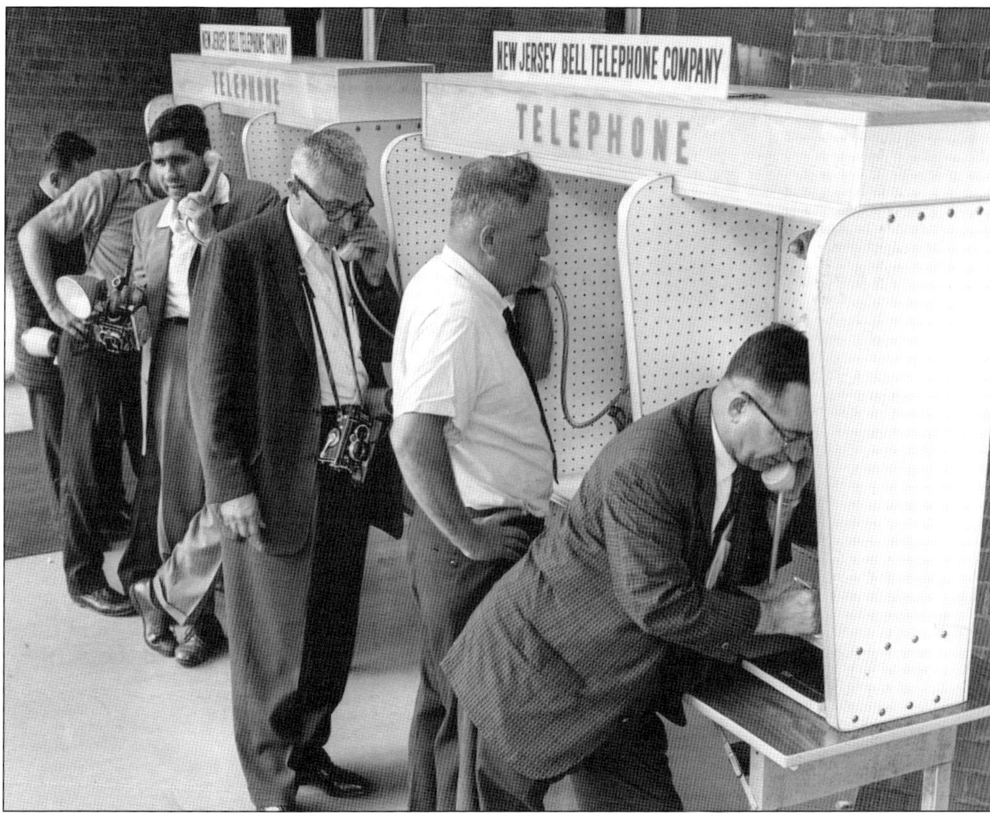

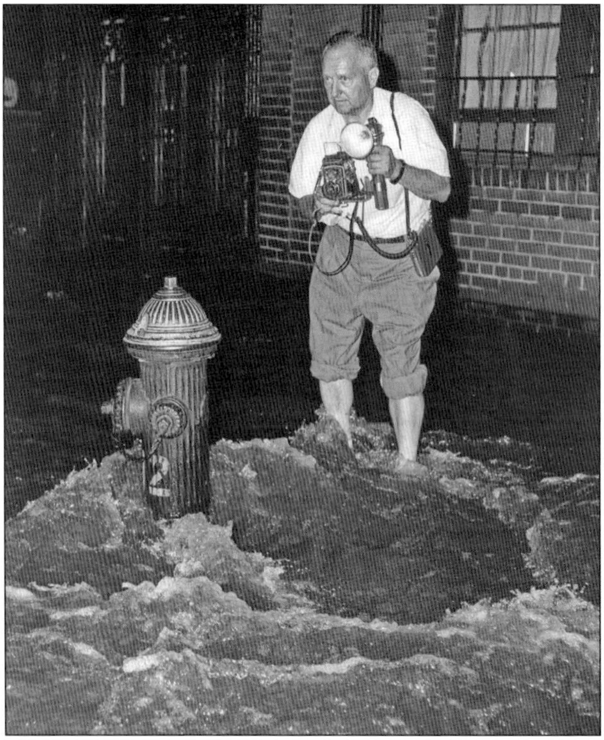

Len Morgan of the *Journal-American* rolls up his trousers and immerses himself in the story. This time, it involves a 4:00 a.m. water main break on the Lower East Side of Manhattan in June 1965.

Herald-Tribune photographer Ira Rosenberg gets the picture of new police commissioner Howard Leary, seated at far right, at his first press conference, held on March 1, 1966. After a turbulent tenure, Leary resigned in 1970. (Photograph by Barney Stein.)

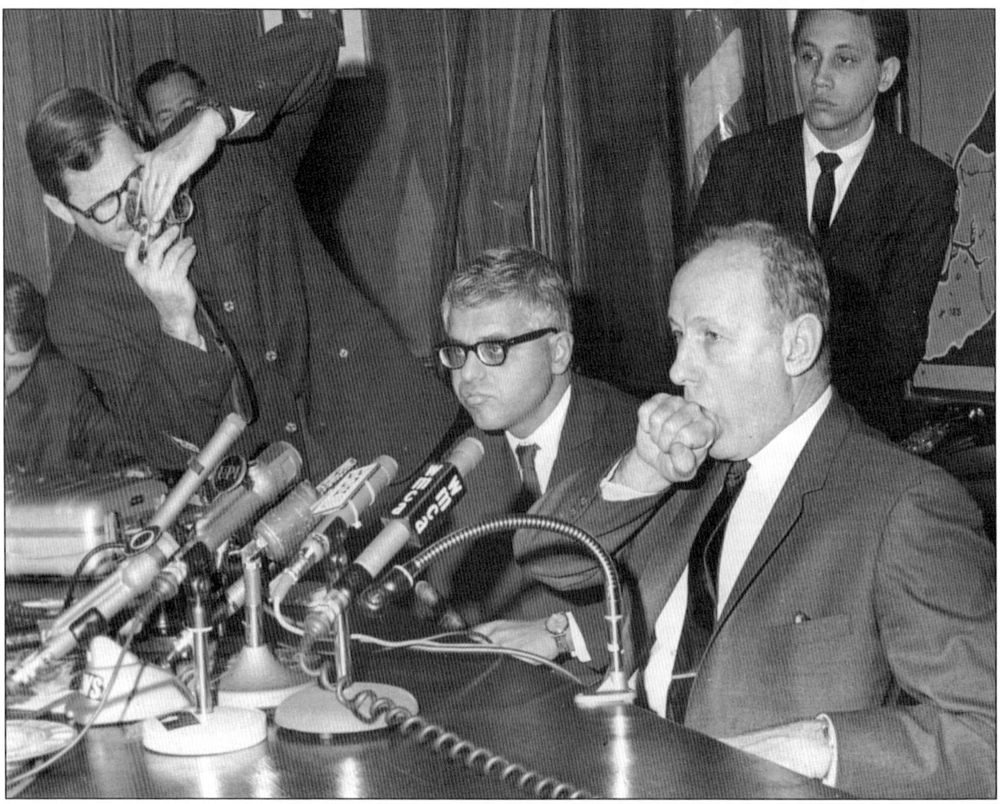

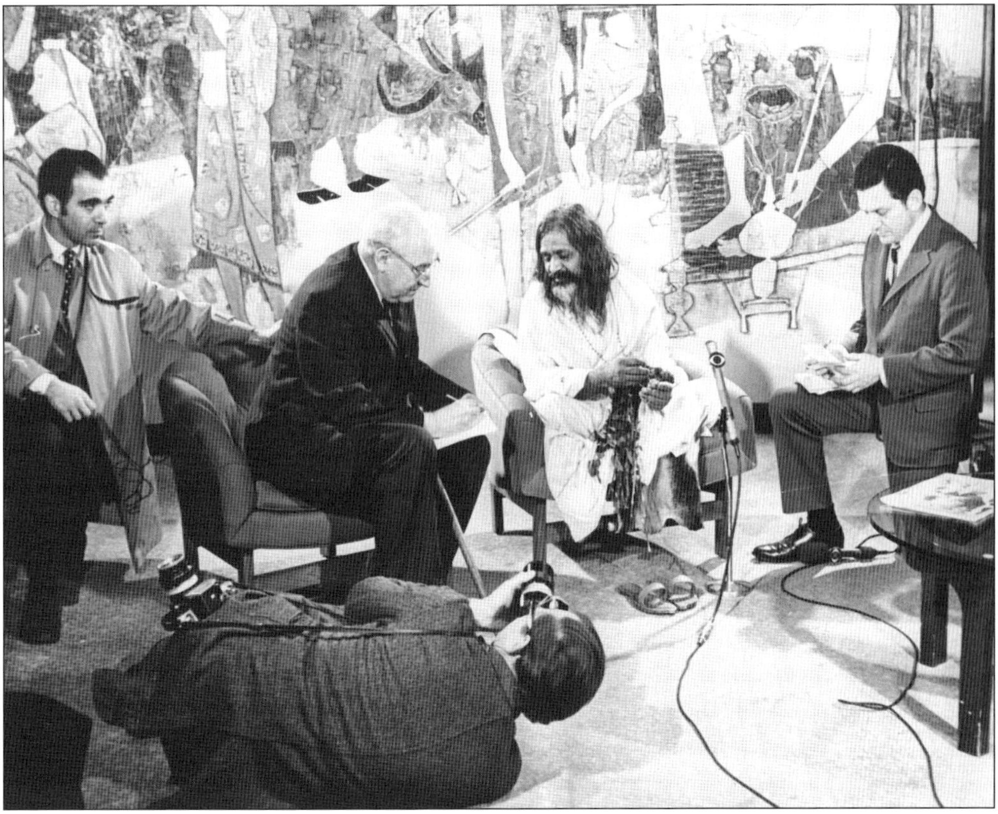

A photographer goes horizontal to get a vertical shot of the Maharishi Mahesh Yogi on January 23, 1968. Along with Mia Farrow, the guru had delivered a lecture to Harvard Law School students before returning to India. (Photograph by Jerry Engel.)

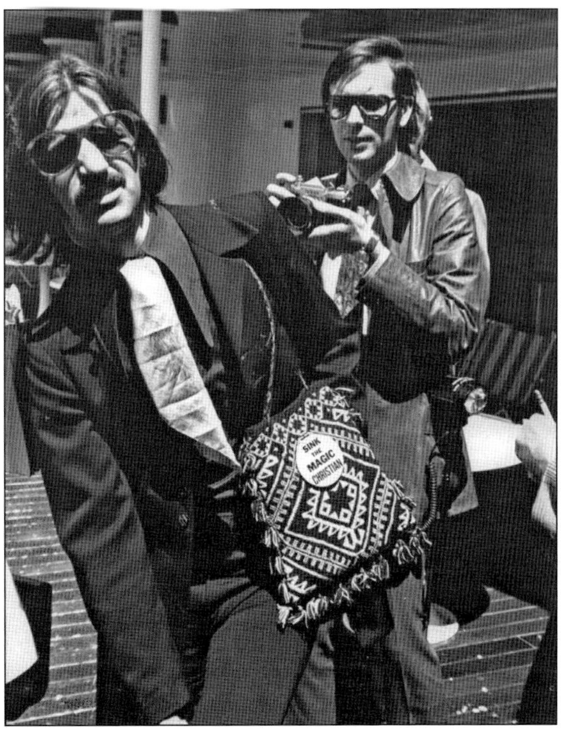

Photographed by Tom Monaster of the *Daily News*, Ringo Starr of the Beatles arrives in New York aboard the *Queen Elizabeth II* in 1969. Monaster is known for his portfolio of portraits of celebrities, many of whom got to know him very well over the years. (Photograph by Frank Hurley.)

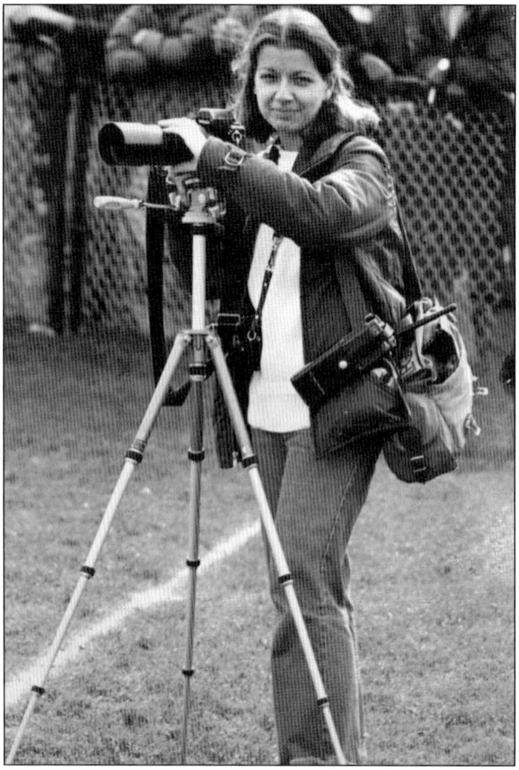

Mary DiBiase is on assignment for the *Daily News* in the 1970s. She carries a portable radio, which allowed the photo desk to communicate with her in the field. In 1979, when mob boss Carmine Galante was shot in the backyard of a Brooklyn restaurant, a cigar still clenched in his teeth, Mary was among the photographers to snap the iconic view from an adjacent roof. (Courtesy of Mary DiBiase Blaich.)

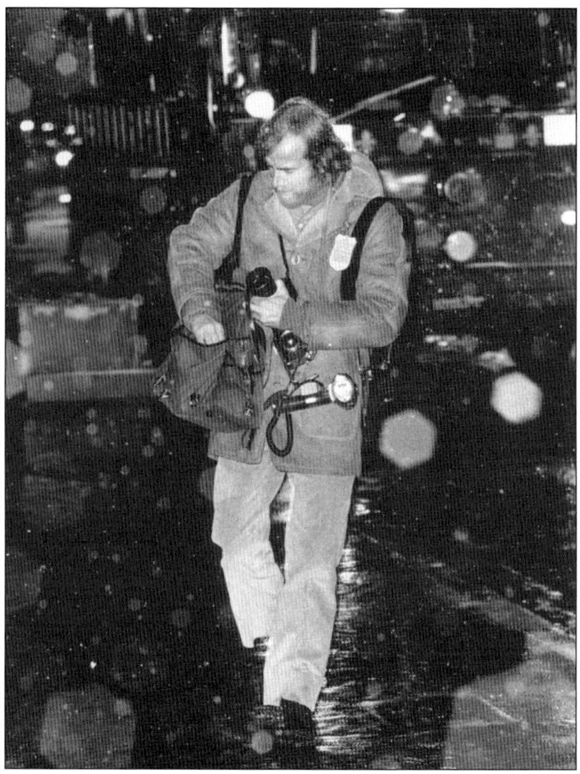

With his press card clipped to the collar of his coat, Vernon Shibla prepares his cameras upon arrival at the scene of a fire in Lower Manhattan in the late 1970s. Shibla served as a combat photographer in Vietnam before joining the *New York Post* in 1968, eventually becoming deputy photo editor. (Photograph by Tom Monaster.)

Former association president and Associated Press photographer Dave Pickoff trains a massive telephoto lens on the World Trade Center as amateur rock climber George Willig scales the south tower on May 26, 1977. (Photograph by Tom Monaster.)

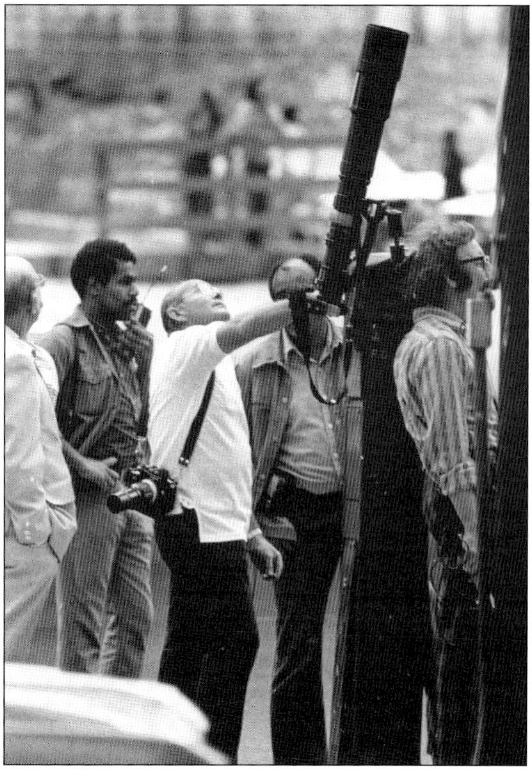

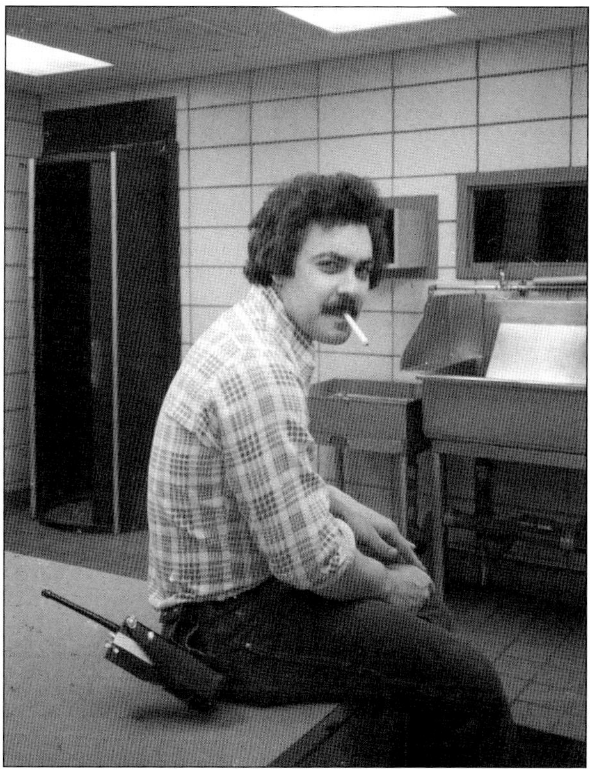

Daily News photographer Michael Lipack takes a break in the photo lab on East Forty-second Street in 1980. Lipack would eventually become director of photography for the paper and delighted in his additional role as a horse racing handicapper. (Photograph by Mary DiBiase Blaich.)

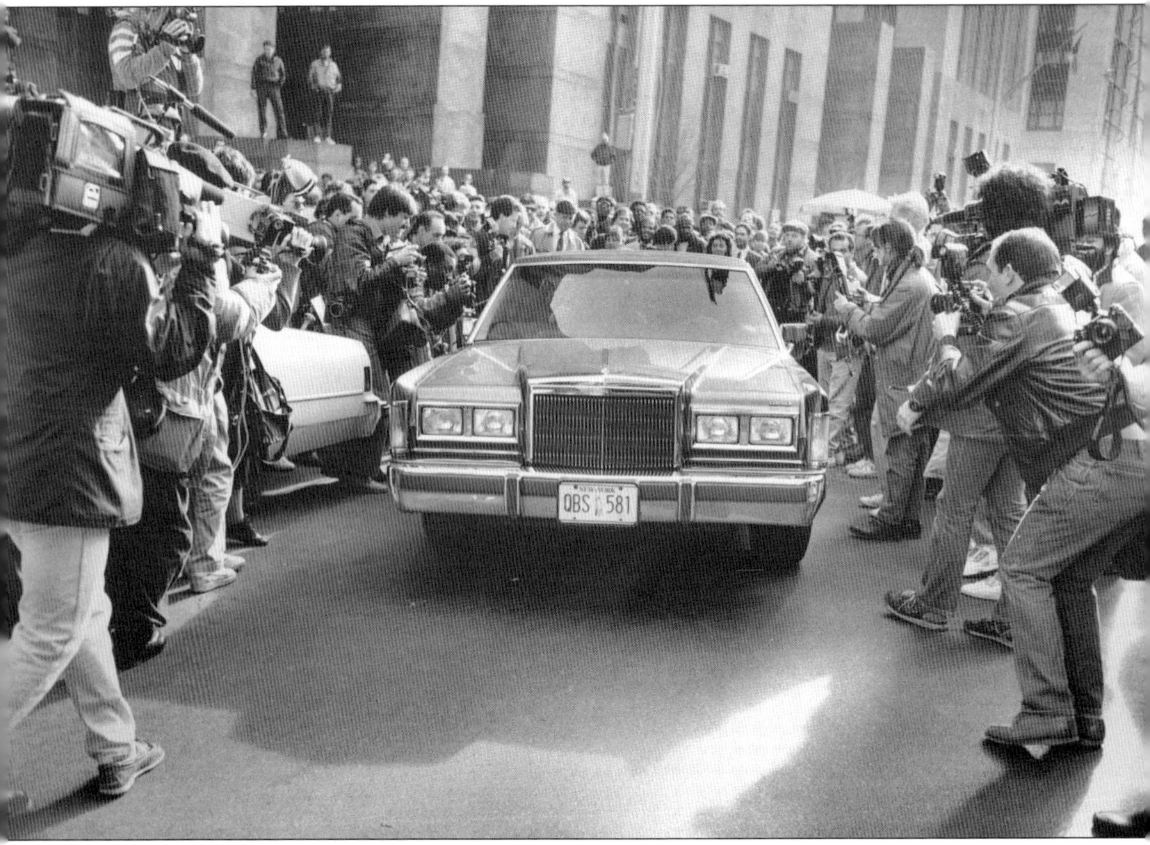

John Gotti, known as "the Dapper Don," is driven away from Manhattan Criminal Court on January 24, 1989, after posting $100,000 bail. Gotti was arrested for the 1986 shooting of a union official. He was later acquitted at trial. Throngs of photographers made it difficult for Gotti's driver to navigate Centre Street, and he supposedly ran a red light to get away. (Photograph by Misha Erwitt; courtesy of the *Daily News*.)

Two

At Leisure

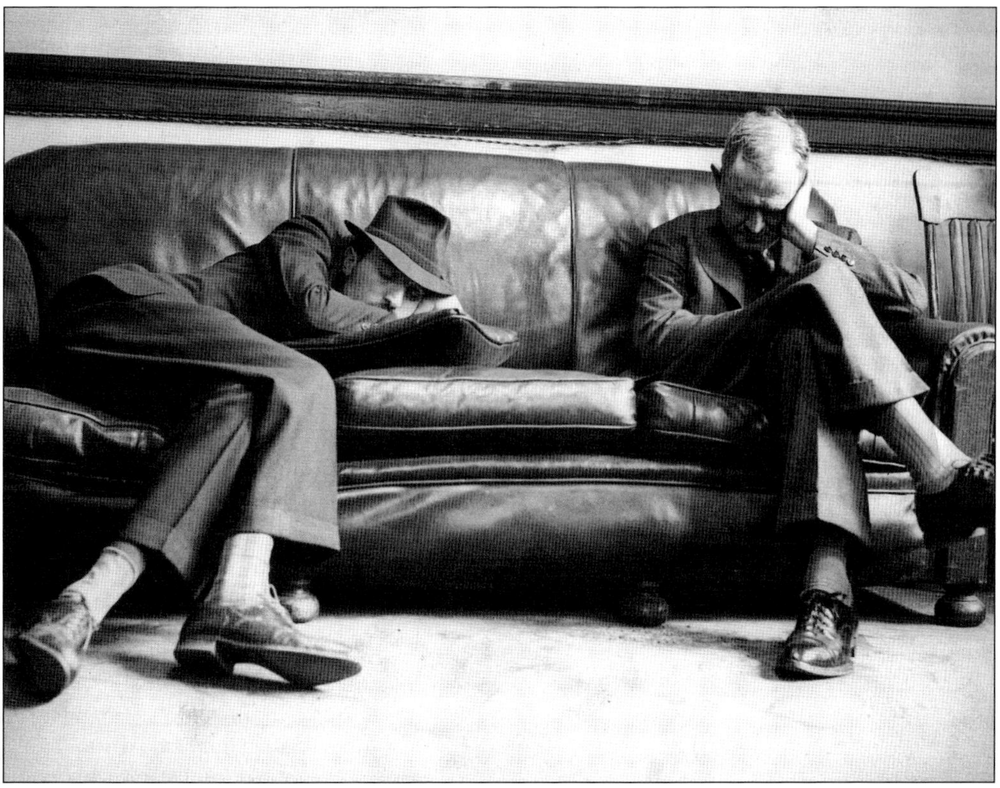

Then, as now, there were moments when the press photographer could take a break. Tony Sande and William "Doc" Skinner take a nap on the couch of the Manhattan Courts building in 1936. An incurable tinkerer, Skinner spent many waking hours perfecting prototypes of cameras and flashguns, for which he was granted at least one patent. (Photograph by John Reidy.)

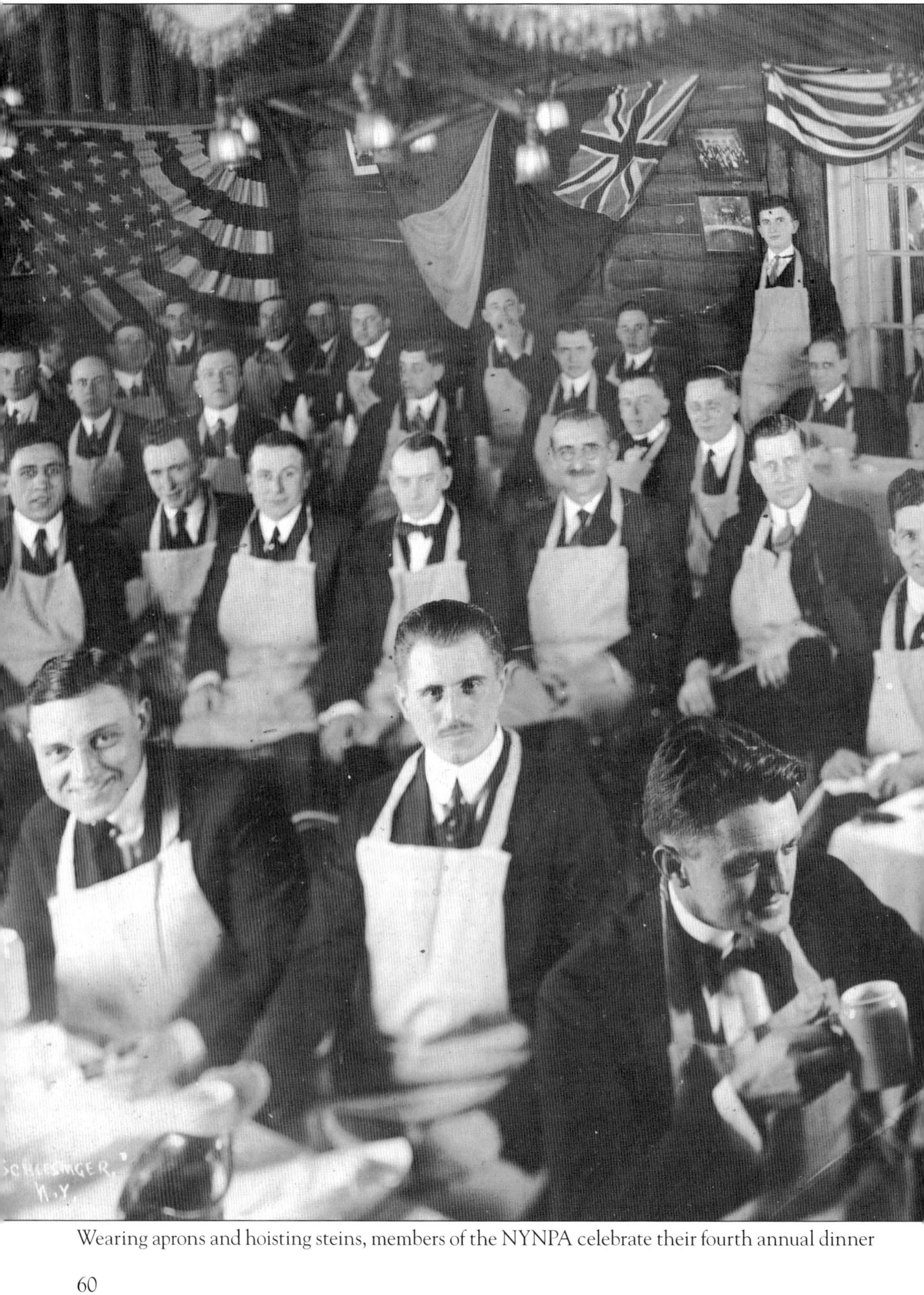

Wearing aprons and hoisting steins, members of the NYNPA celebrate their fourth annual dinner

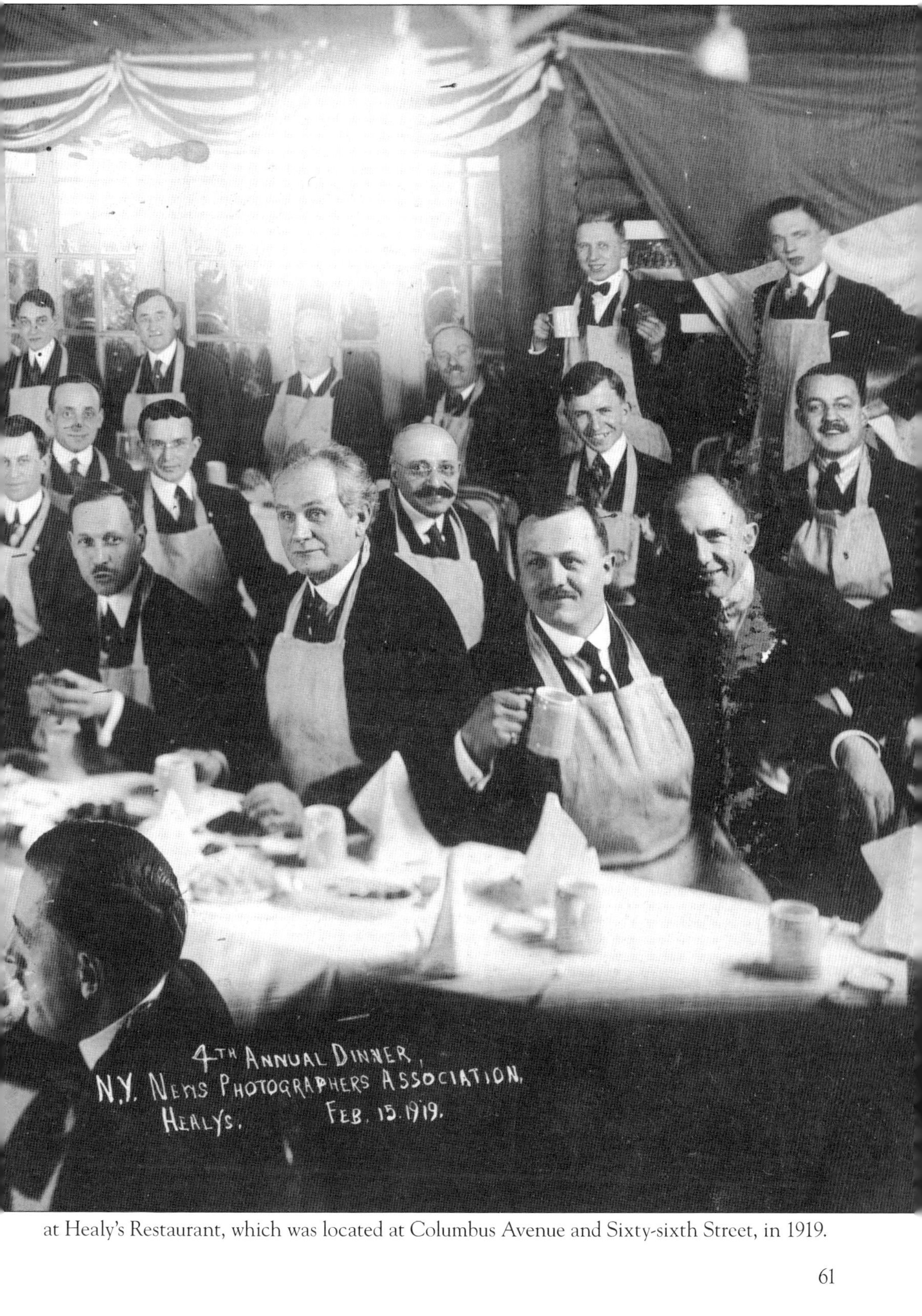

at Healy's Restaurant, which was located at Columbus Avenue and Sixty-sixth Street, in 1919.

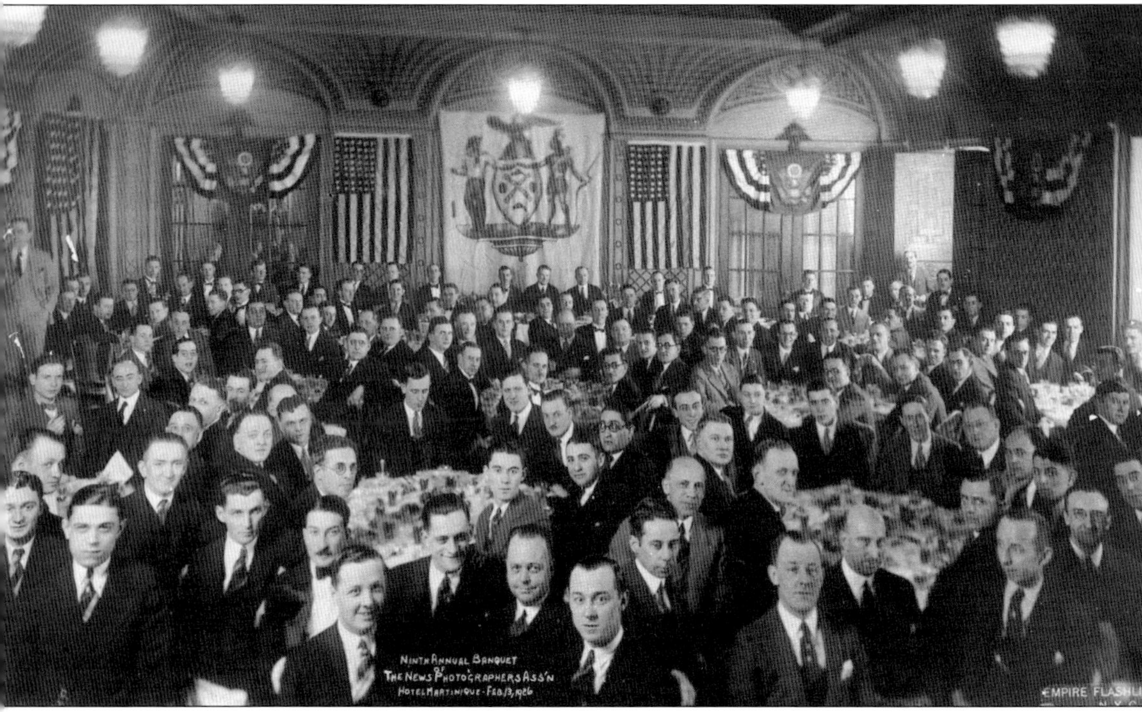

A much more formal affair than that on the previous page, this banquet was held at the Hotel Martinique near Herald Square in 1926. The association would return to the Martinique many times over the years.

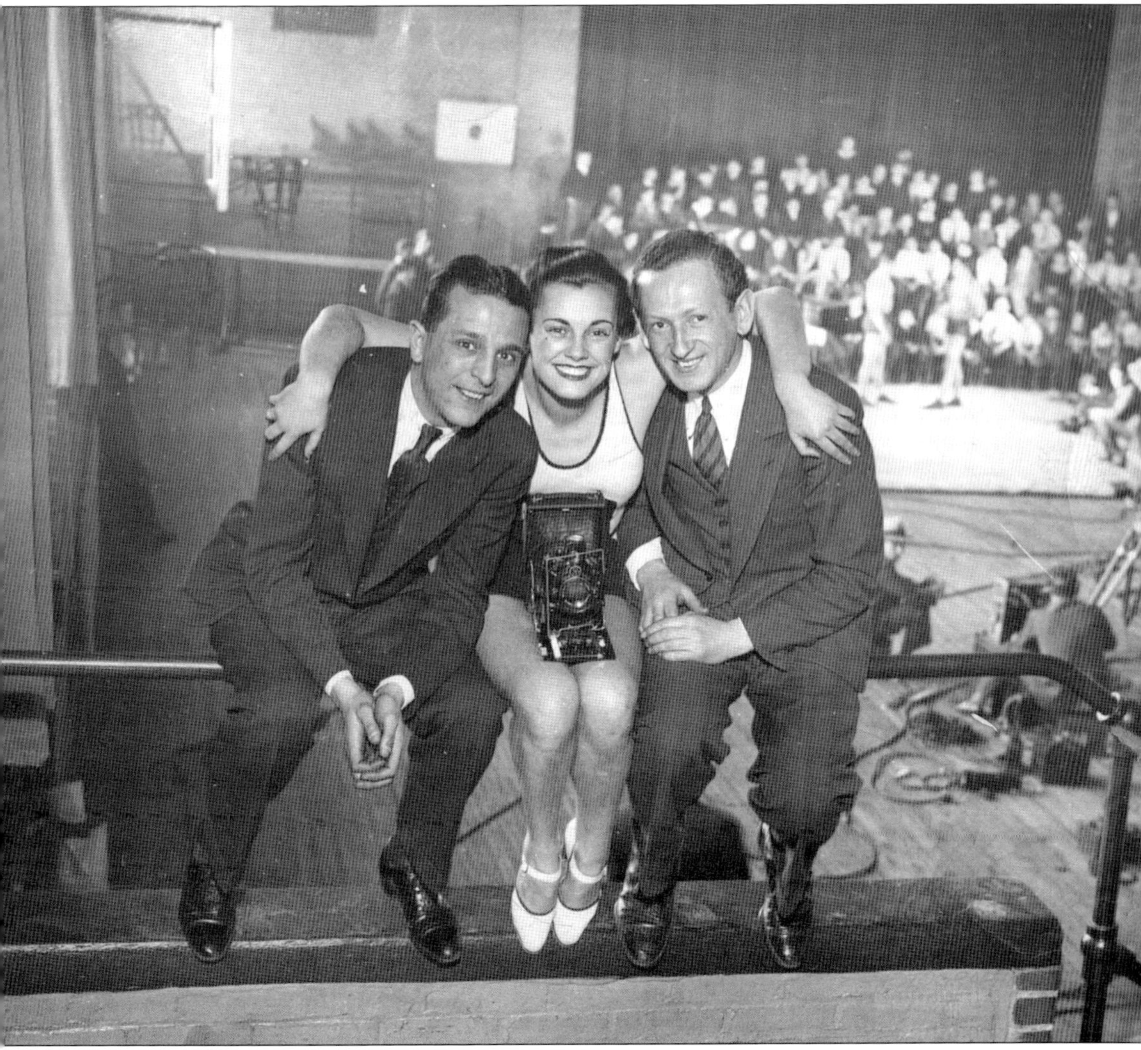

Sam Andre (left) of *Pic Magazine* and Sam Falk (right) of the *New York Times* flank Olympic swimmer and Brooklyn native Eleanor Holm, who was working on a movie in 1930.

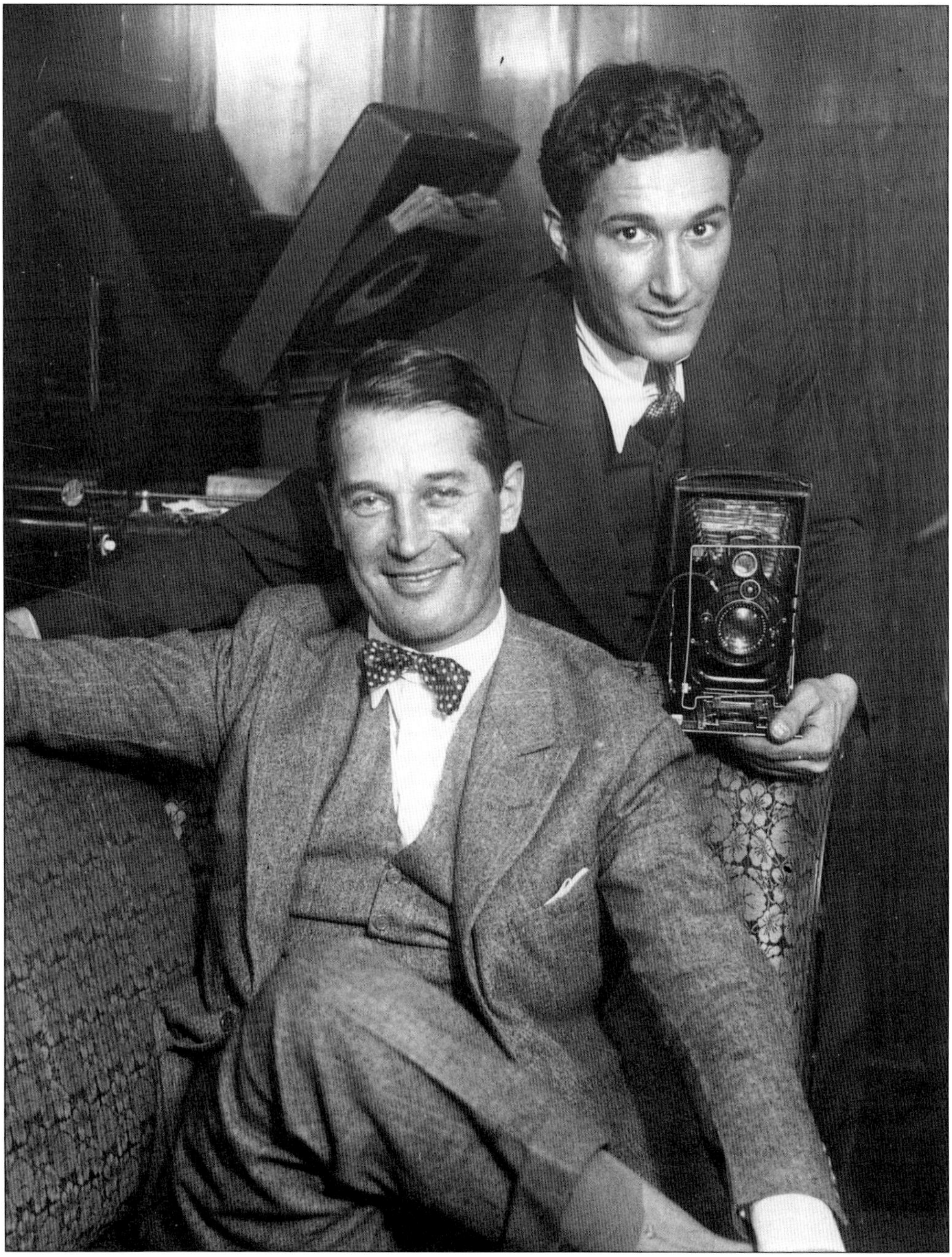

Maurice Chevalier obliges photographer Dan Grossi for a picture aboard the SS *Paris* in August 1930.

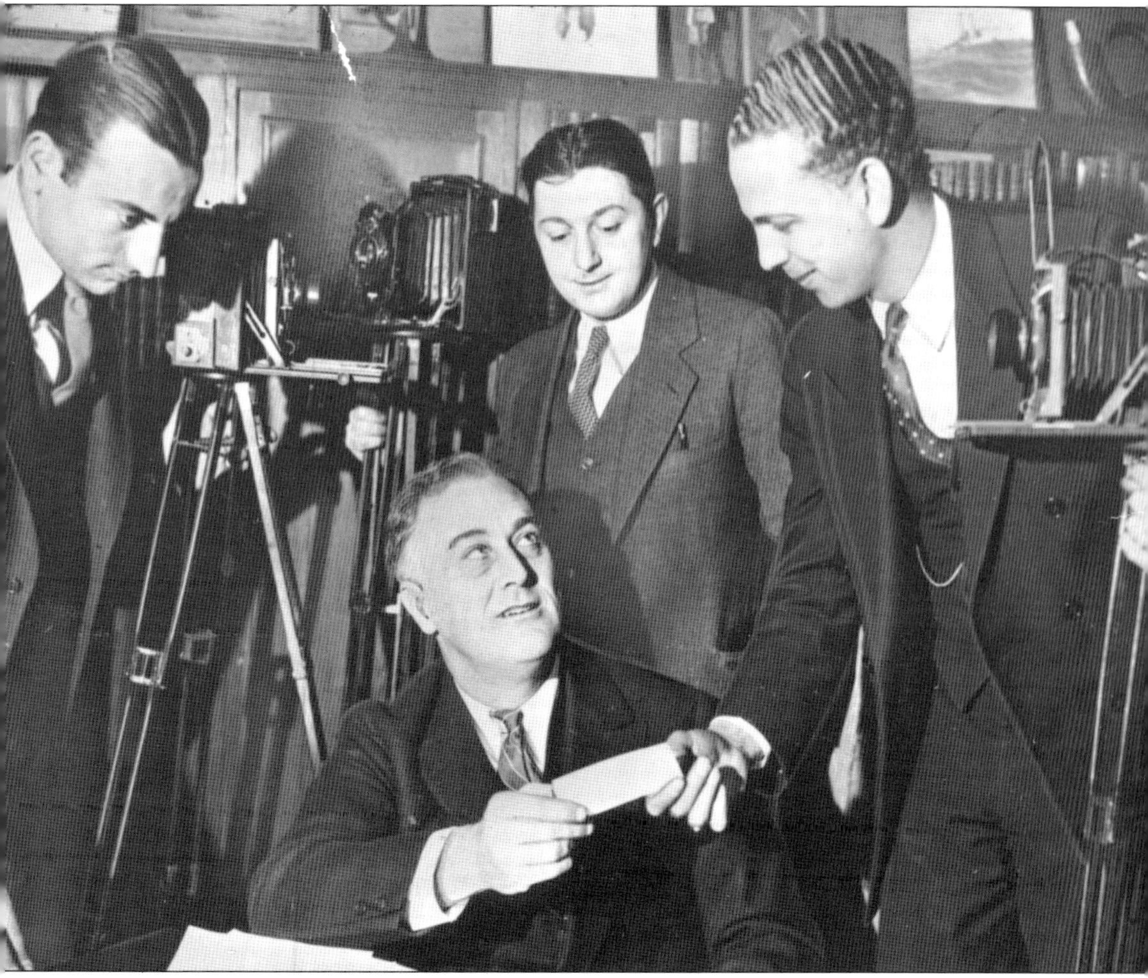

President-elect Franklin D. Roosevelt, seated, receives a hand-delivered invitation to the Press Photographers' Ball from, from left to right, Murray Becker, Al Amy, and Bill Greene on January 18, 1933. Throughout his presidency, Roosevelt sent congratulatory notes to the association for its various occasions even if he could not attend.

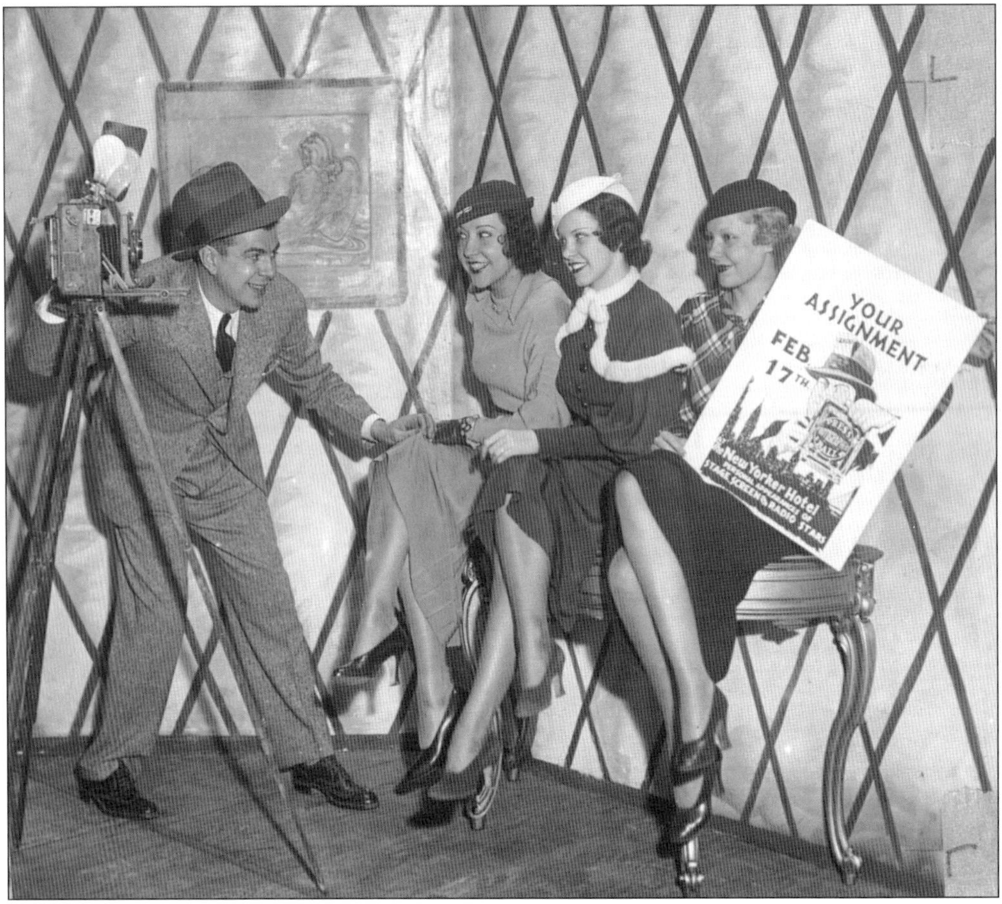

Seated from left to right, Ethel Merman, Mitzi Mayfair, and June Knight pose for comic Ken Murray, who himself poses as a photographer. The quartet was at the Hotel New Yorker to promote the 1933 Press Photographers' Ball, at which Murray was the master of ceremonies.

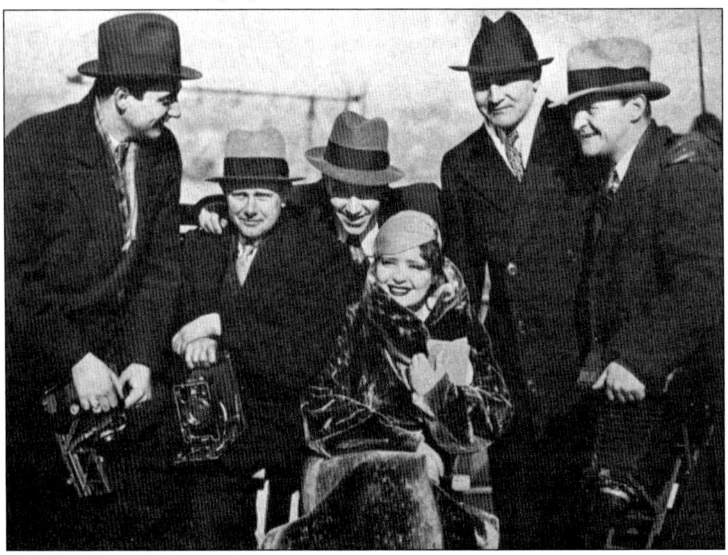

Aboard the SS *Roma* in 1934, Clara Bow is delighted to pose with, from left to right, photographers Vincent Lopez, Ed Pickwoad, Tony Quintieri, Michael Barron, and Tommy Flanagan.

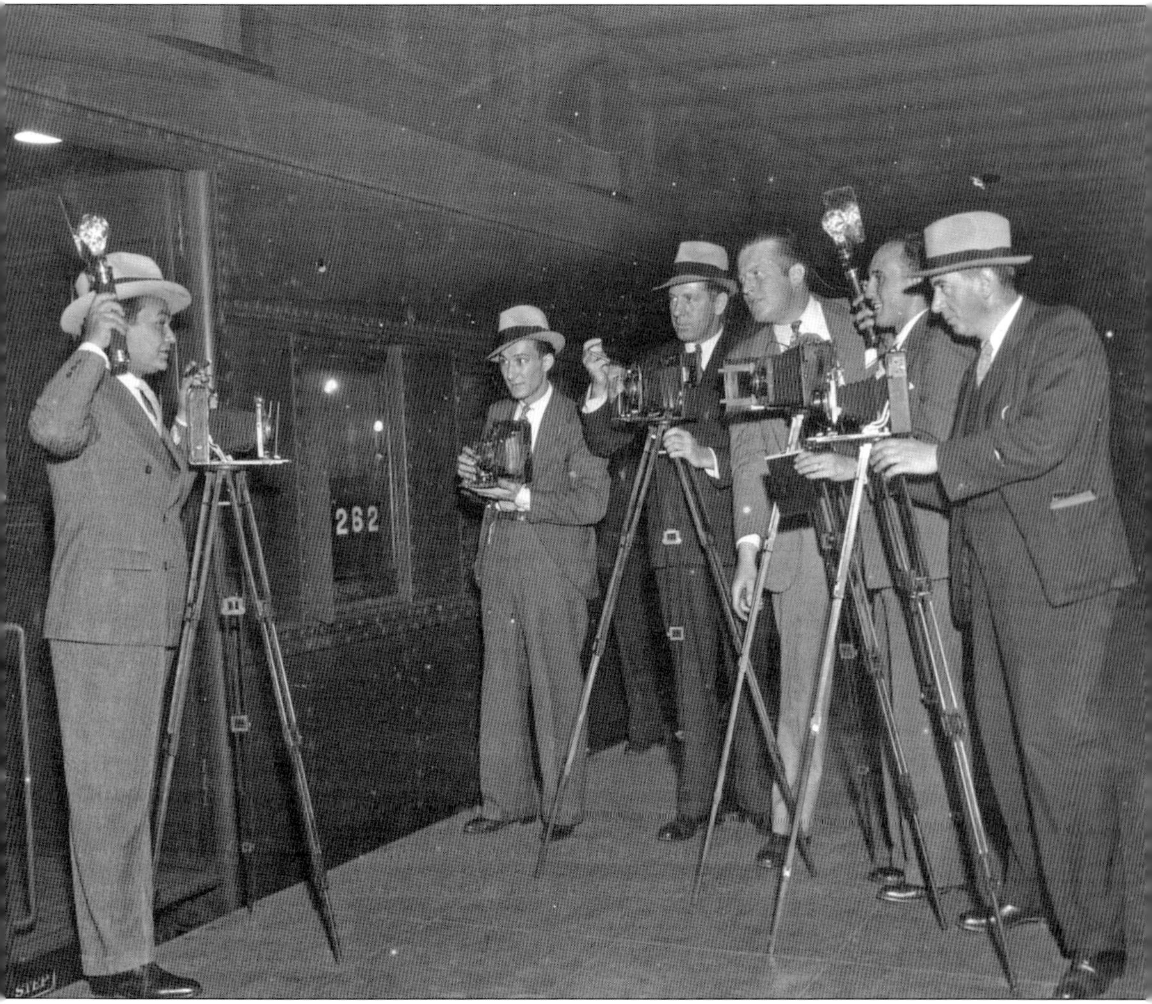

At left, Edward G. Robinson turns the tables on, lined up from left to right, Dan Grossi, George Reidy, John Reidy, Tony Sande, and Vic Twyman in 1934 when he arrives at Grand Central Station aboard the *20th Century Limited*. Of note are the early flashguns that had not yet been synchronized with camera shutters as a one-step process. The shutter was held open until the photographer fired the bulb separately.

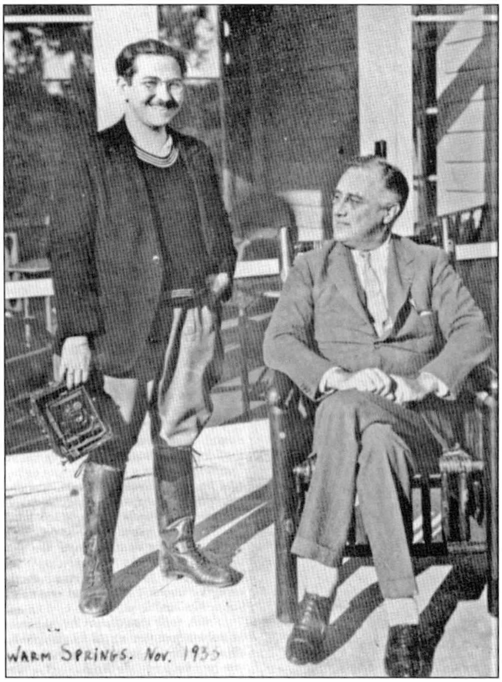

Sammy Schulman is pictured with Pres. Franklin D. Roosevelt in 1935. From as early as 1931, the diminutive photographer of International News Pictures was Roosevelt's favorite cameraman. Roosevelt would often invite Schulman to his private quarters for conversation. At a press conference, Roosevelt famously began by asking, "Where's Sammy?"

Starting in 1935, the Press Photographers Association held an annual photograph contest to promote the craft and recognize its members. Here, in 1938, from left to right, contest winners Anthony Lanza, Carl Thusgaard, Vincent Lopez, Charles Hoff, Jack Frank, Sam Falk, and Hugh Broderick surround WOR radio host Dave Driscoll at the microphone.

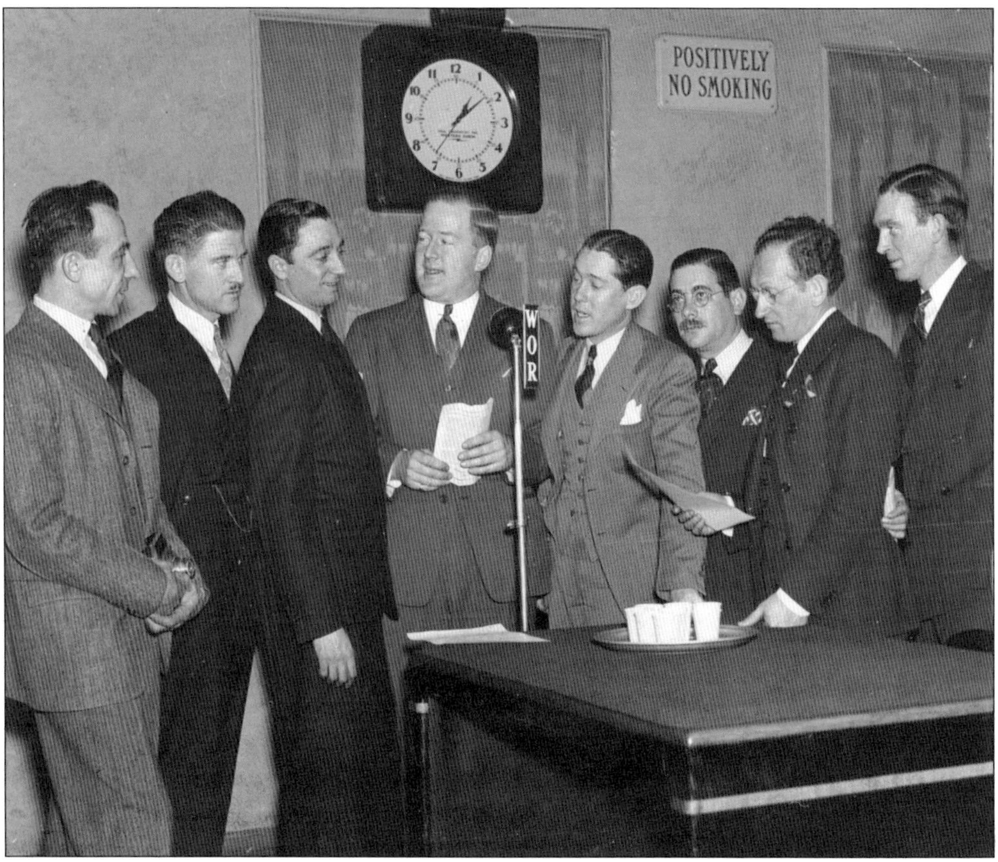

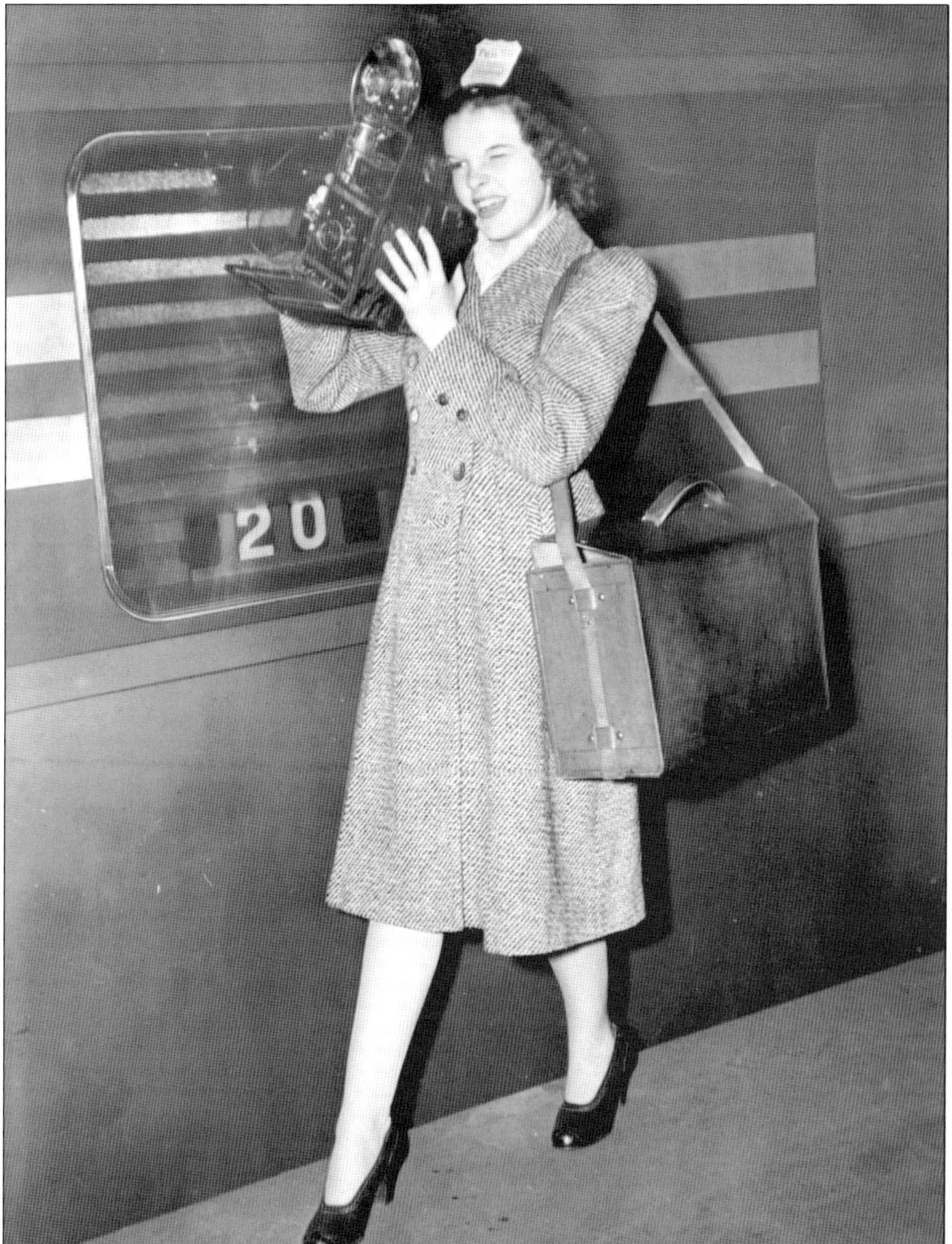

Fresh from the set of *The Wizard of Oz* in 1939, Judy Garland borrows a hat and camera to mimic a press photographer at Grand Central Station, part of a personal appearance tour. (Author's collection.)

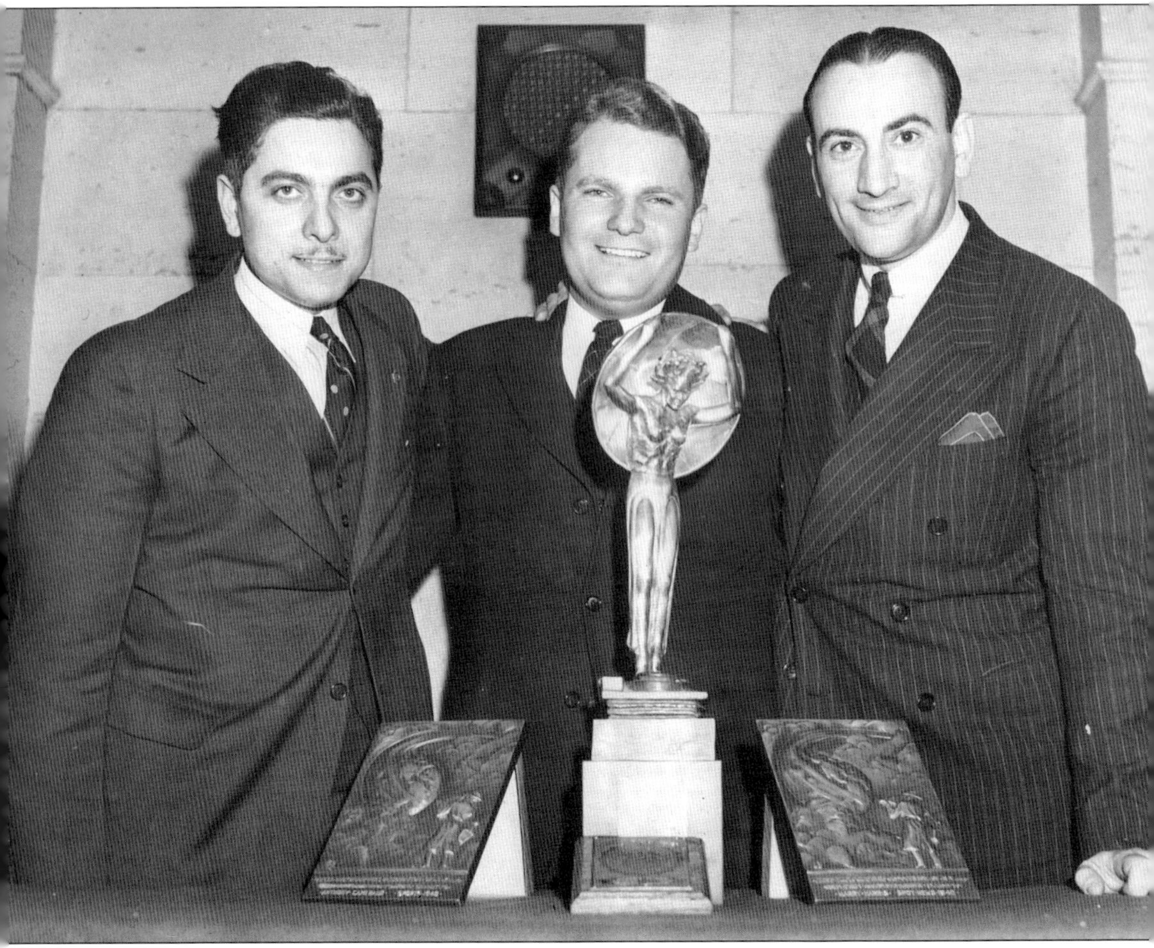

From left to right, Associated Press photographers Tony Camerano, Harry Harris, and Murray Becker are pictured in February 1940 with the awards they received for the sports and spot news categories of the 1939 contest.

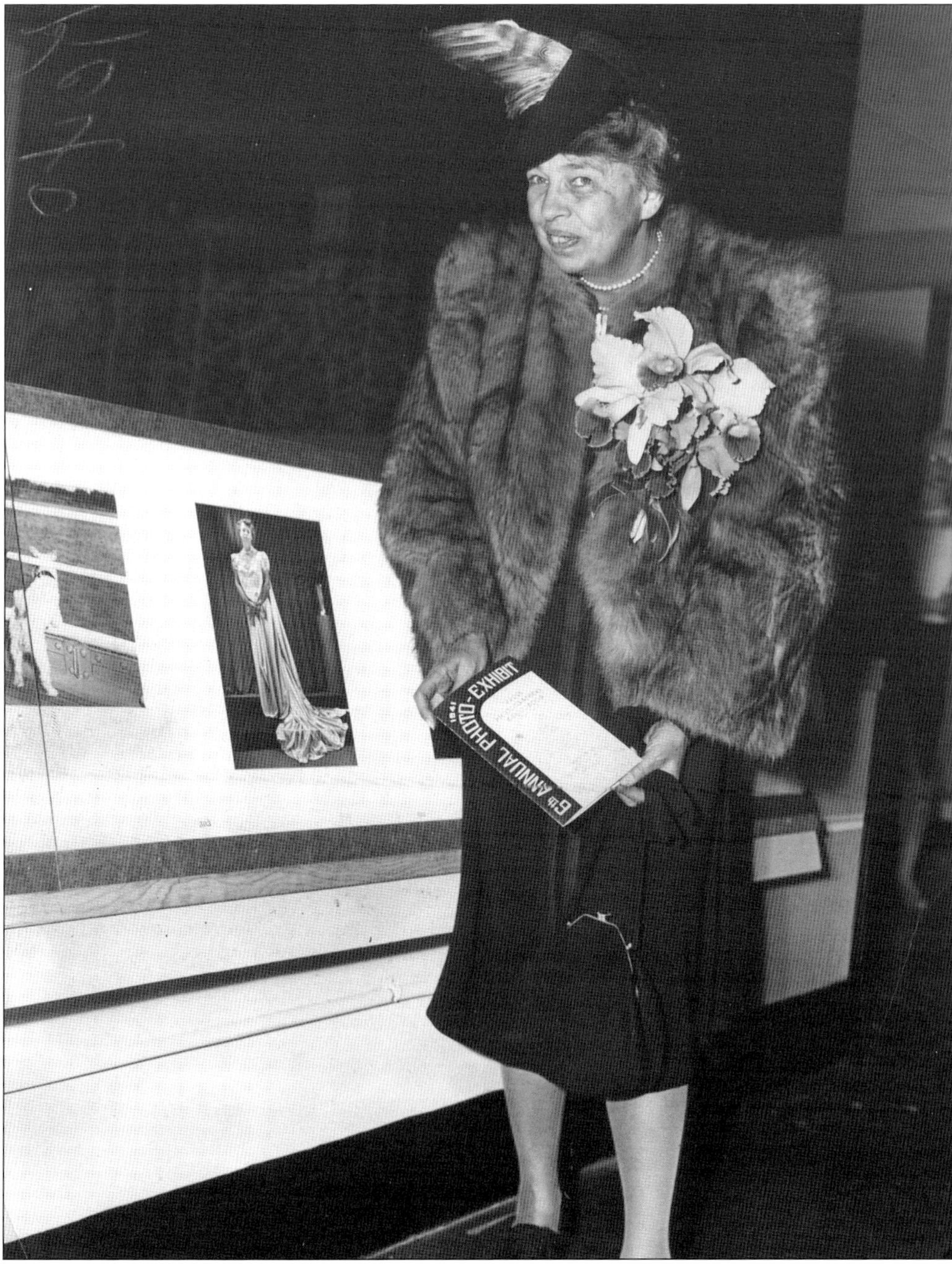

Eleanor Roosevelt sees a familiar face among the exhibits at the association's sixth annual photograph exhibit in 1941. Her portrait was among the year's contest winners, displayed at the Museum of Science and Industry in Rockefeller Center. (Photograph by Walt Kelleher; author's collection.)

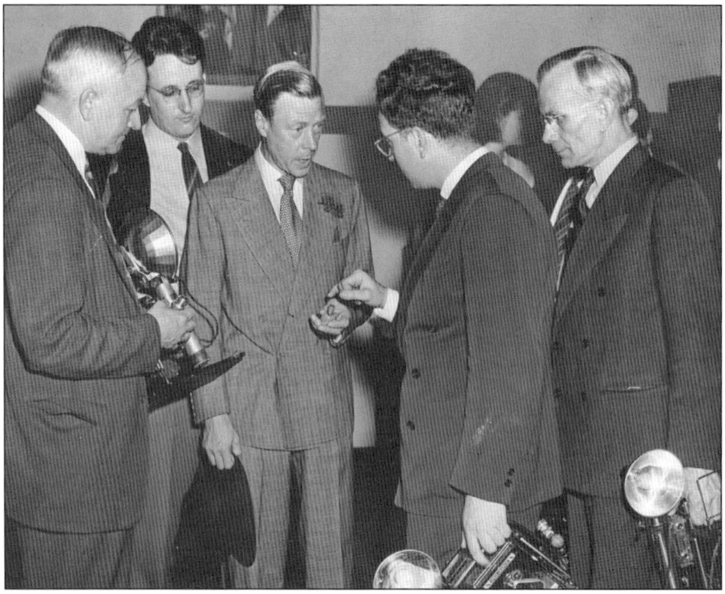

At center, the Duke of Windsor seems to be getting a lesson from Ken Lucas on the new breed of small flashbulbs as, from left to right, John Hemmer, Charles Haacker, and C.M. Stieglitz look on.

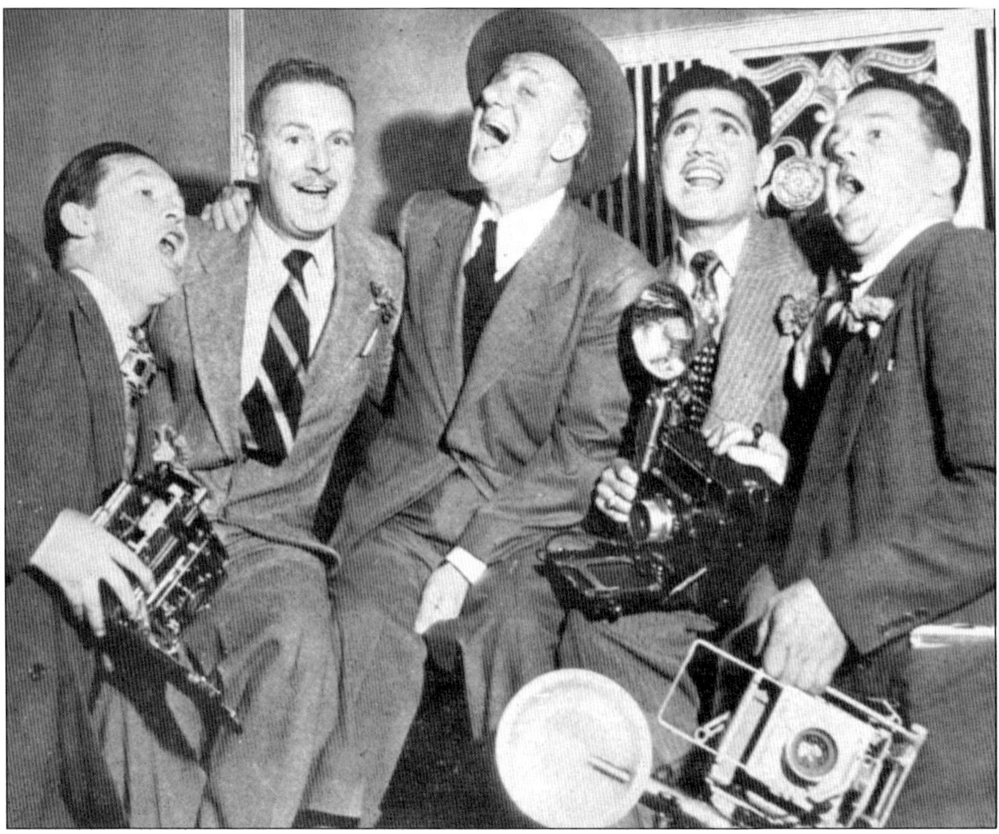

A longtime friend to the press photographers, Jimmy Durante (center) takes time to clown around with, from left to right, Pat Burns, John Lindsay, Herb Schwartz, and Charlie Seawood during the American Newspaper Publishers Association convention at the Waldorf-Astoria Hotel. (Photograph by Jimmy Collings.)

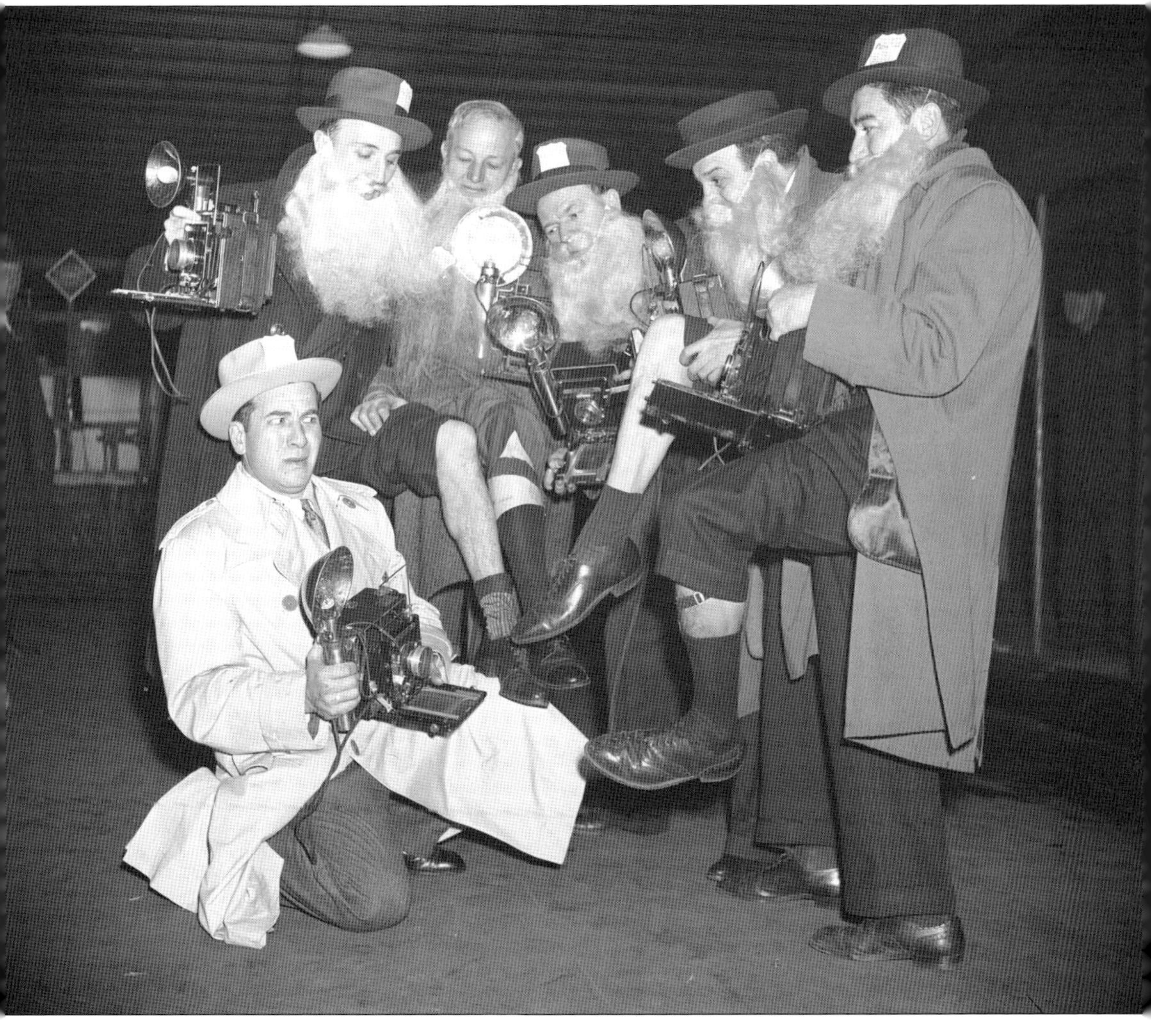

In 1944, former *Daily News* photographer turned radio actor Artie Auerbach is greeted by his old pals, whose beards represent Artie's 10-year absence from the local scene. He originated the character "Mr. Kitzel" on *The Jack Benny Program* but passed away in 1957, just before making the switch to Benny's television show. (Courtesy of the *Daily News*.)

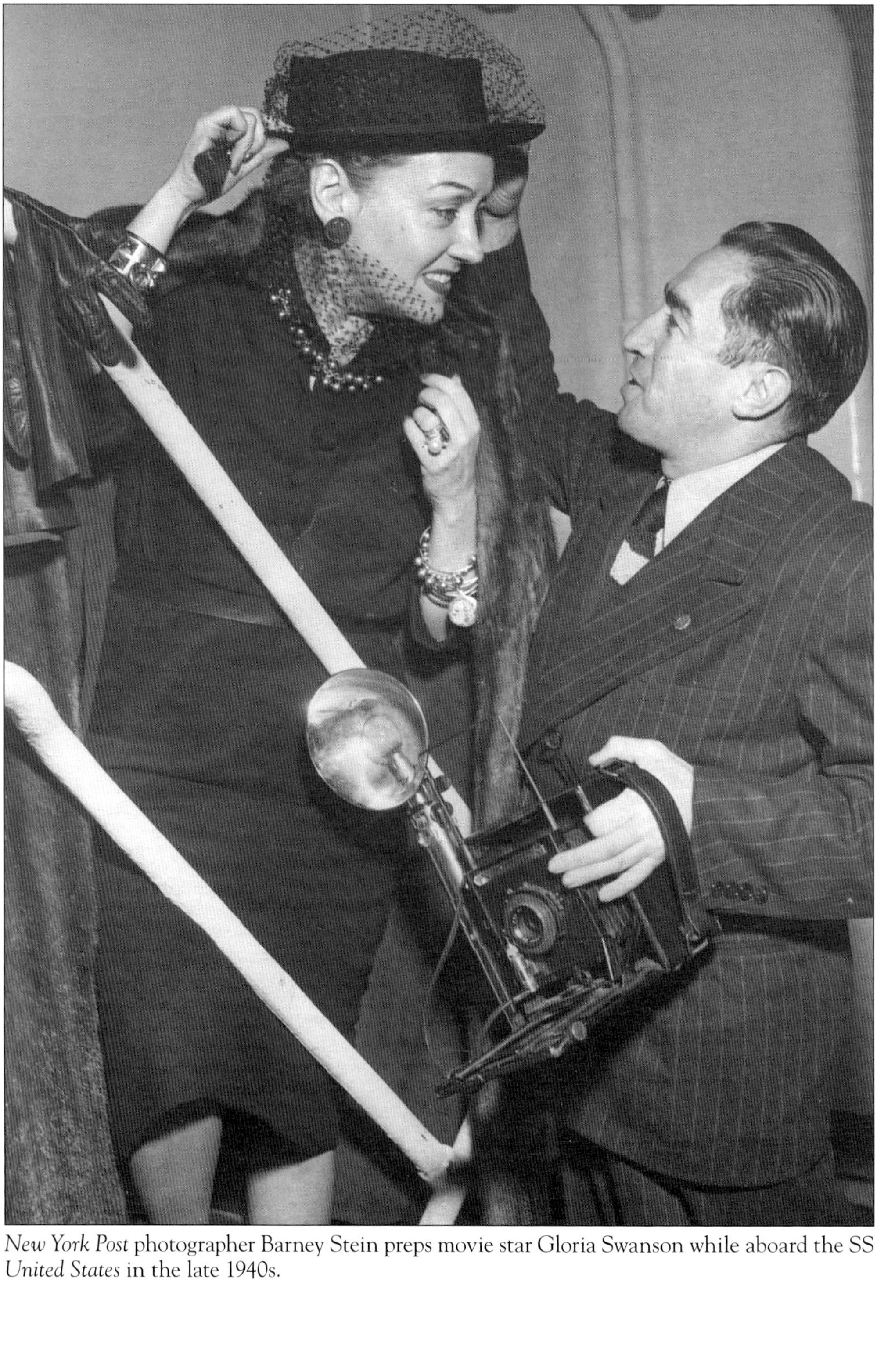

New York Post photographer Barney Stein preps movie star Gloria Swanson while aboard the SS *United States* in the late 1940s.

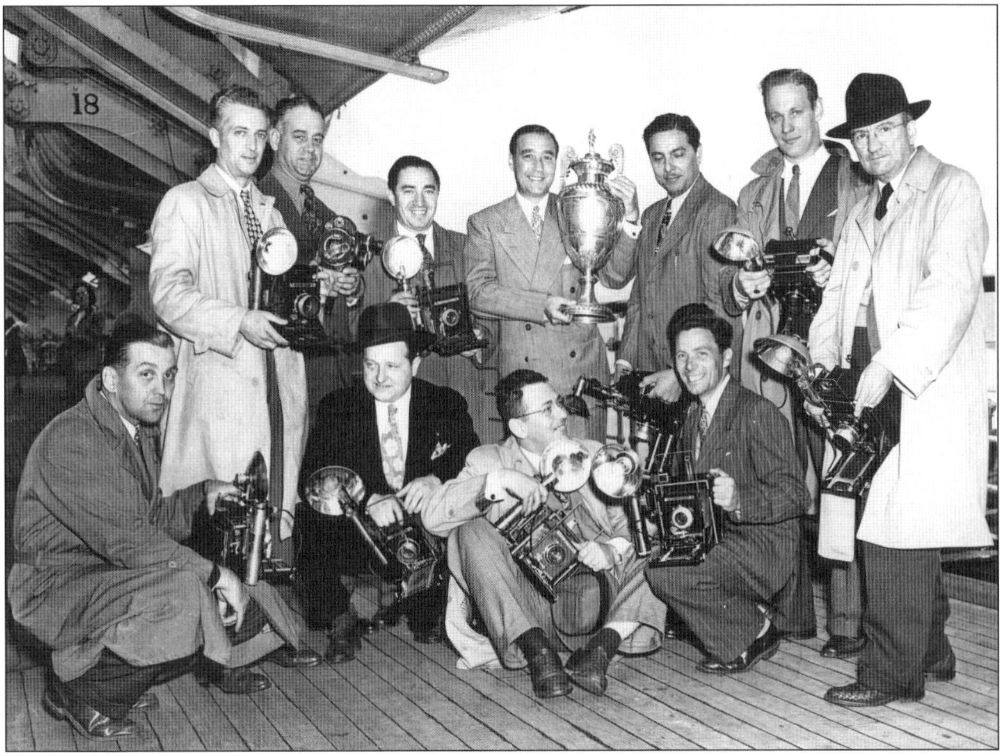

Golf champ Willie Turnesa, winner of the British Amateur in 1947, is pictured with the press aboard the *Queen Elizabeth*. From left to right are (first row) Frank Jurkowski, Len Morgan, Maurice Morrell, and Arthur Brower; (second row) Art Abfier, Al Mingalone, Barney Stein, Turnesa, Tony Camerano, George Mattson, and Pat Mulligan.

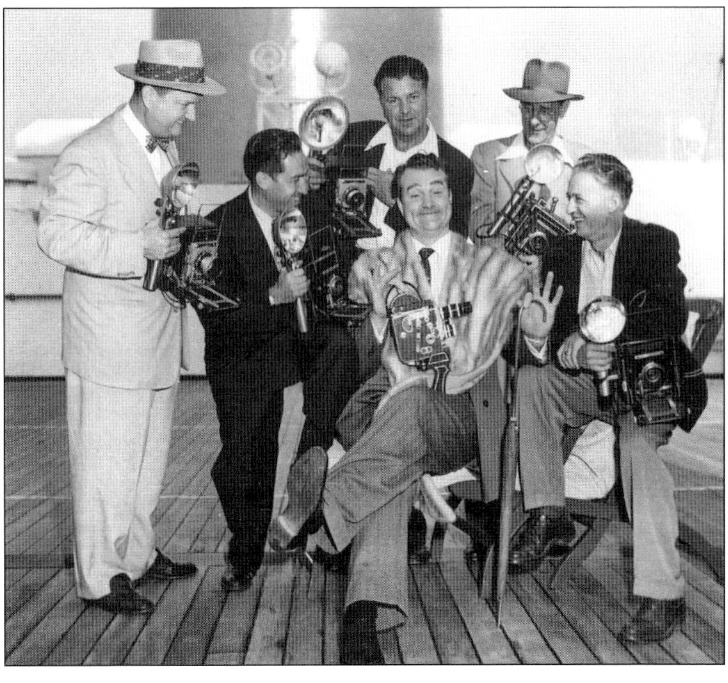

Similarly drawing a crowd of lensmen is Richard Bernard "Red" Skelton aboard the SS *United States*. From left to right are (first row) Fred Morgan, Barney Stein, Skelton, and Art Abfier; (second row) Charlie Seawood and Joe Lyons.

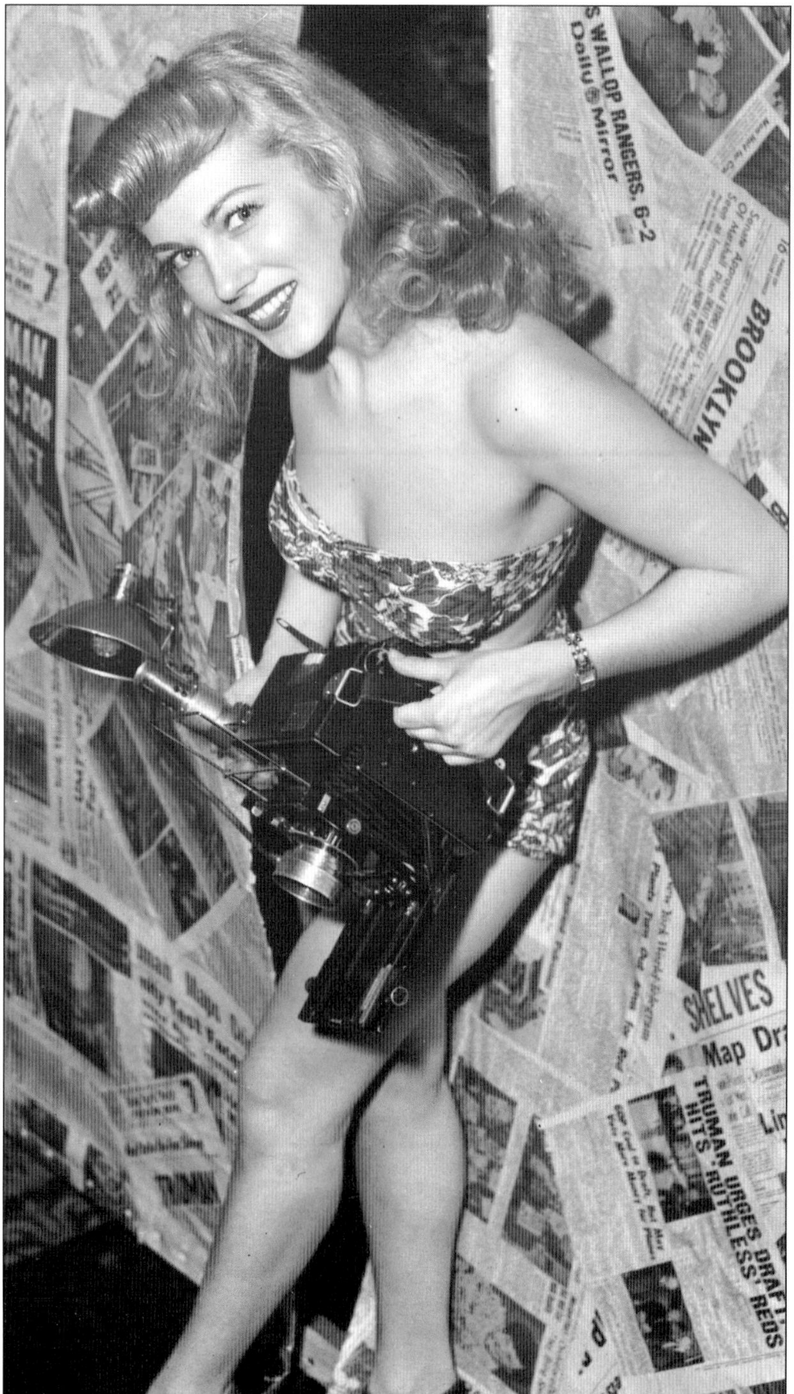

From the 1940s until 1970, the association sponsored a beauty contest for aspiring actresses and models. The winner would be crowned "Queen of the Press Photographers Ball," then later, "Miss New York Press Photographer." Here, Karen Lewis poses after winning the 1948 contest. (Author's collection.)

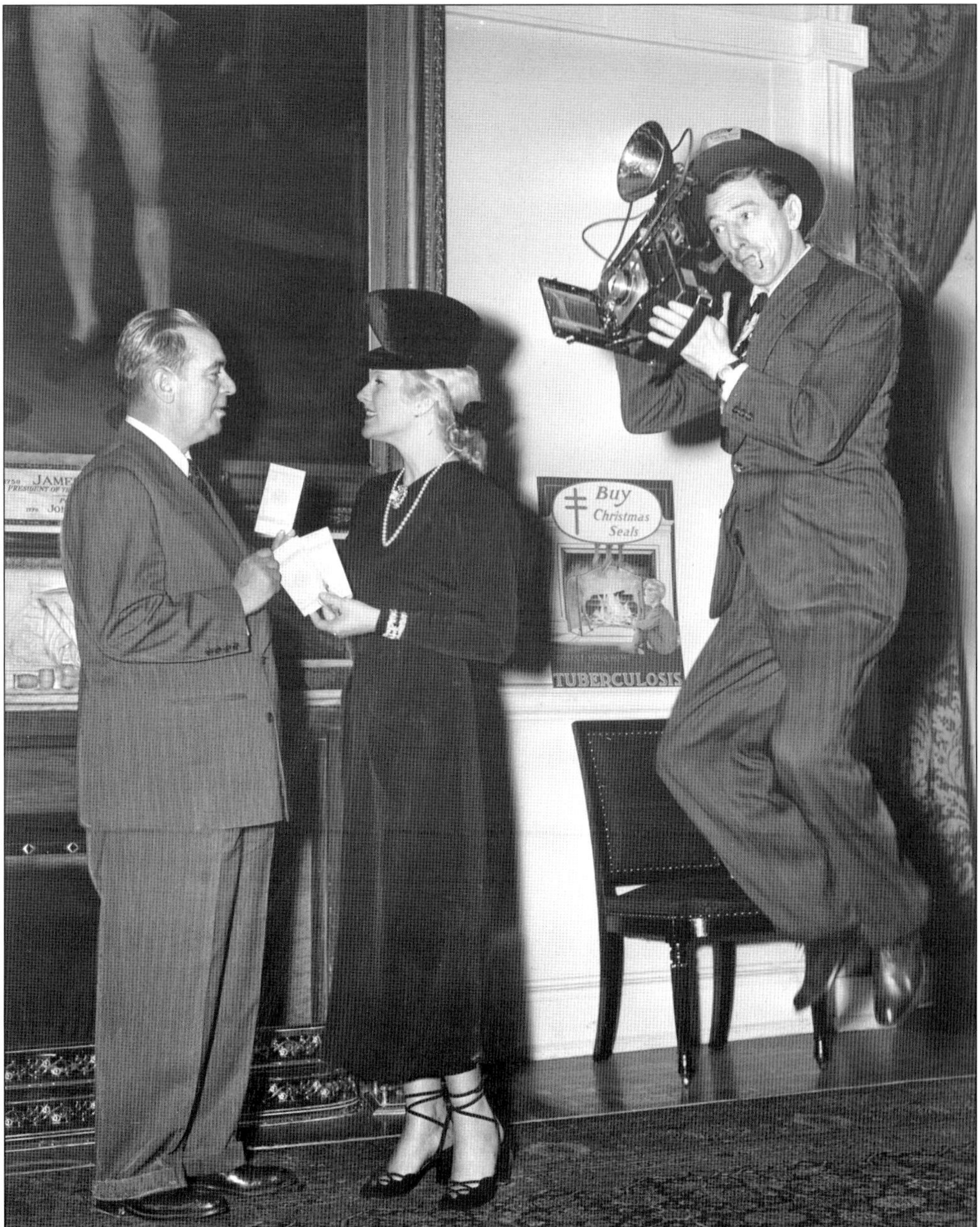

Mayor William O'Dwyer receives his tickets to the 1949 Press Photographers' Ball from actress Ilona Massey, while Ray Bolger gets an aerial view of the presentation. (Author's collection.)

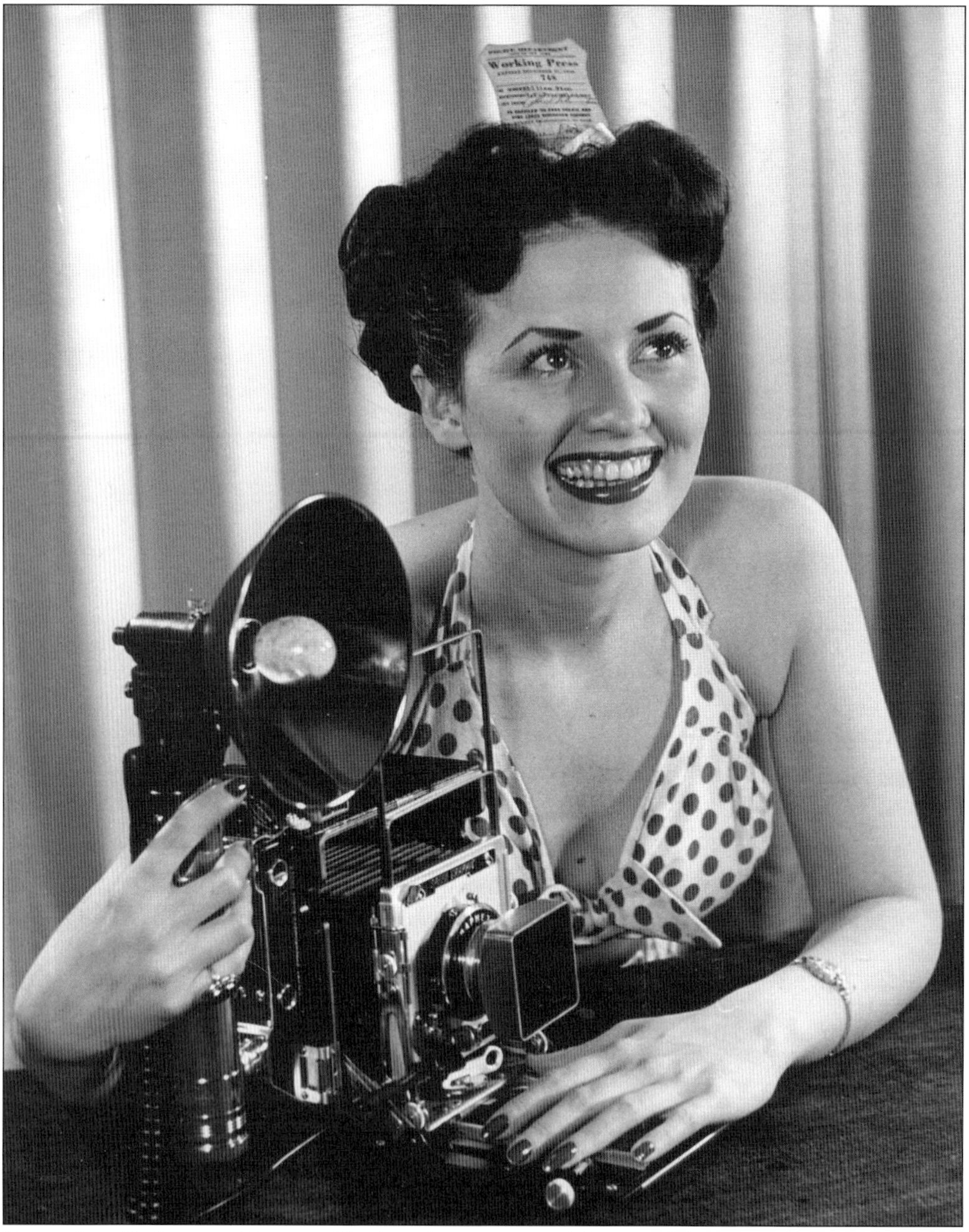

Donna Lee Hickey was 22 years old when she was named Queen of the Press Photographers Ball in 1950. Seen here with photographer William Finn's press card as her crown, Hickey would later appear in movies under her new name of May Wynn. (Author's collection.)

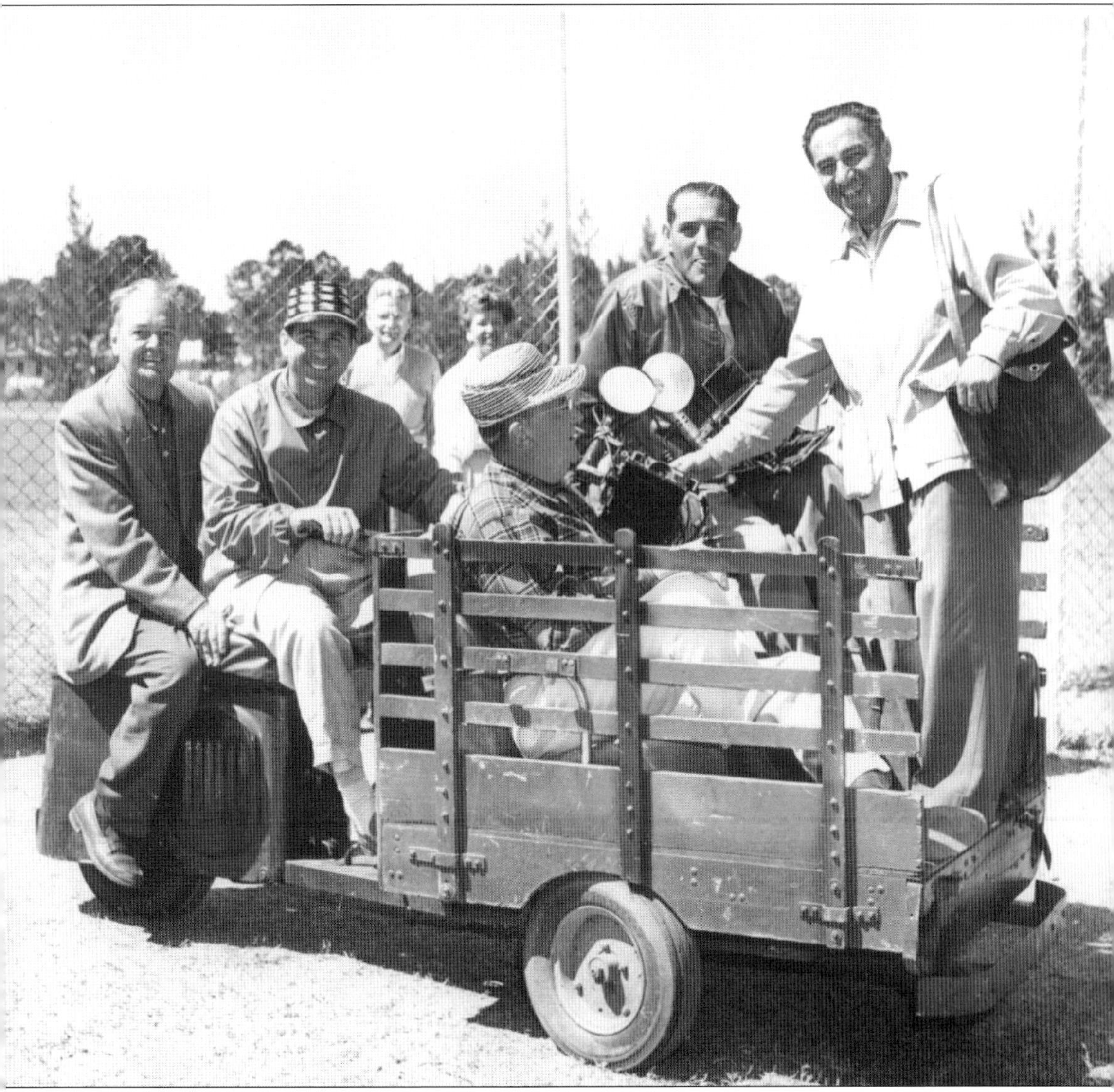

On the road with the Brooklyn Dodgers at spring training in Vero Beach, Florida, are, from left to right, Brooklyn borough president John Cashmore, photographer Herb Scharfman of International News Pictures, Dodgers owner Walter O'Malley, and photographers Harry Hirsch and Barney Stein.

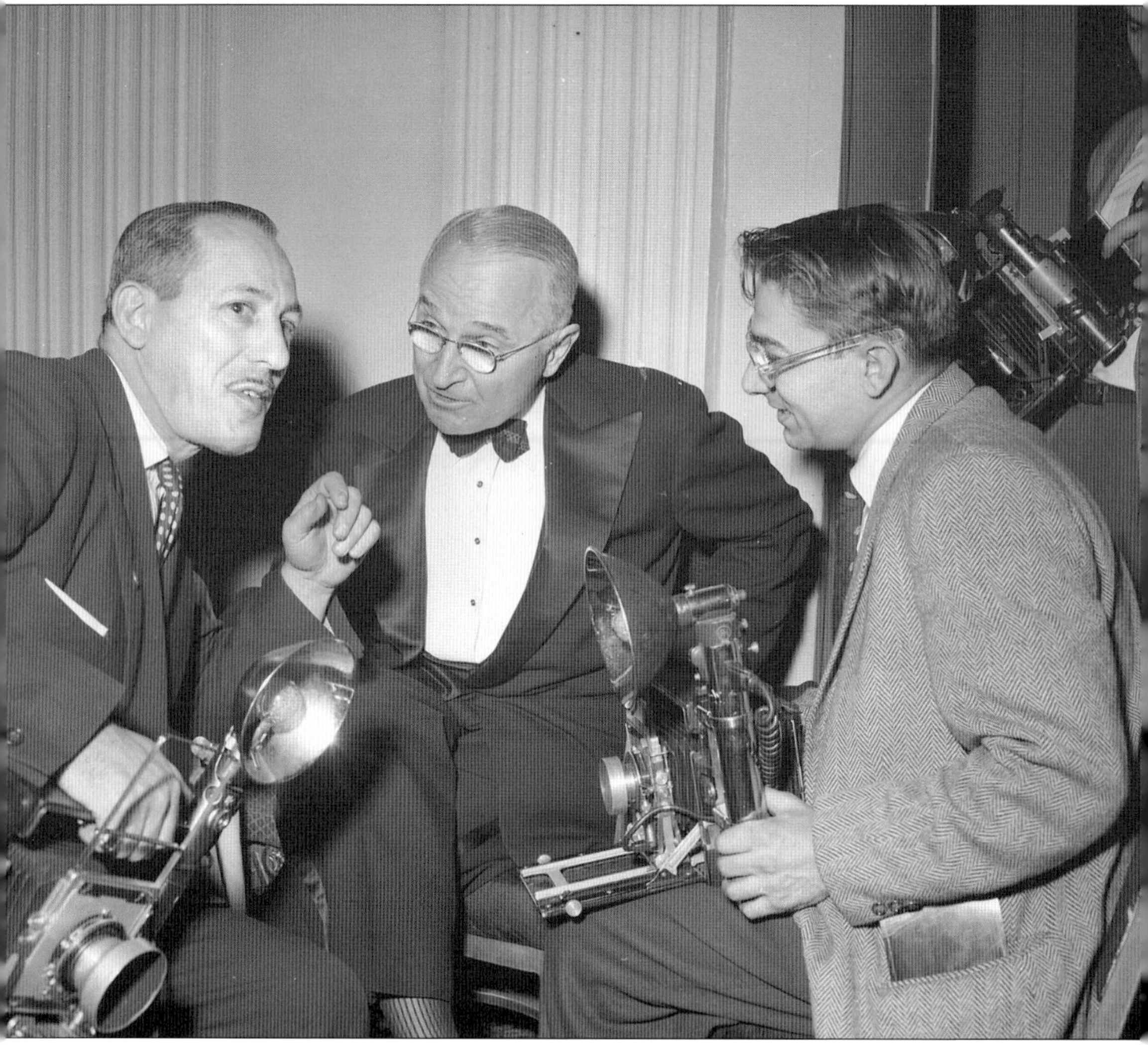

Although he was unable to attend the ceremony, Pres. Harry S. Truman was given the association's first Award of Merit in 1947 for his interest in the craft and his cooperation with its practitioners. Despite his absence, Truman later managed to spend time with New York's photographers.

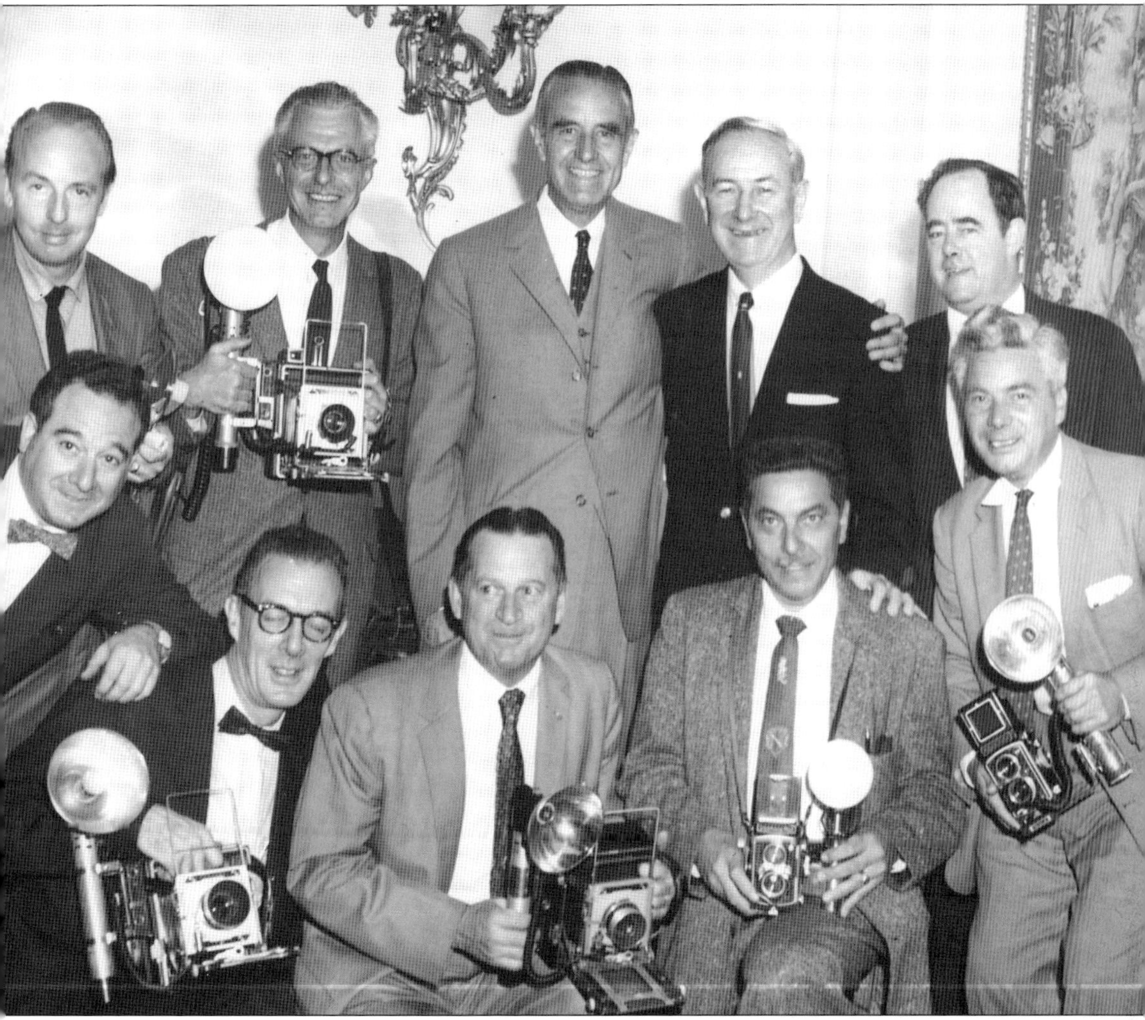

Members of the association gladly pose for guest photographer President Truman on September 17, 1958. Gov. W. Averell Harriman, standing in the middle, has his arm around Manhattan district attorney Frank Hogan. (Photograph by Harry S. Truman.)

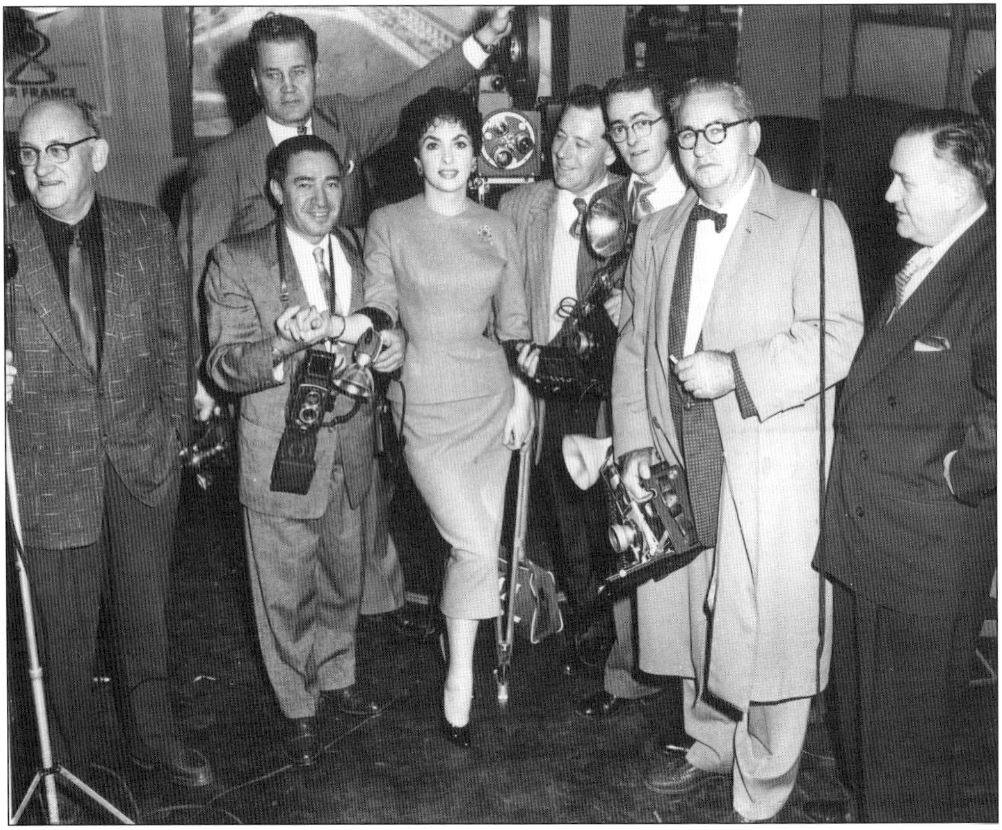

Actress Gina Lollobrigida (center) is greeted by photographers at Idlewild Airport on December 4, 1956. She is flanked by Barney Stein on the left and Jack Clarity (third from right) and Jack Layer (second from right) on the right. Various "movie men" get in on the picture too.

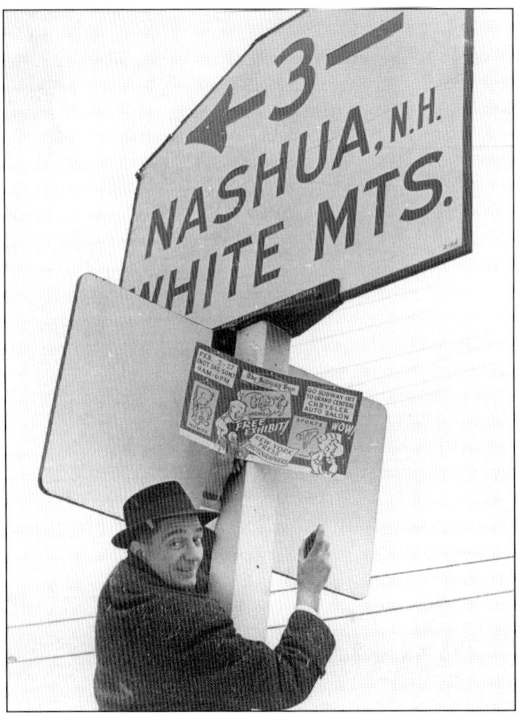

Vincent Lopez of the *Journal-American* does his part in promoting the 1958 press photographers' exhibit by posting a flyer on a road sign along Highway 3 in Massachusetts.

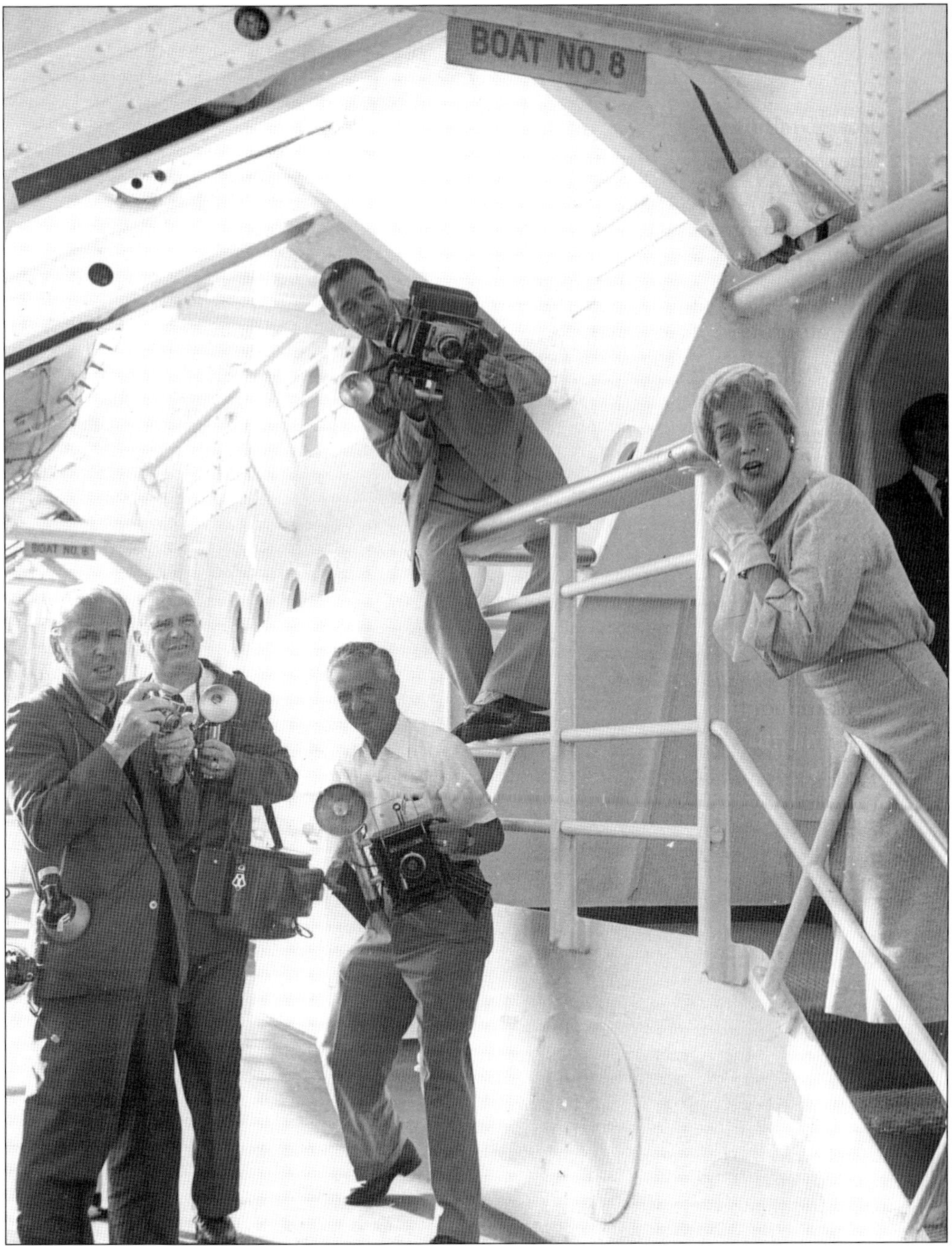

Actress Jeanette MacDonald seems pleasantly surprised by the attention she is receiving from, from left to right, Joe Schuppe of United Press International, John Lindsay, Art Abfier, and Vincent Lopez in 1959.

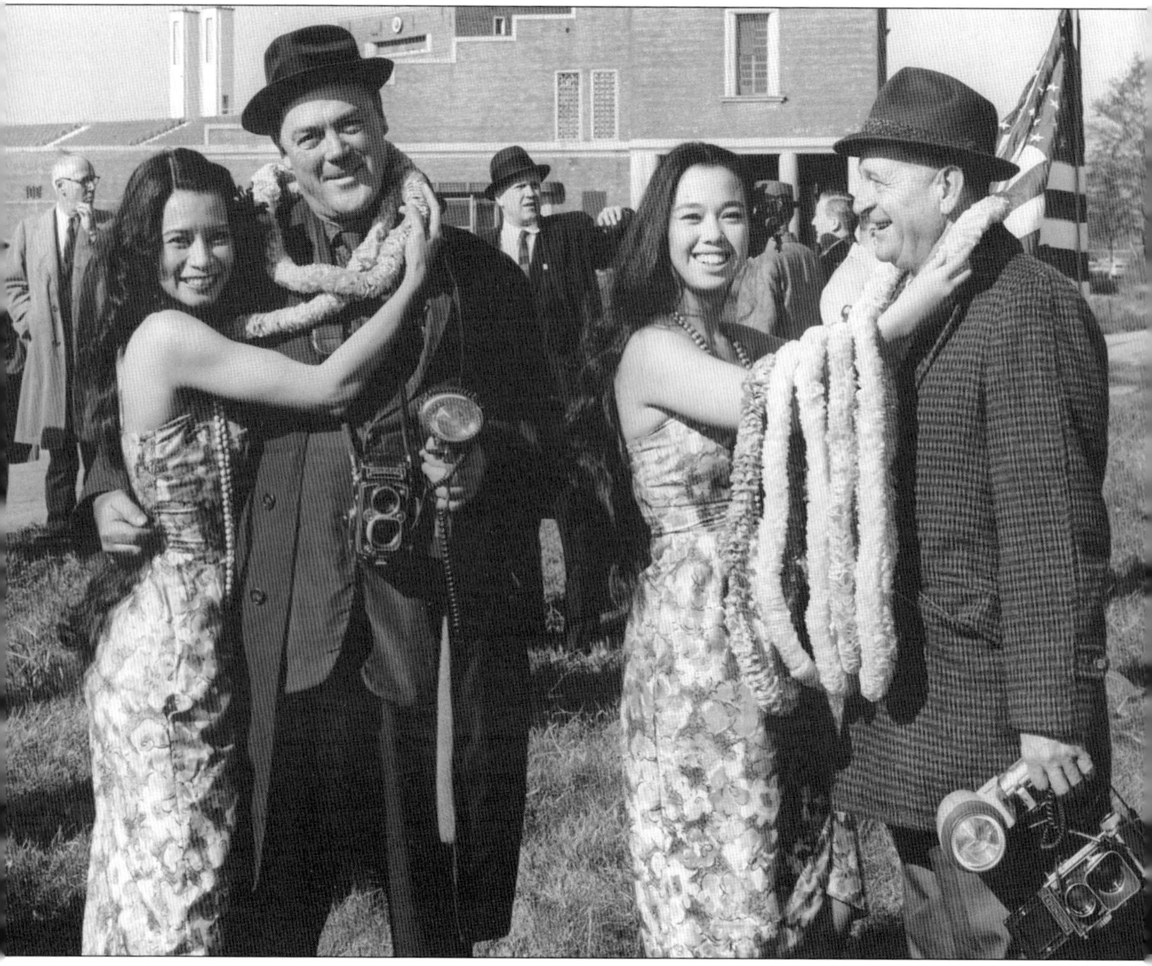

World's Fair excitement returned to New York in the 1960s. On March 1, 1962, ground was broken at the Hawaiian Pavilion. Bruce Hopkins (second from left) of the *Daily Mirror* and Charley Carson (right) of the *Journal-American* came away with souvenirs of the occasion.

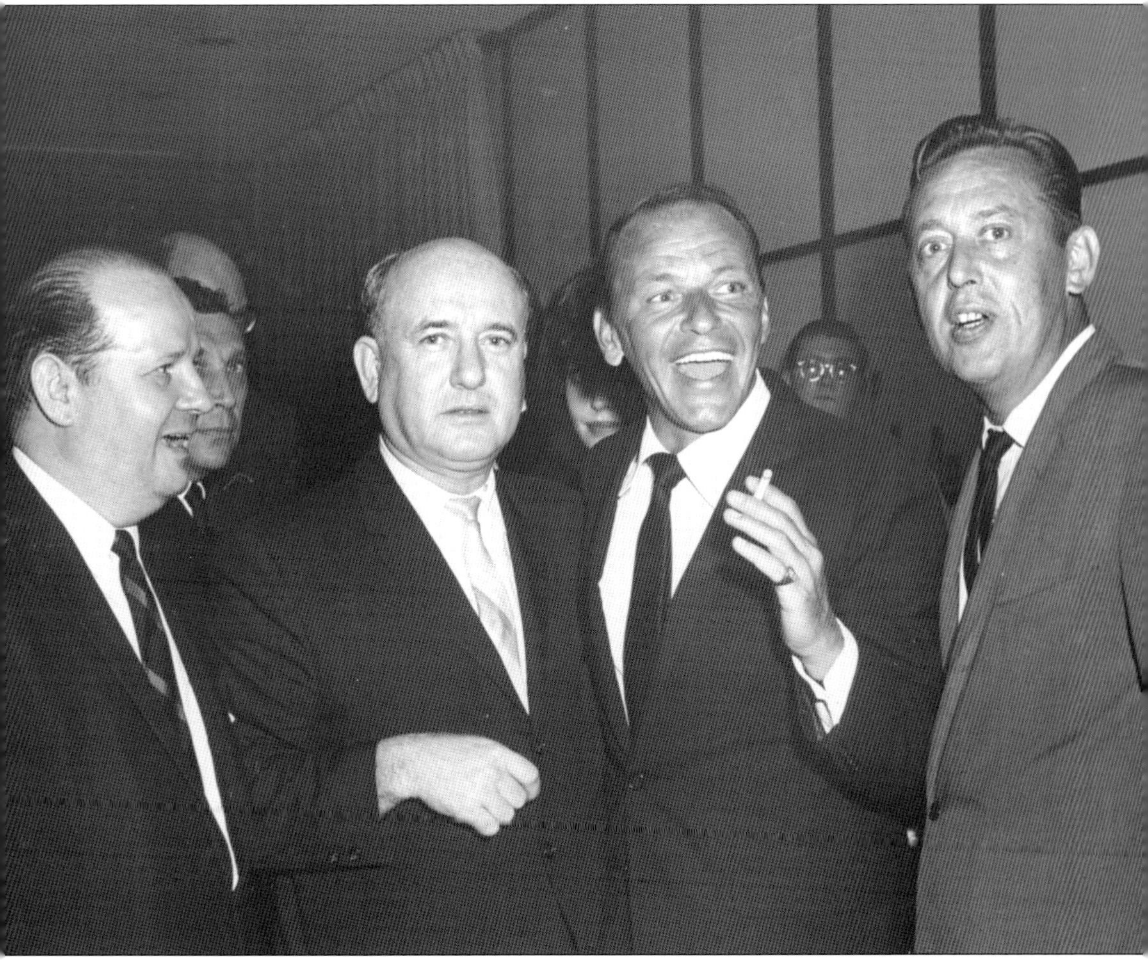

Ol' Blue Eyes, Frank Sinatra (second from right), was a friend of the association and a regular guest at its functions. He is pictured with, from left to right, Al Clark and Jim Ritchie, both of the Newspaper Reporters Association, and NYPPA president Ellsworth Schell in June 1963. (Photograph by Ed Sullivan.)

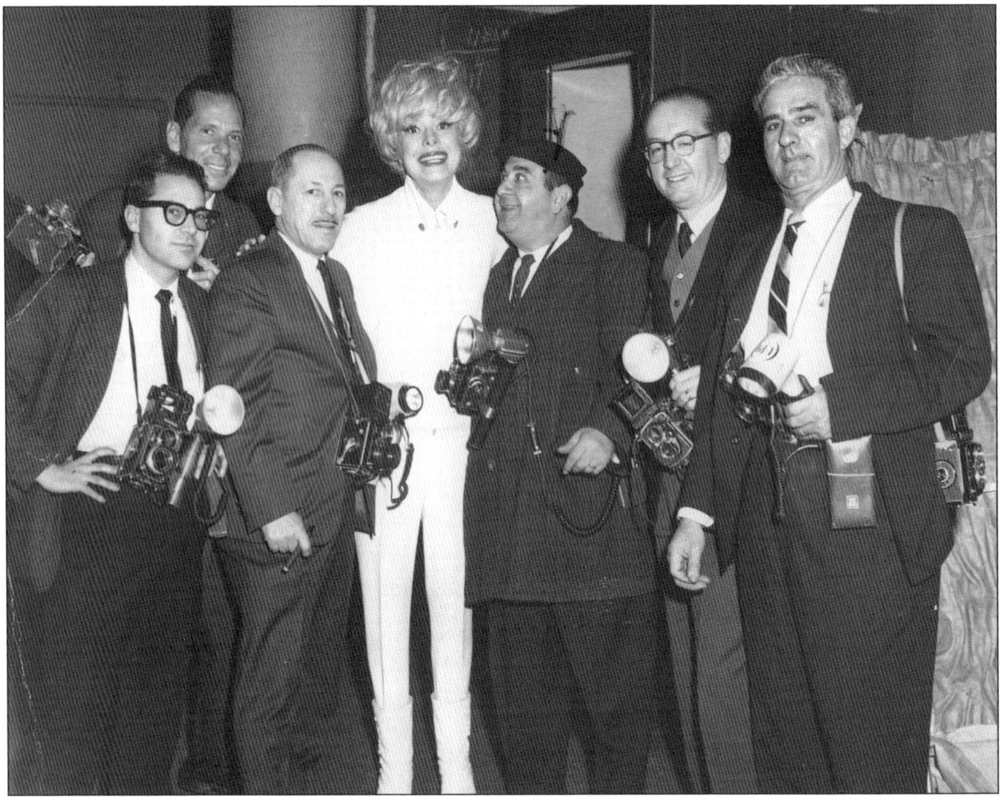

Carol Channing is pictured backstage at the St. James Theatre with press photographers in April 1965 during the run of *Hello, Dolly!*

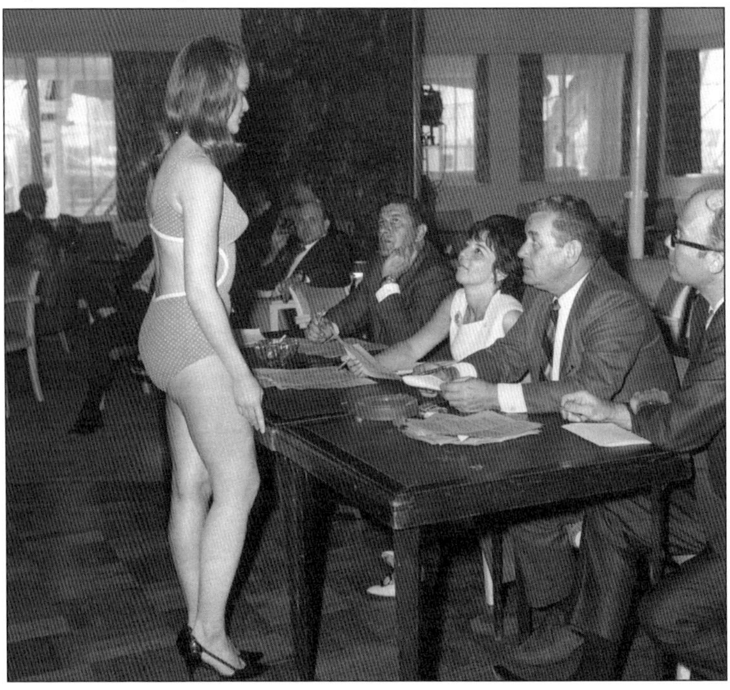

At the table, from left to right, Nick Sorrentino, an unidentified woman, and Harold Matthewson are among those who were tasked with interviewing candidates for the Miss New York Press Photographers contest.

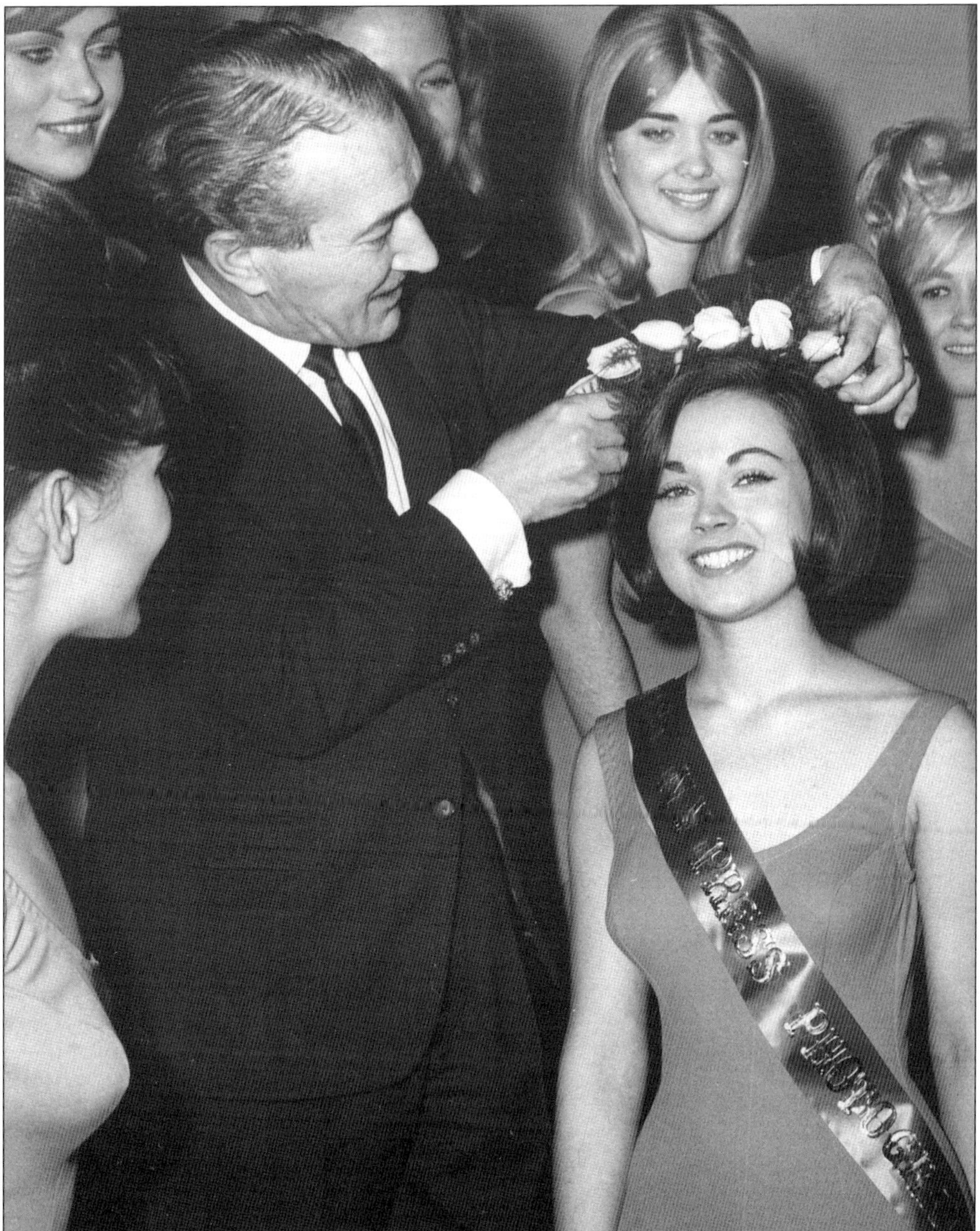

Association president Dan Grossi crowns Gisa Kothe as Miss New York Press Photographer in 1965. The crown was made of yellow roses to commemorate the group's 50th anniversary. Kothe was a TWA flight attendant who had the privilege of accompanying the Beatles on their flight to the United States that year. In 2015, she attended the association's centennial celebration as a special guest and received a replica of her crown of roses.

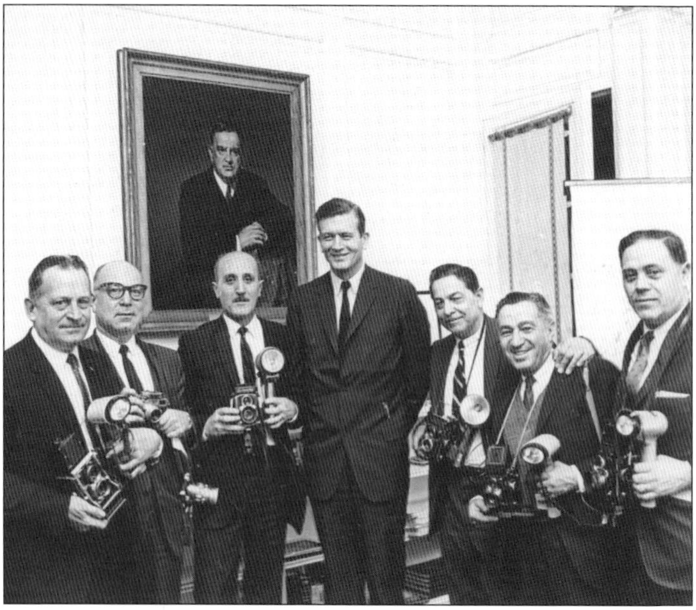

A group of photographers is seen at city hall with Mayor John Lindsay, who served from 1966 to 1973. From left to right are Charley Carson, Ted Kell, Tony Sande, Lindsay, Tony Camerano, Barney Stein, and Ed Giorandano. (Photograph by Stanley Wolfson.)

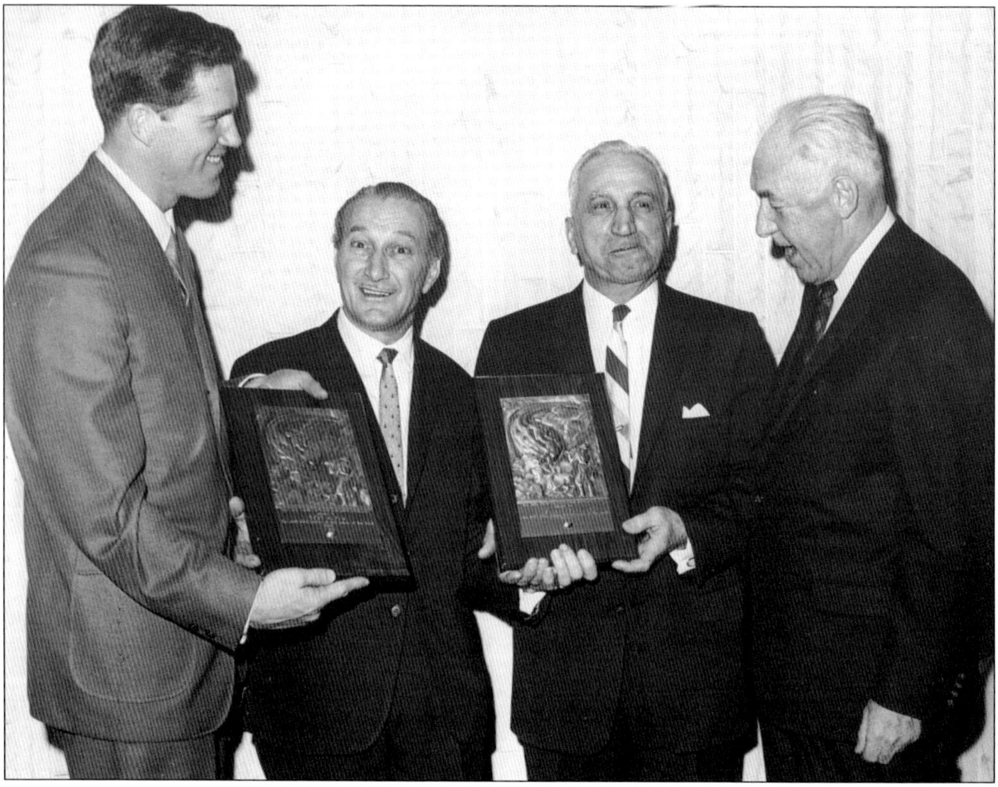

For a time, the association sponsored a Sports Awards dinner at which members of the athletic community received tokens of thanks from the photographers. In 1966, president Dan Grossi (second from left) presents awards to former New York Yankee Tony Kubek (left) and Columbia University football coach Buff Donelli (second from right). Retired baseball commissioner Ford Frick looks on from the right.

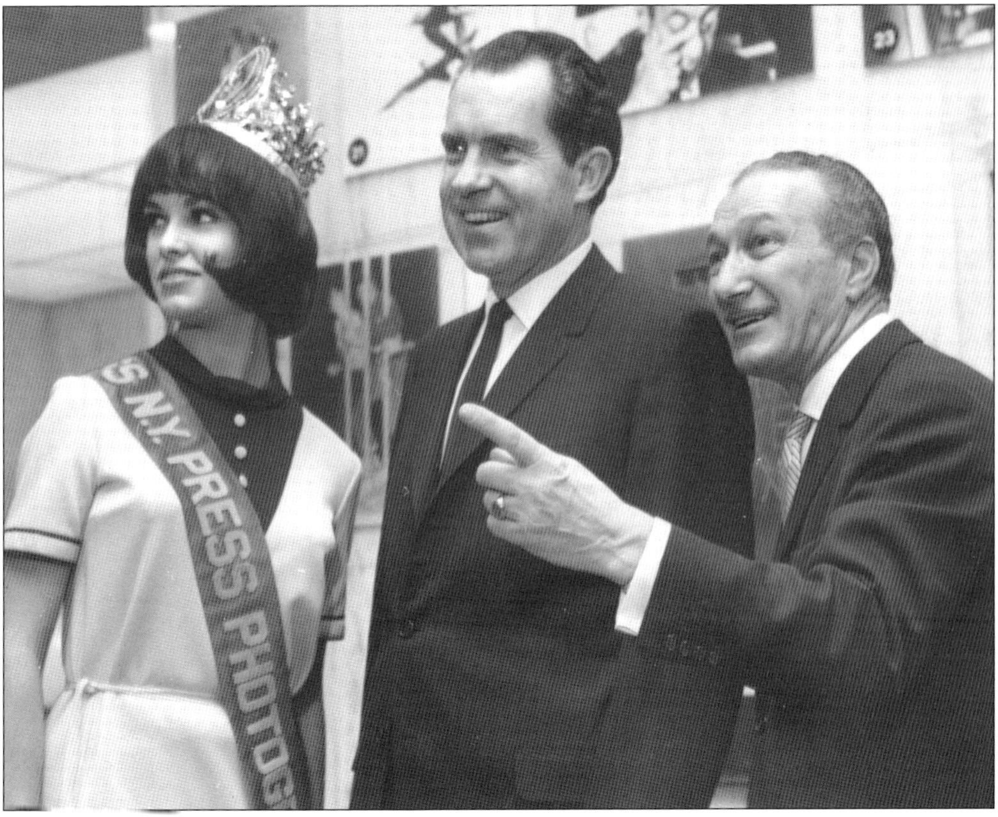

Future president Richard Nixon gets a personal tour of the 1966 press photographers' exhibit from Miss New York Press Photographer Eileen Beatty and association president Dan Grossi. By the next decade, a change in social mores had resulted in the abandonment of the Miss Press Photographer contest.

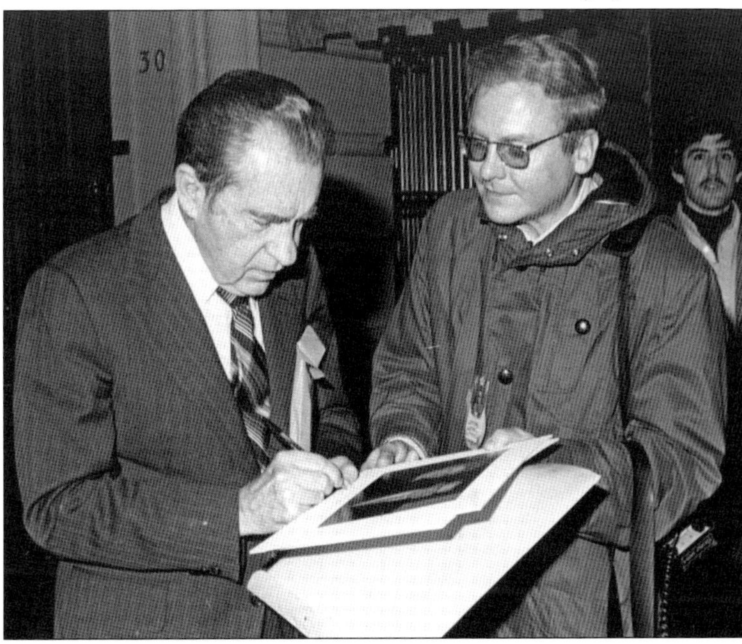

Daily News photographer and association president Charlie Ruppmann has President Nixon autograph a picture he had taken of him some years before. (Photograph by C.J. Zumwalt.)

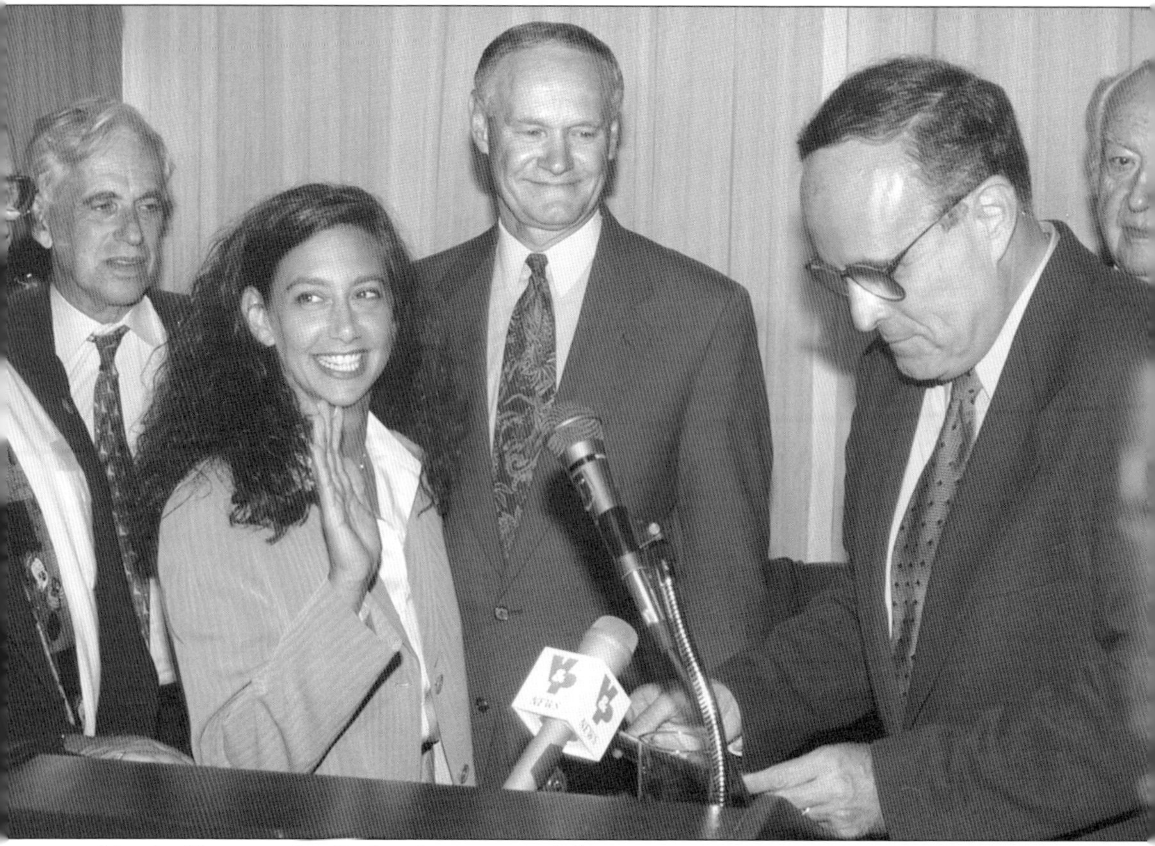

Nearly 50 years after Evelyn Straus joined the association, Mayor Rudolph Giuliani swears in *Daily News* photographer Susan Watts as the first female president of the NYPPA while parks commissioner Henry Stern (left) and police commissioner Howard Safir (center) look on. (Photograph by Ken Murray.)

Three

In Harm's Way

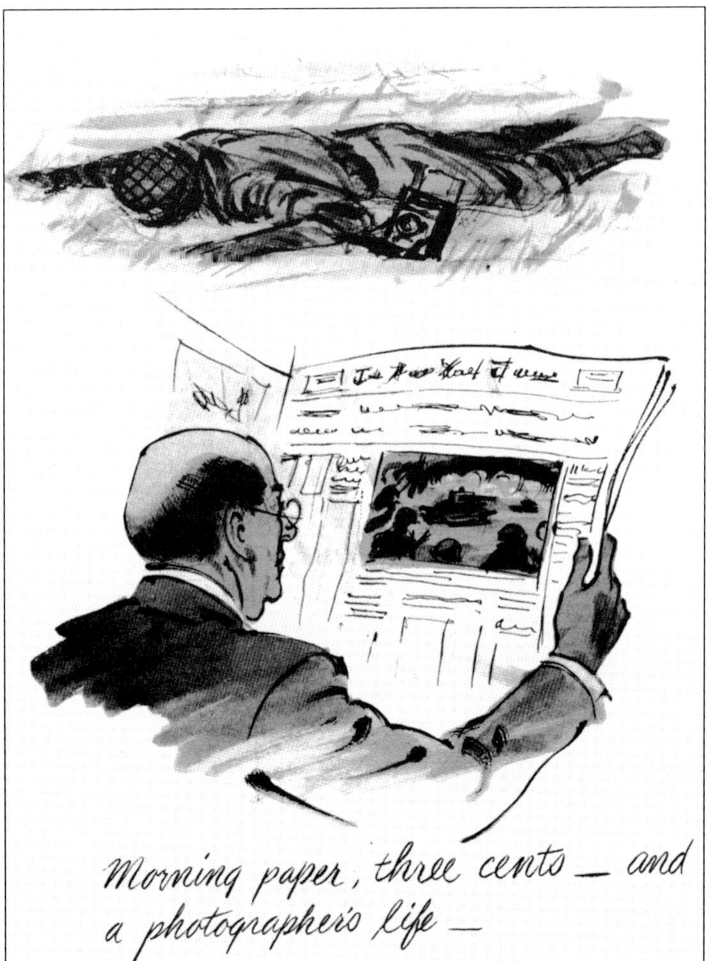

A poignant editorial illustration, sponsored by Lord & Taylor, reminded newspaper readers of the human cost sometimes necessary to bring the public the stories of war.

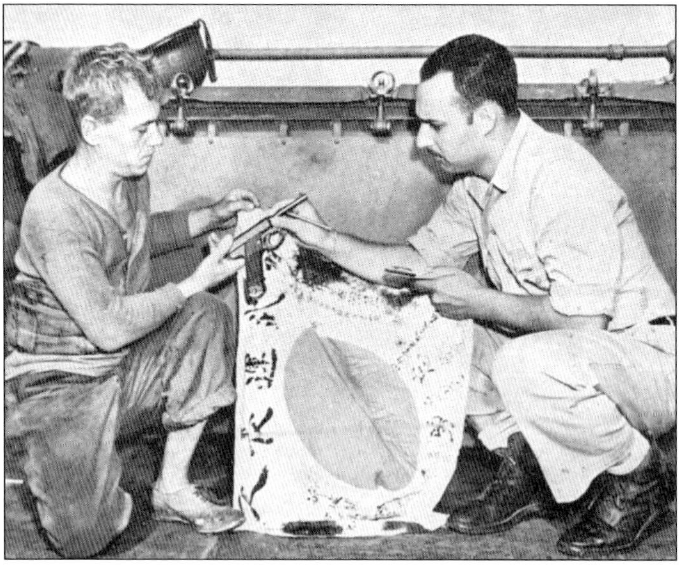

Pvt. Nicholas Timmens, left, makes a trade with photographer Ray Platnick at Makin Island. Platnick, one of the few Coast Guard combat photographers in the Pacific, was among the first wave to hit the beaches at Makin in August 1942. He would take home the battle flag pictured here as a souvenir. Two years later, he distinguished himself by scouting gun emplacements at Eniwetok Atoll and signaling to Marine riflemen if he found them occupied by the enemy.

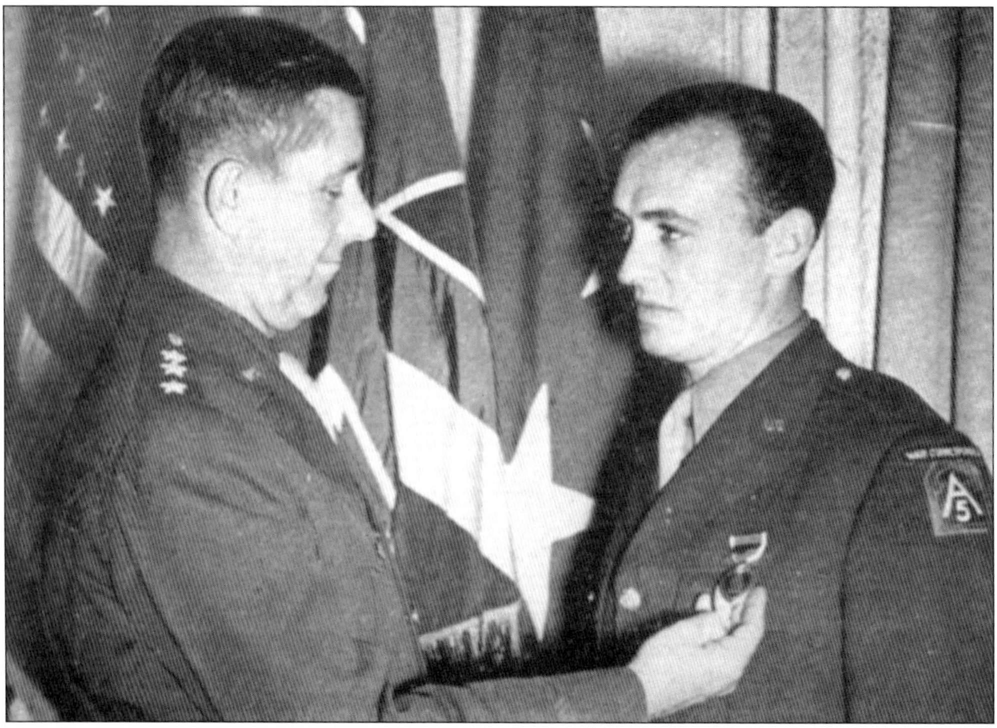

Charles Corte (right) receives the Purple Heart from Gen. Jacob Devers on November 27, 1943. Corte was wounded at Kasserine Pass earlier that year. The 5th Army patch on his sleeve is surmounted by a war correspondent tab. Between 1942 and 1992, civilians wounded while participating in military operations, such as embedded war correspondents, were eligible to receive the Purple Heart.

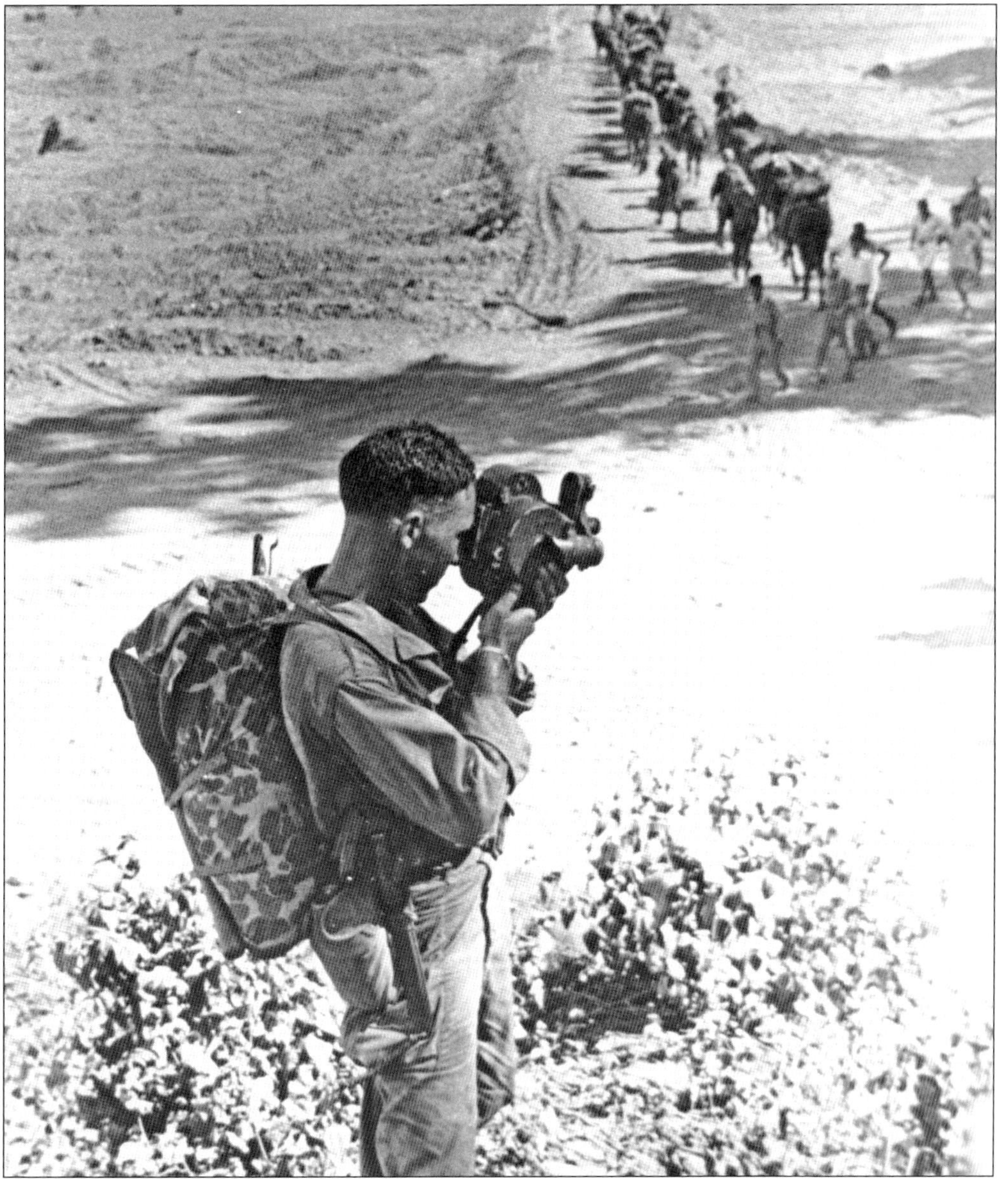

Local cameramen, like Jackson Pokress, were thrilled when the Army chose to establish the Signal Corps pictorial training school in Astoria, Queens—he was able to go home each night. Life wasn't as easy once he went overseas. Here, as a member of the 164th Signal Photo Company, Pokress documents the exploits of "Merrill's Marauders" in Myitkyina, Burma. Initially, he wasn't allowed to keep a personal record of the film he shot, but he later convinced the army to sell it to him at 10¢ per foot. (Courtesy of Jackson Pokress.)

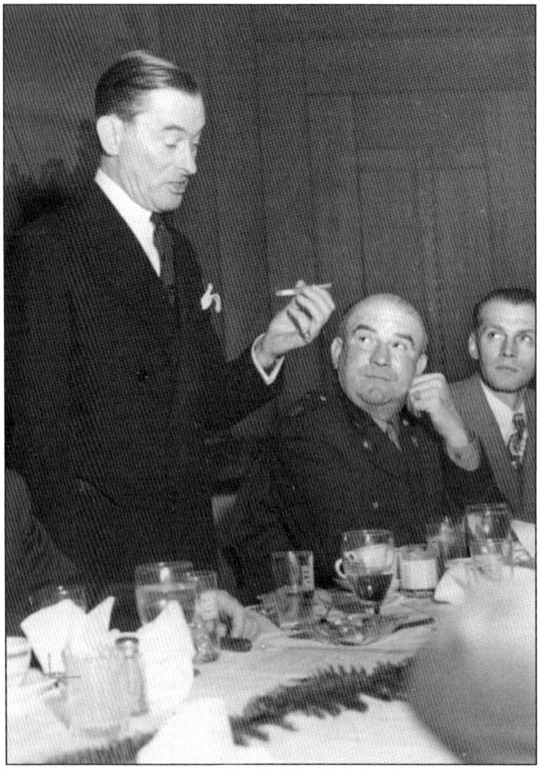

Former mayor James J. Walker speaks at a 1942 send-off dinner for Capt. Martin J. McEvilly, picture editor of the *Daily News*, now tasked with training Signal Corps photographers for service at the front.

Promoted to major, Martin McEvilly stands at far right with a group of other combat photographers, including Andy Lopez (second from right). Lopez would be wounded later that year when his jeep came under fire, though he would recover and go on to win a Pulitzer Prize in 1960. McEvilly escaped injury from a nearby explosion while coordinating operations. His son Cpl. Martin McEvilly Jr. was not as lucky. Formerly a photographer with *PM Magazine*, Corporal McEvilly was mortally wounded on the Guam beachhead. His father would travel there to visit his grave before returning home.

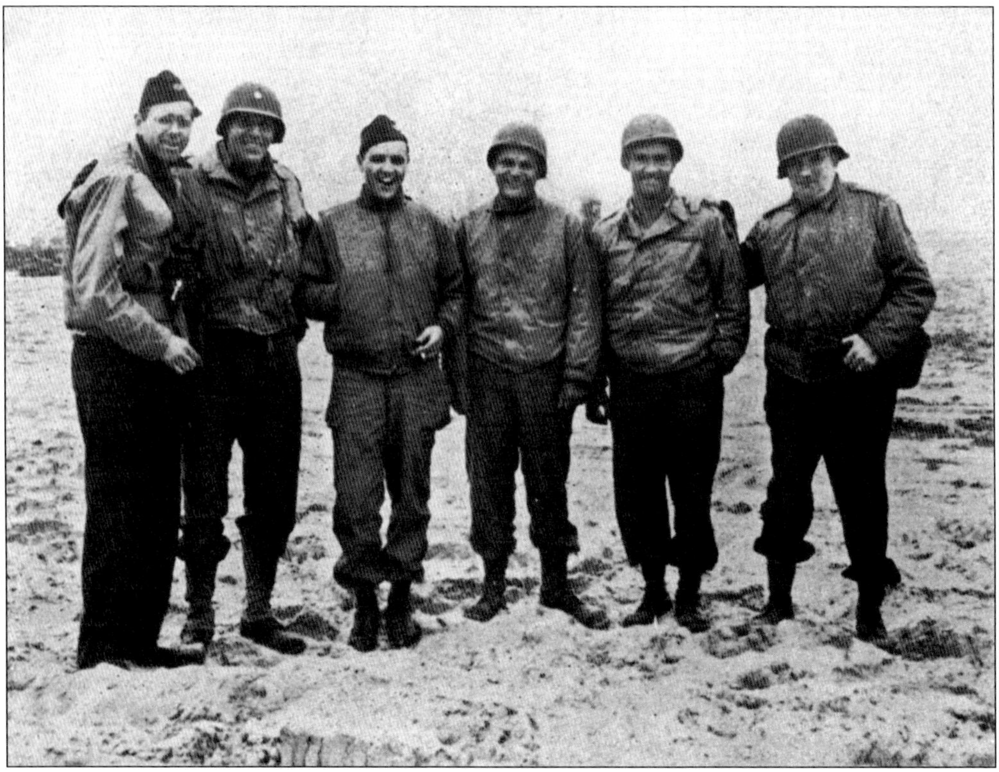

Harry Harris of the Associated Press wears a helmet emblazoned with a hand-lettered correspondents emblem and carries a newly produced Speed Graphic camera featuring blackened metal parts to decrease conspicuousness in combat. Writing about Harris and his comrades, one news writer said, "Not even the photo desk in New York knows exactly what these boys have been going through to get the pictures they have been shipping home. And the days when there are no pictures often are tougher than those which produce smash play stuff." Harris died at age 88 in 2002.

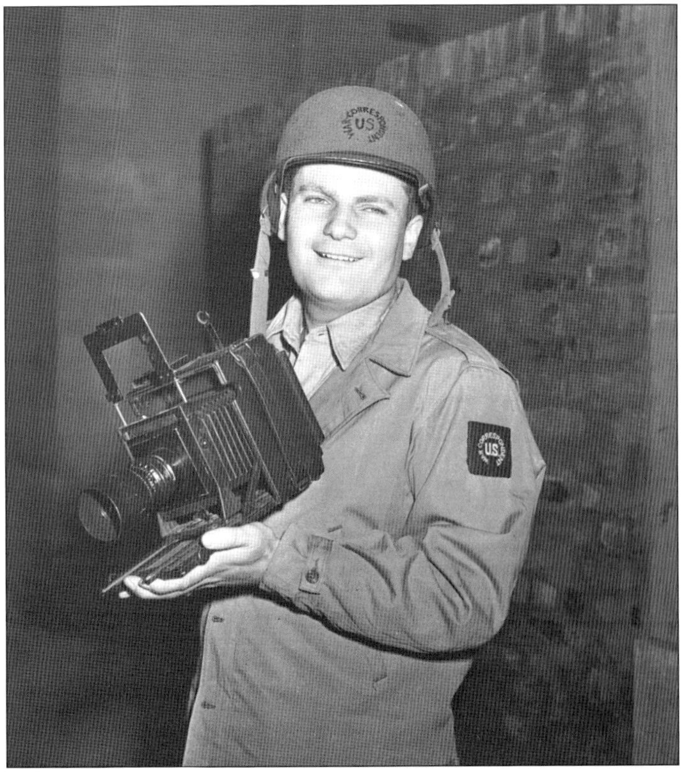

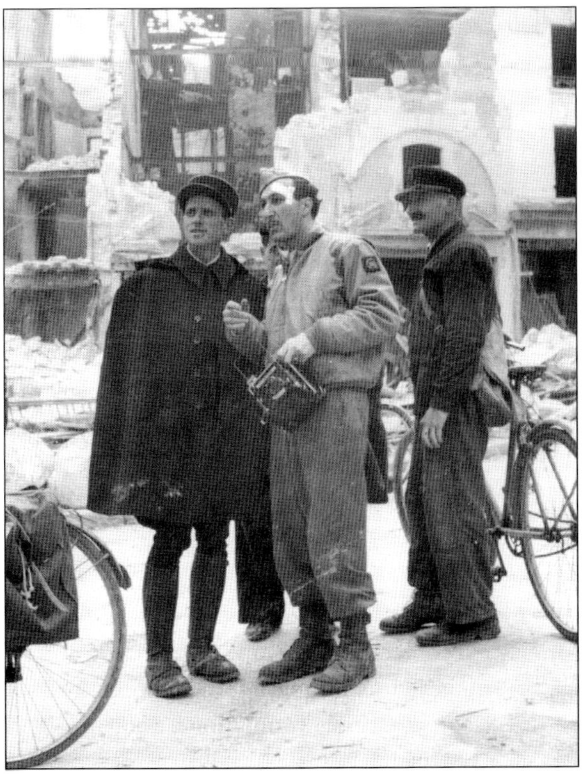

Sporting bandages on his face from shrapnel wounds, Dan Grossi, on assignment for the Associated Press, chats with French gendarmes. Coming under intense fire at Carentan in 1944, Grossi's colleagues urged him to take cover, but he refused, not wanting to dirty his uniform. While nursing six crushed ribs, Grossi was only able to lie down in the back of a truck as Americans victoriously paraded down the Champs-Élysées, but from this vantage point, he created an iconic photograph that was later used on a postage stamp.

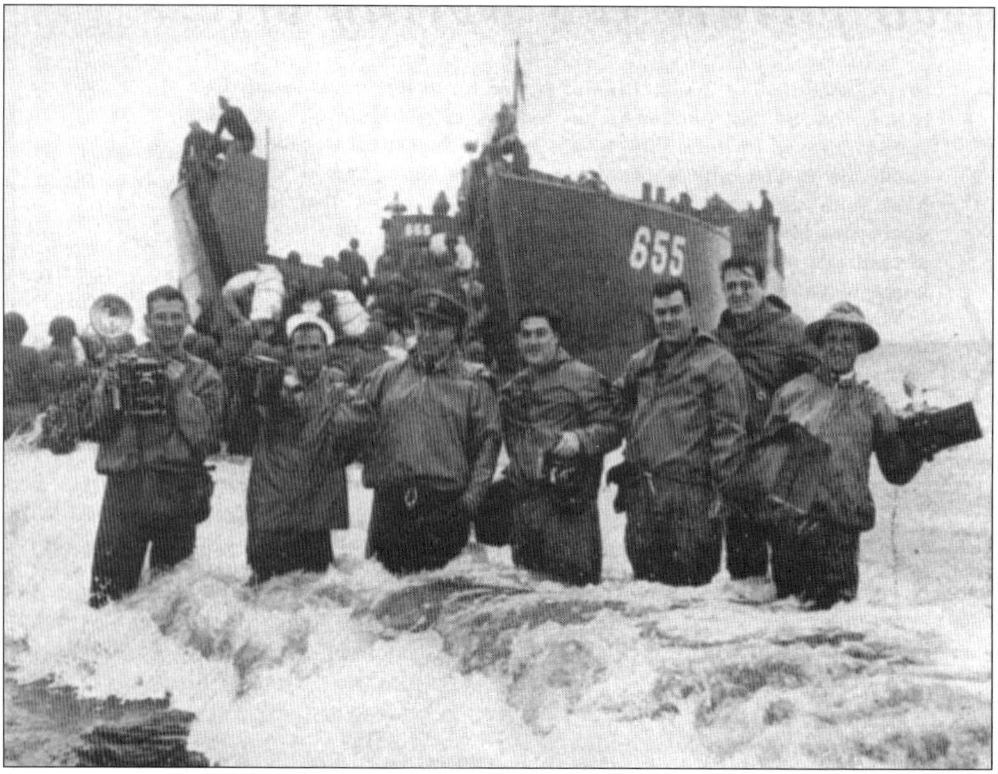

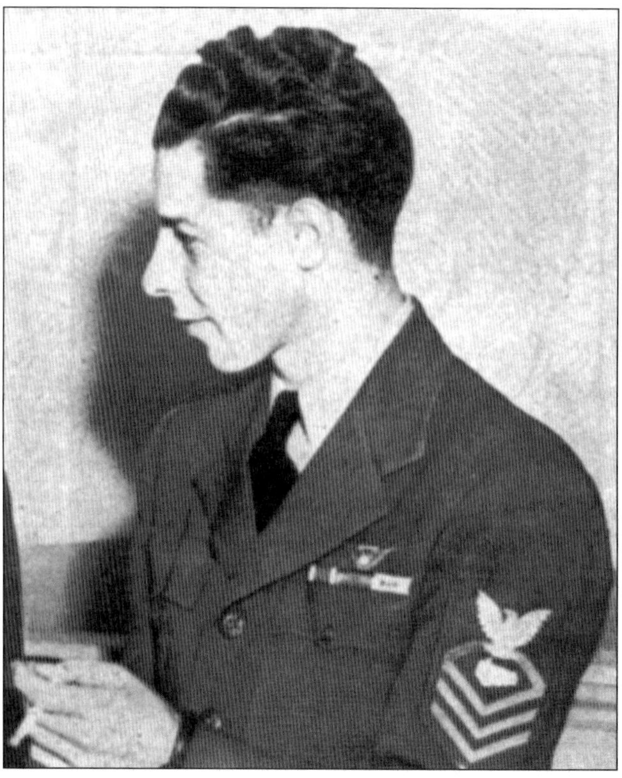

New York photographers Marty Black (far right) and Walter Kelleher (center) are knee deep in water but keep their cameras dry as they take part in an amphibious landing exercise.

CPO Ben Mancuso managed to make it back home to New York for the 1945 Press Photographers' Ball, albeit 20 pounds lighter than when he left and with decorations on his chest that told of his exploits while away in the Pacific. Formerly a photographer on the society scene for *Cosmo-Sileo*, Mancuso's picture assignments with the Navy earned him two Presidential Unit Citations, the Air Medal, the Good Conduct Medal, and three battle stars on his Naval Aircrew Wings.

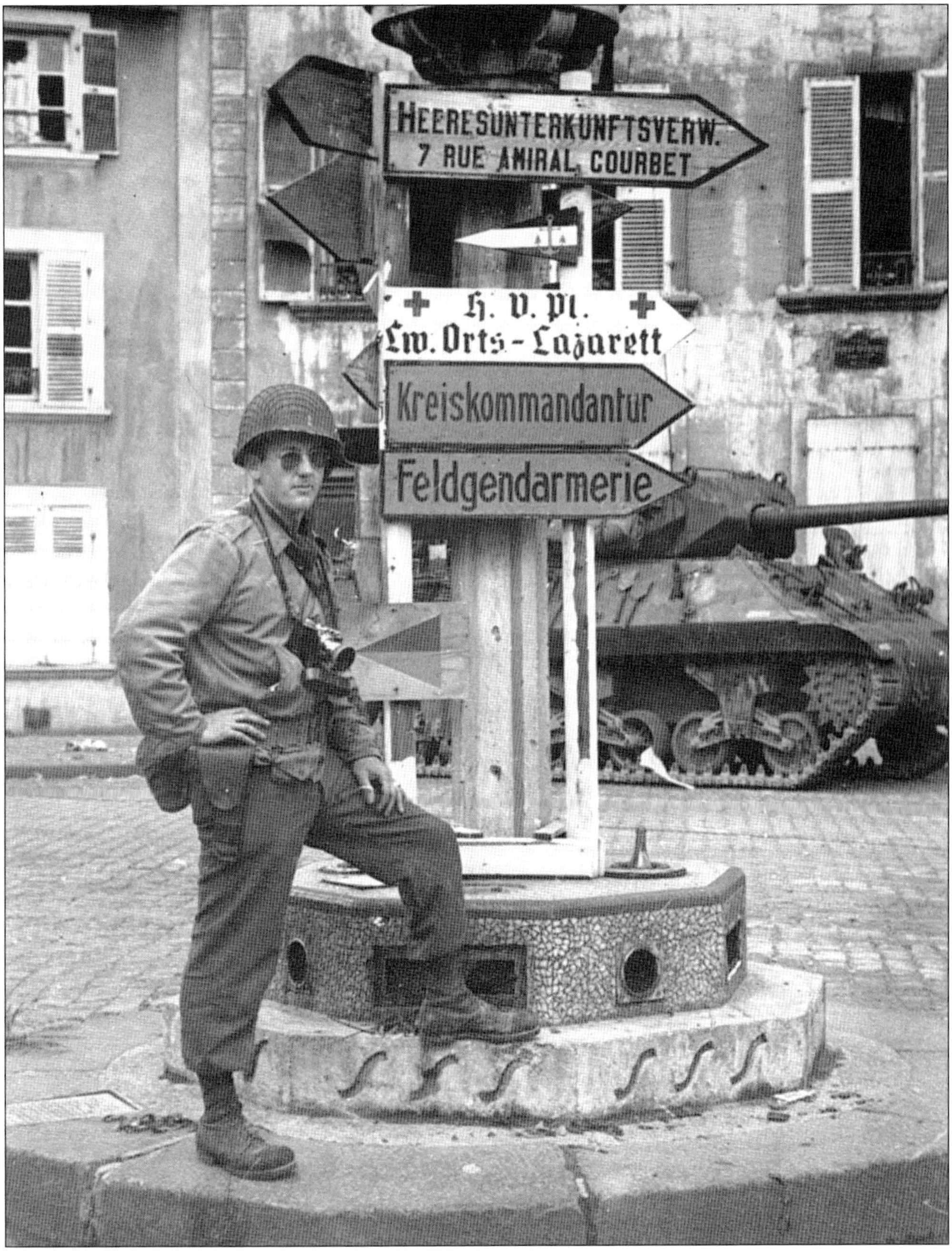

When the Normandy invasion was postponed 24 hours due to bad weather, no one considered how the extra day in captivity would affect the carrier pigeons, which the Army still relied on to fly rolls of exposed 35-millimeter film back to headquarters. Lt. Martin Lederhandler of the 165th Signal Photo Company landed on Utah Beach, photographing with his Leica camera and later affixing his film to one of two pigeons he carried. The disoriented bird flew toward the German lines. Some time later, Lederhandler, a Jewish native of Brooklyn, was shocked to see a German military magazine featuring one of his pictures, complete with a byline. Lederhandler returned to New York, where he worked for the Associated Press until his retirement in 2001.

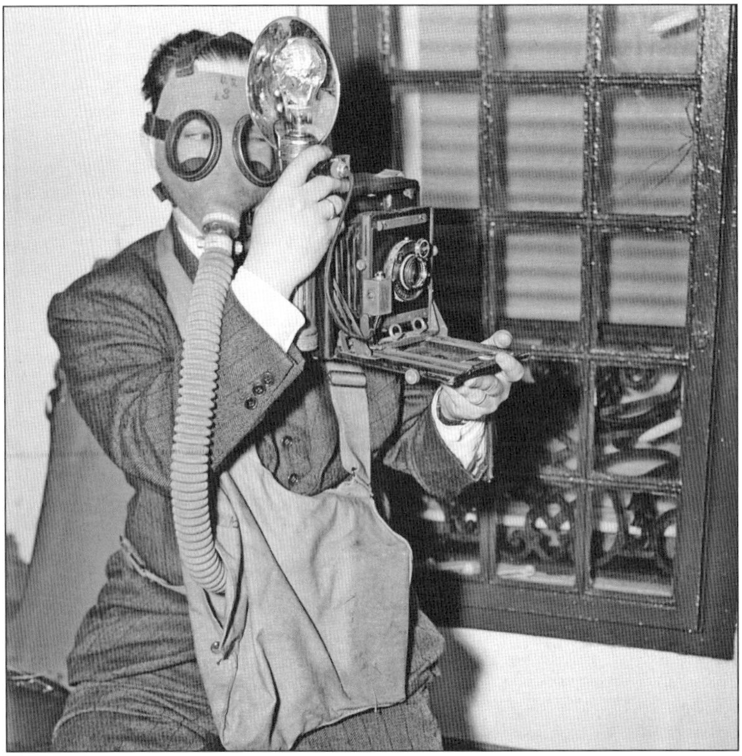

President Roosevelt's favorite photographer, Sammy Schulman, seems to delight in demonstrating his gas mask while en route to Europe in 1939 to manage International News Pictures' Paris bureau. He would end up on the front lines of the Allied invasion of Africa in 1942 and would once more be warmly greeted by the commander-in-chief at the Casablanca Conference in 1943. (Courtesy of the Associated Press.)

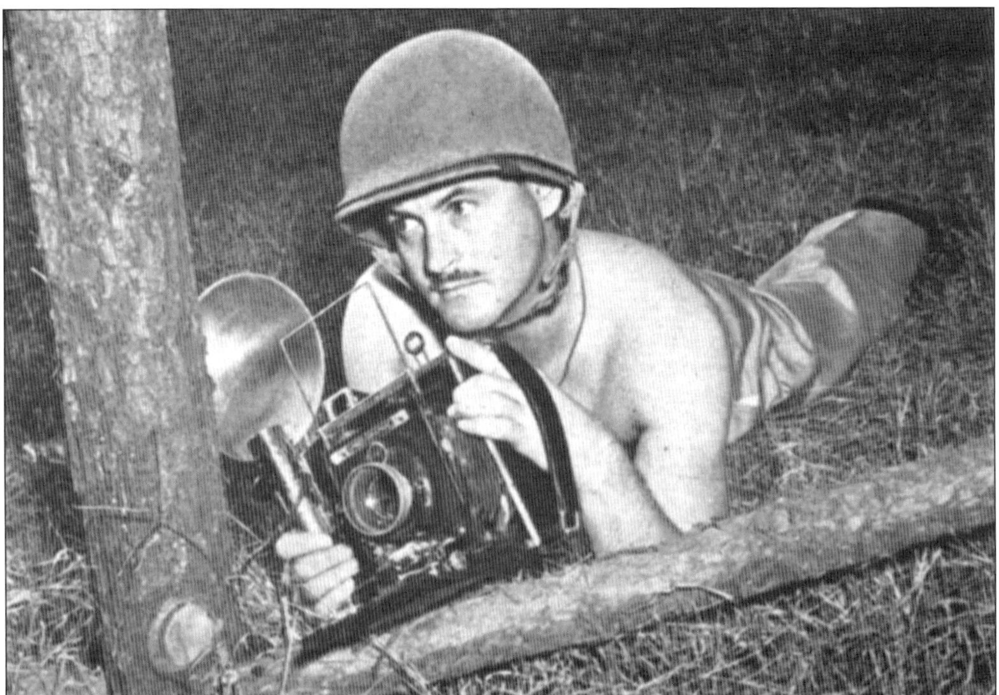

After training at Camp Peary, Virginia, *Daily News* photographer Leroy Jakob, seen here shirtless, accompanied the Seabees into action.

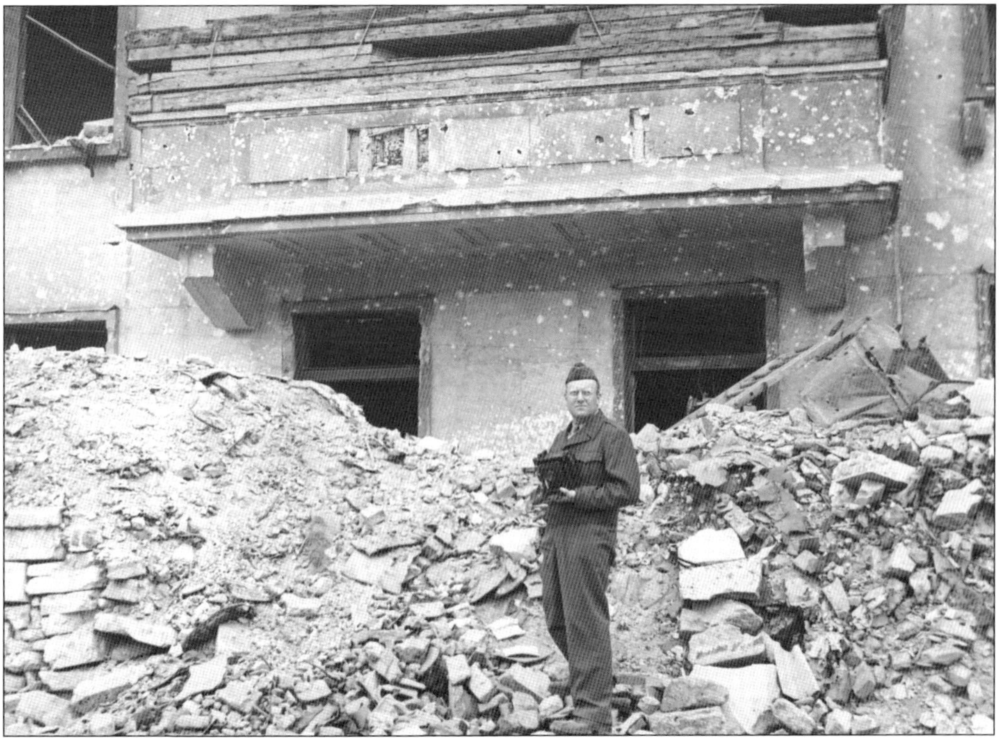

John Reidy had a long career at the *Daily Mirror* and was part of the 113th Regimental Combat Team's Service Company when World War II got under way. Stateside, he excelled in a carbine-firing competition, likening weapon skills to camera skills. His photographic talents were put to use during the occupation of Berlin. Here, Reidy stands under the balcony of the Reich Chancellery, which has been hastily turned into a defensive machine gun position.

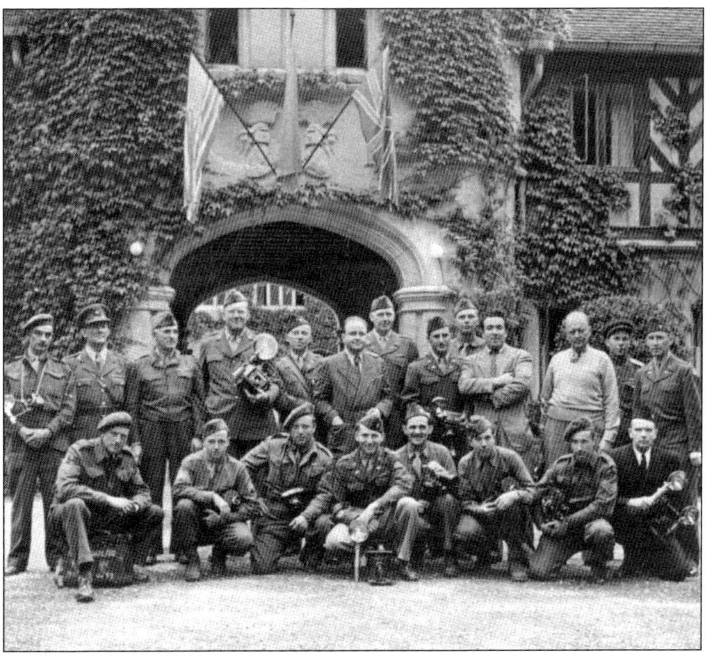

Reidy (second row, fourth from left) appears among the photographers and correspondents covering the Potsdam Conference in 1945. Other metropolitan newsers are Edward Stiso of the *Newark Star-Ledger* (first row, fourth from left), Robert Wands of Wide World Photos (second row, far right), and Jack Harris of the Associated Press (second row, sixth from right). The feeling of a reunion among friends after a long ordeal did not escape these photographers.

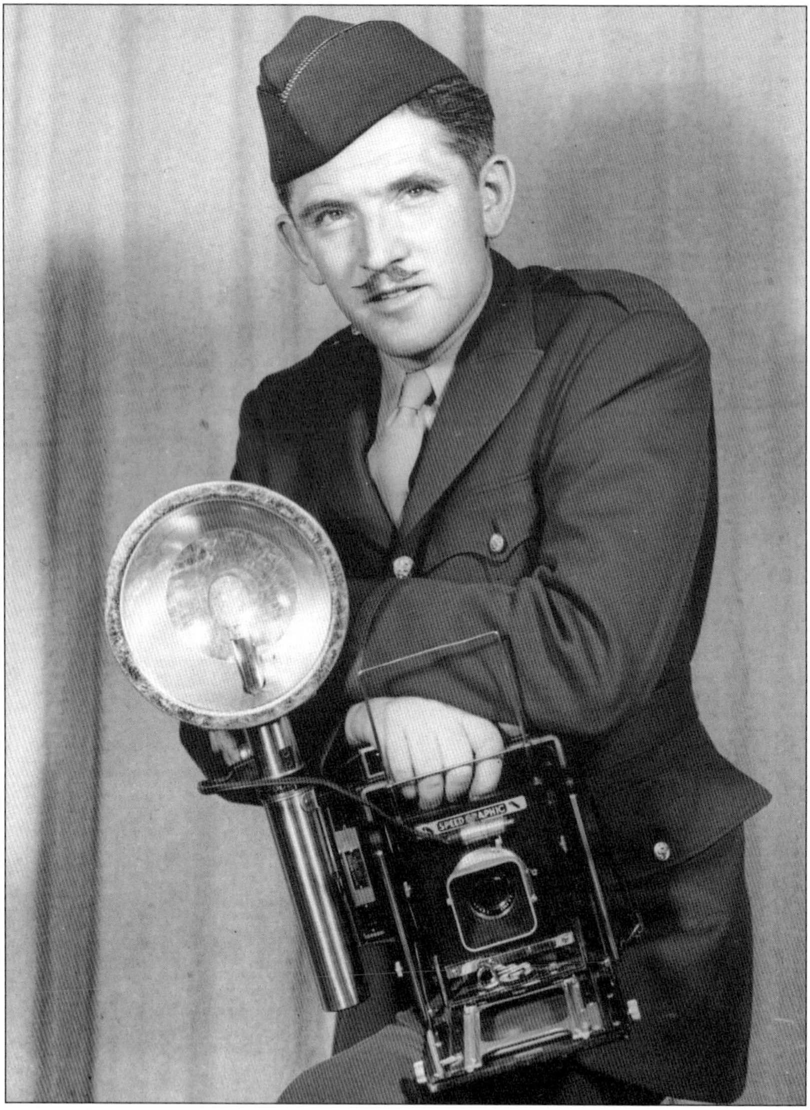

Born in Denmark in 1904, Carl Thusgaard came to America in 1927, then went to work as a messenger for Acme Newspictures in 1930, becoming a photographer a short time later. With the onset of World War II, Thusgaard jumped at the chance to cover the action. Soon after arriving in New Guinea in 1943, however, he received word that his son had died of peritonitis. Acme offered him the chance to return home, but he declined. "I have seen a lot of sad things here caused by the war and, when I compare our lot with the lot of others, we are not so bad off after all," he said. "I can assure you this sad event has not in any way altered my determination to stay here and do the job I was sent out to do." At Nassau Bay, Thusgaard jumped into a foxhole to avoid aerial fire, but as he said, "I got some good pictures of the attack." On July 20, 1943, Thusgaard was aboard a B-24 from the 5th Air Force on a bombing mission when it came under fire. Reportedly suspended over the open bomb doors, Thusgaard continued to man his camera until the plane exploded in a ball of fire. The only survivor, the nose gunner, was blown away from the wreckage. Thusgaard's body was never recovered. On December 17, 1943, Press Photographers Association president Joseph Costa joined Thusgaard's widow, Madeline, and daughter, Anne, for the launching of a floating tribute—a Liberty ship christened the SS *Carl Thusgaard*.

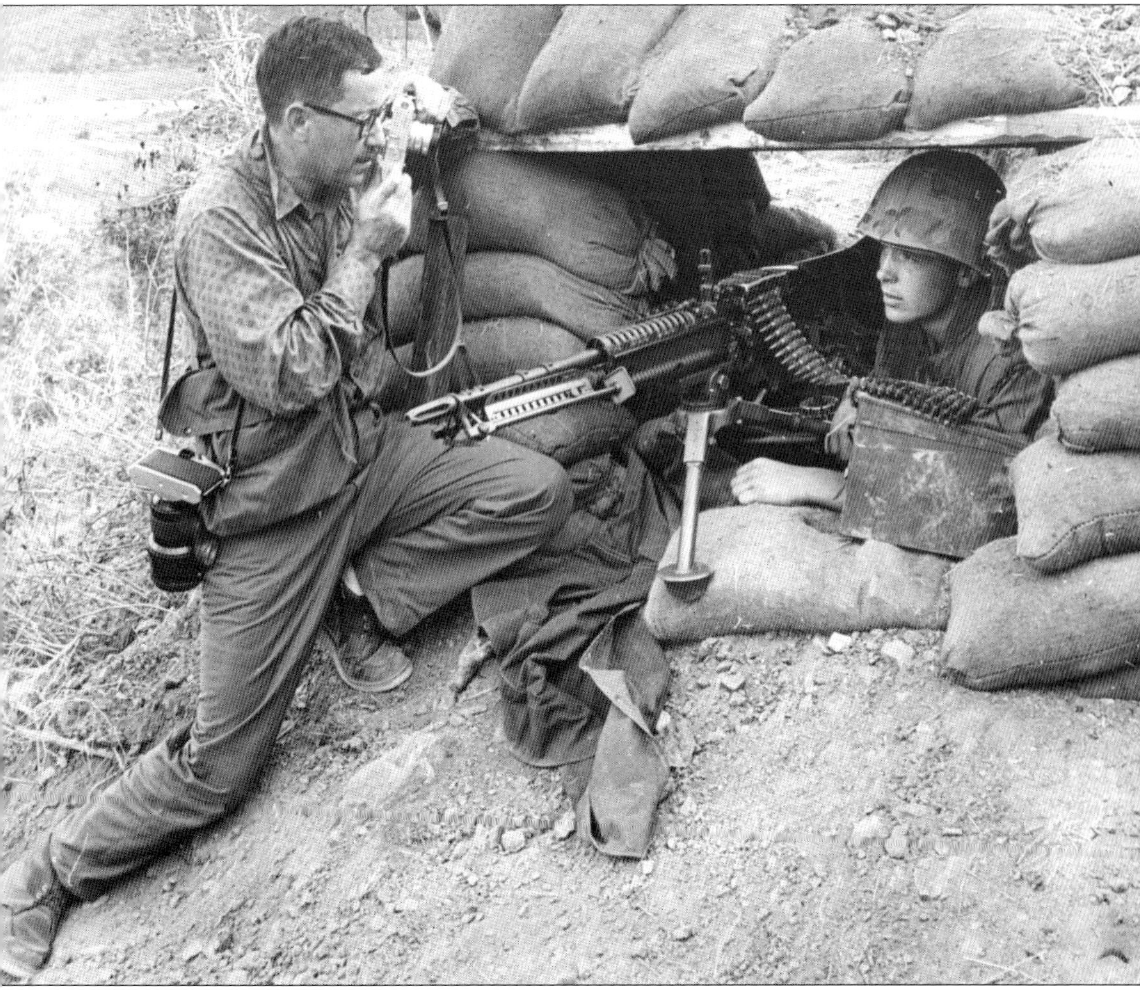

At the height of the Cold War, New York's photographers raced to the scene of the conflict. Here, Ira Rosenberg photographs an American soldier manning a machine gun at Guantanamo Bay during the Cuban Missile Crisis in 1962.

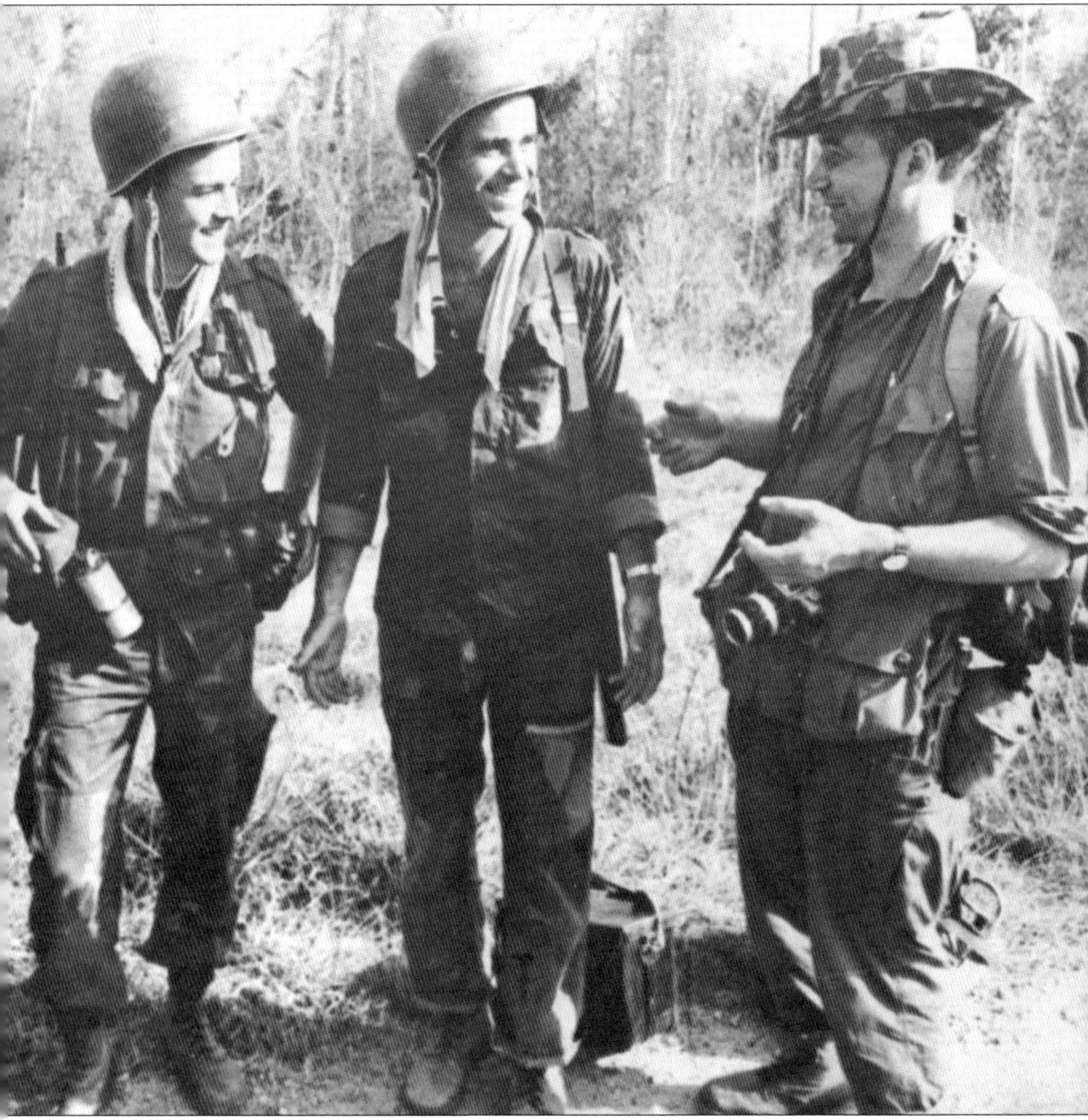

Seen here in 1965, Eddie Adams (right) is arguably the best-known American photographer to cover the Vietnam War. Operating from the New York bureau of the Associated Press, Adams also served as a combat photographer for the Marine Corps during the Korean War. Winner of the 1969 Pulitzer Prize, his photograph of the execution of a Vietcong prisoner is one of the iconic images of the century.

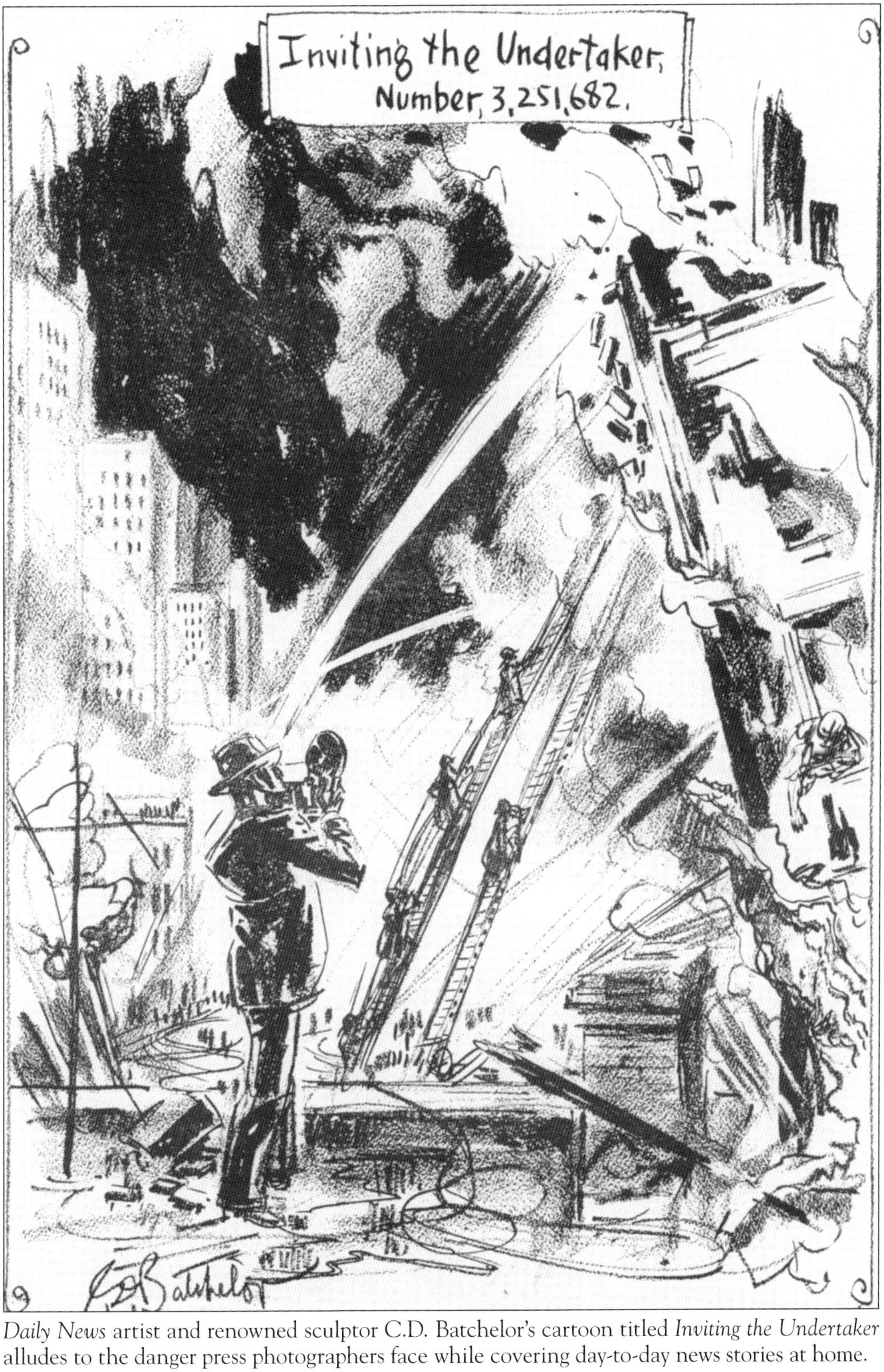

Daily News artist and renowned sculptor C.D. Batchelor's cartoon titled *Inviting the Undertaker* alludes to the danger press photographers face while covering day-to-day news stories at home.

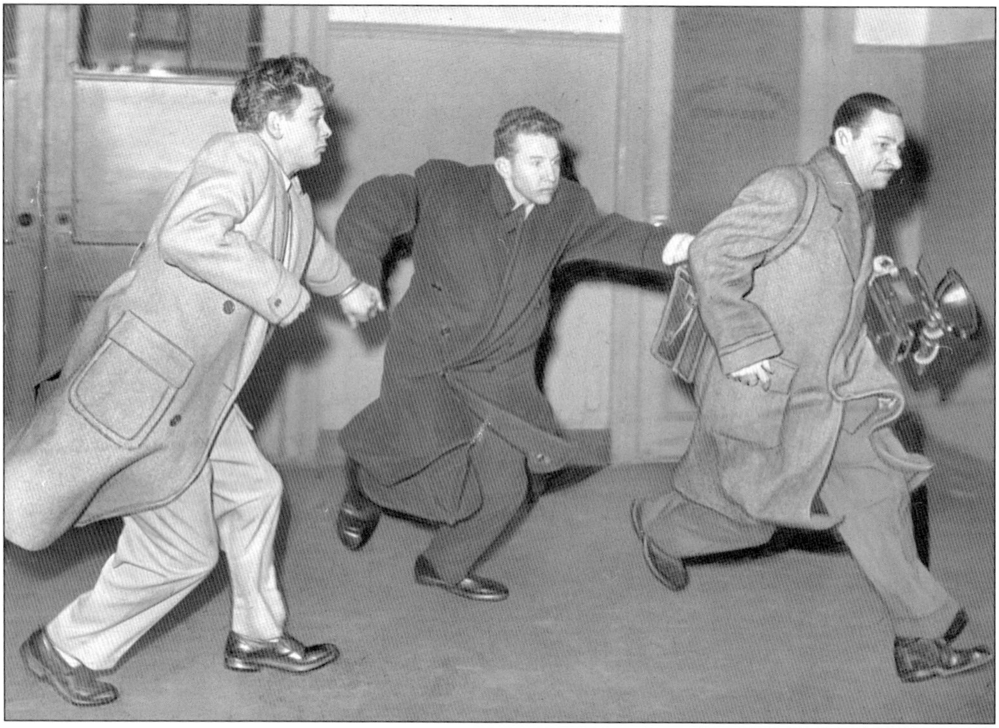

Photographers have often dealt with uncooperative subjects, many of whom have lashed out verbally and some physically. Broken cameras and broken bones were such an occupational hazard that New York State lawmakers passed legislation making it a crime to assault a press photographer. It was little deterrent, however, as seen in these two incidents from the mid-1950s, and eventually, the law would sunset. (Above, courtesy of the *Daily News*.)

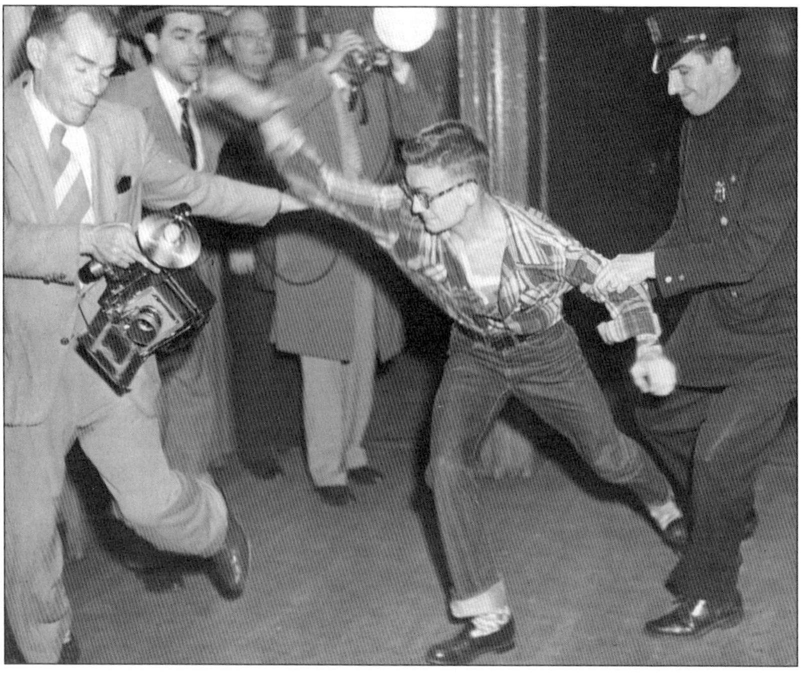

On June 25, 1958, a catastrophic collision between the freighter *Nebraska* and tanker *Empress Bay* occurred in the East River, near the Manhattan Bridge. Among the photographers who raced to the scene was William Finn of the *Journal-American*. Finn, who was described by reporter Jeanne Toomey as "a lovable redheaded Irish-American," had served several terms as president of the Press Photographers Association. While photographing the scene, 52-year-old Finn collapsed and died of an apparent heart attack. His final photograph, however, received national distribution. (Both, author's collection.)

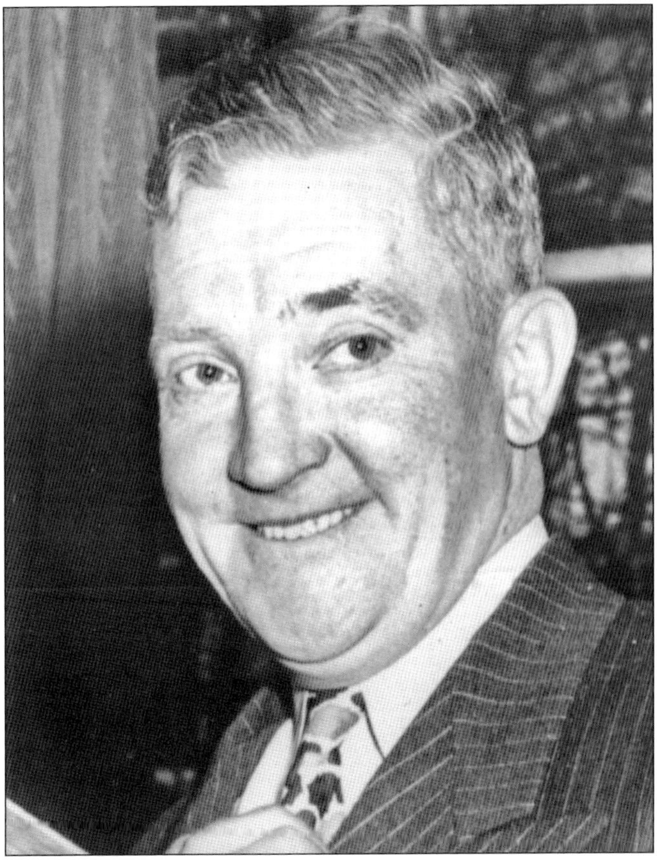

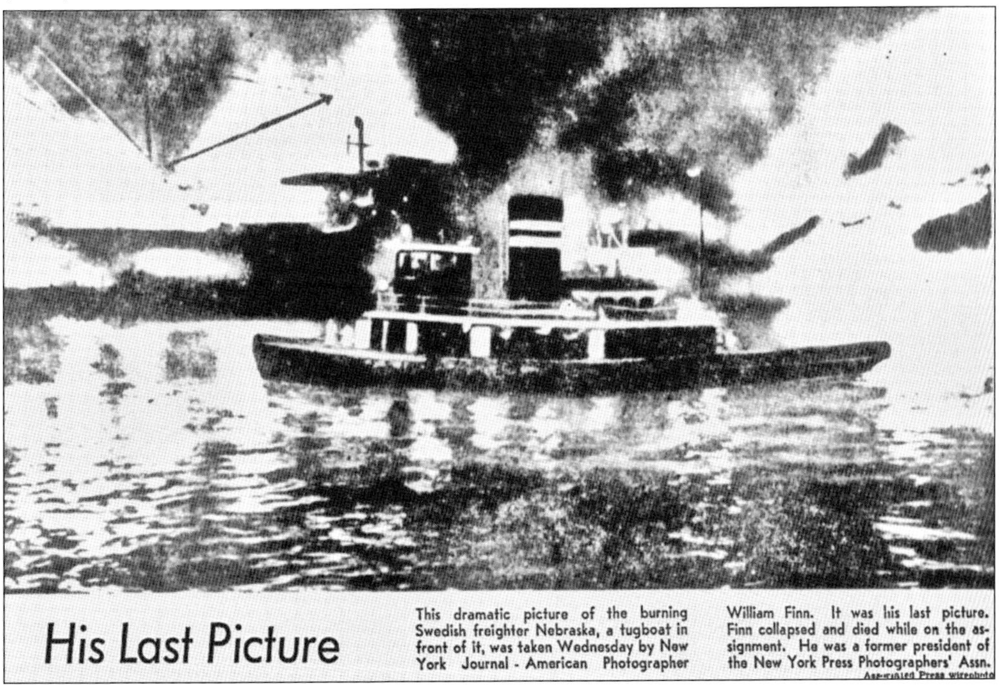

His Last Picture

This dramatic picture of the burning Swedish freighter Nebraska, a tugboat in front of it, was taken Wednesday by New York Journal - American Photographer William Finn. It was his last picture. Finn collapsed and died while on the assignment. He was a former president of the New York Press Photographers' Assn.

Associated Press wirephoto

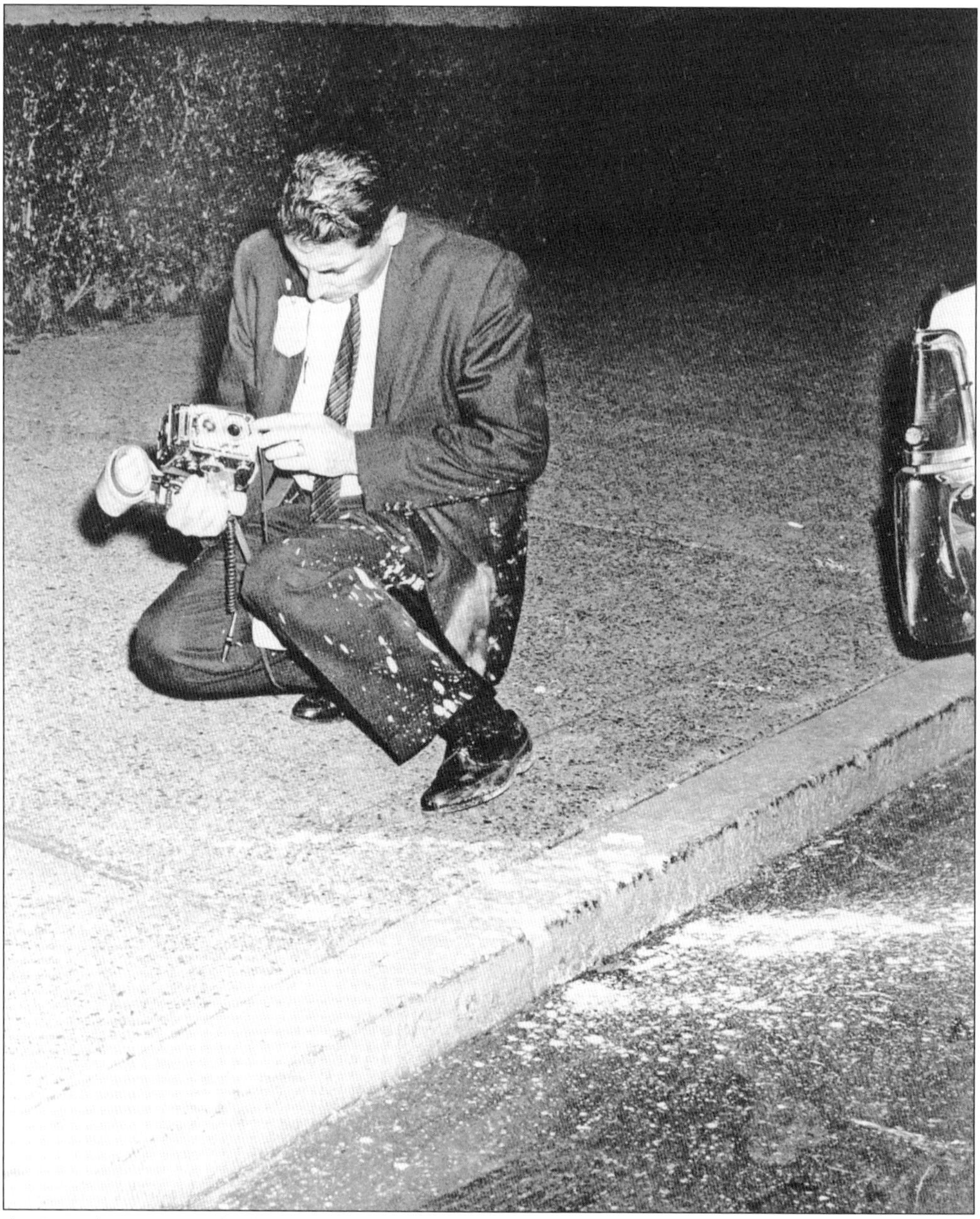

As President Kennedy dined in a Fifth Avenue apartment on September 19, 1963, a station wagon occupied by shouting teenagers pulled alongside the presidential limousine and hurled a plastic egg filled with white paint at Secret Service driver William Greer. Next to him was *Mirror* photographer Bob Wendlinger, pictured, who was himself doused. A true professional, however, Wendlinger was more concerned about the welfare of his equipment. (Courtesy of the Associated Press.)

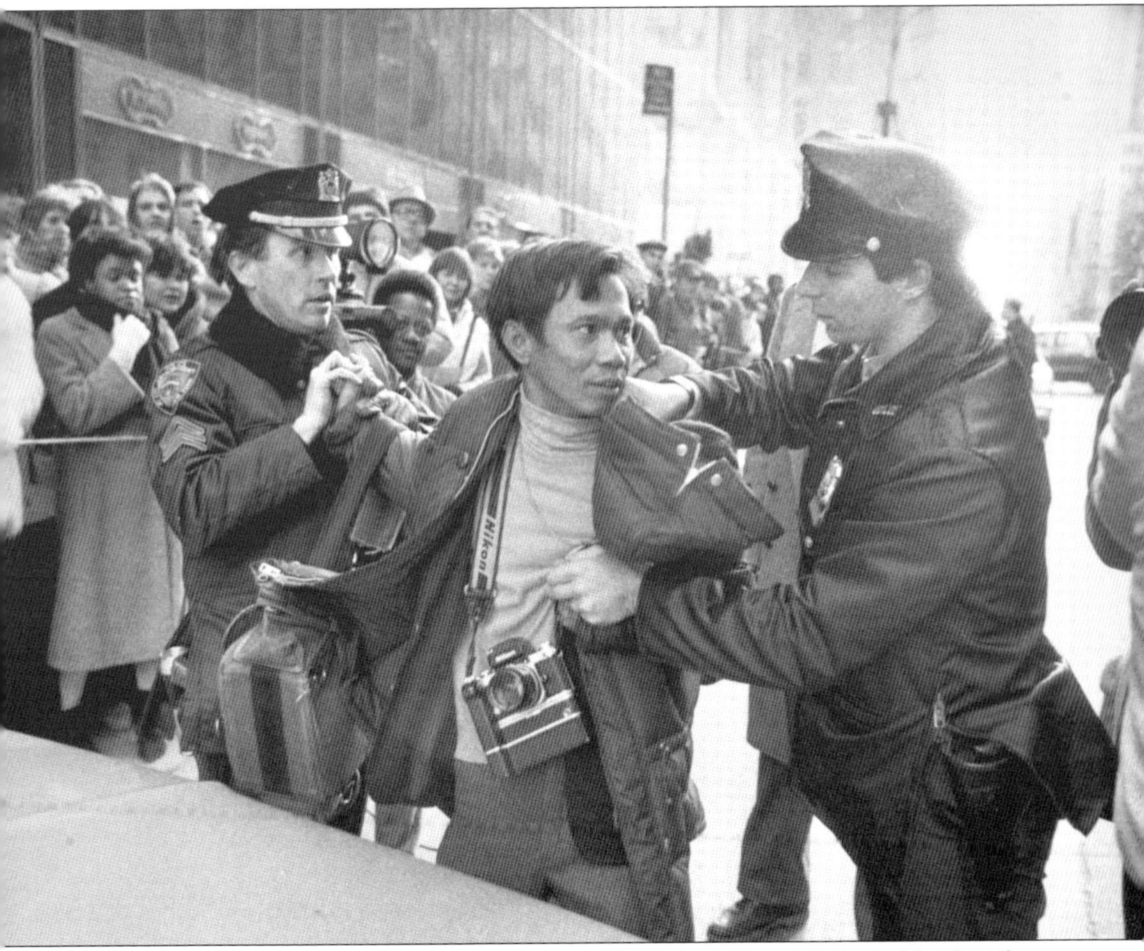

Born in Cambodia in 1942, Dith Pran was witness to the genocide perpetrated by the Khmer Rouge in the 1970s. Linking up with *New York Times* correspondent Sydney Schamberg, Dith photographed as much of the turmoil around him as he could before being taken prisoner himself. He managed to escape in 1979 and immigrated to the United States. Working for the *Times*, Dith was not exempt from the trials of the New York City press photographer, as seen here while he is detained by two police officers, but his resilience made him a success. Dith died in 2008.

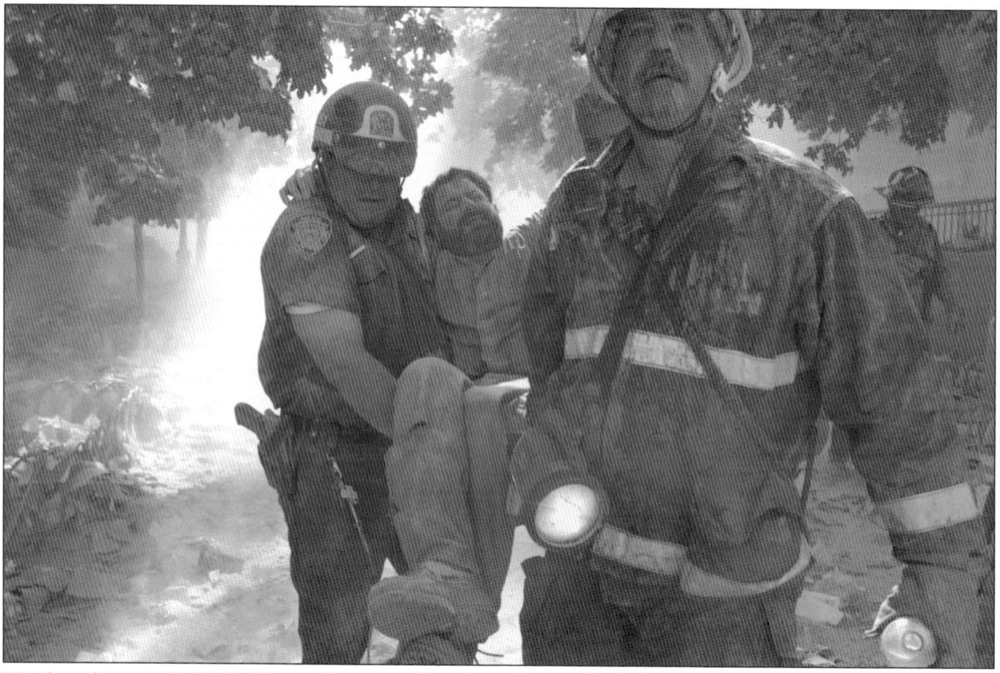

His leg shattered, *Daily News* photographer David Handschuh is carried from the scene of the World Trade Center collapse. A veteran of many fire scenes in his career, Handschuh followed the ill-fated Rescue Company No. 1 down the West Side Highway to the scene. After the collapse, Handschuh's colleague Todd Maisel helped get him to safety and took custody of his cameras, ensuring that his pictures were seen. After a long recovery period, Handschuh returned to work in 2002 and became an advocate for journalists suffering from post-traumatic stress disorder and other health problems from their time covering the World Trade Center. *New York Post* photographers Bolivar Arellano and Don Halasy were also among those who were struck by debris. (Photograph by Todd Maisel; courtesy of the *Daily News*.)

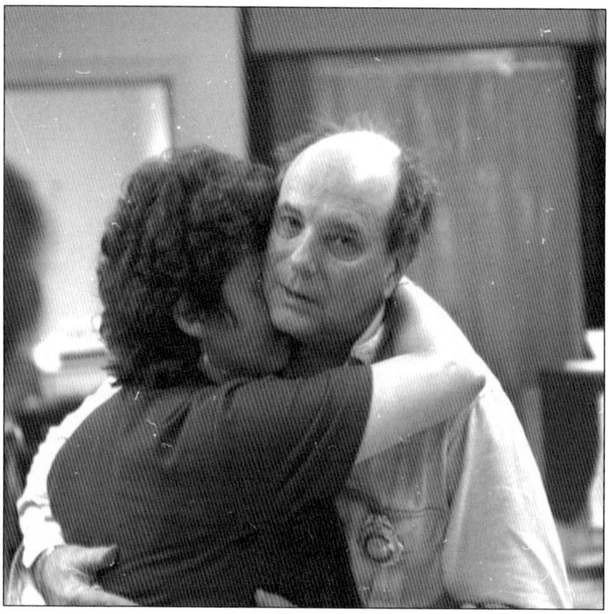

After surviving the collapse of the World Trade Center, *Daily News* photographer Tom Monaster is hugged by photo editor Jo Barefoot as he returns to the office. Monaster, who wears an honorary fire chief's badge, narrowly escaped the cascading debris from the second tower by ducking under a fire engine. "Whatever the motivation was for me as a young photographer when I first started out in photojournalism, 9/11 put the cap on it," he would later say. (Photograph by the author.)

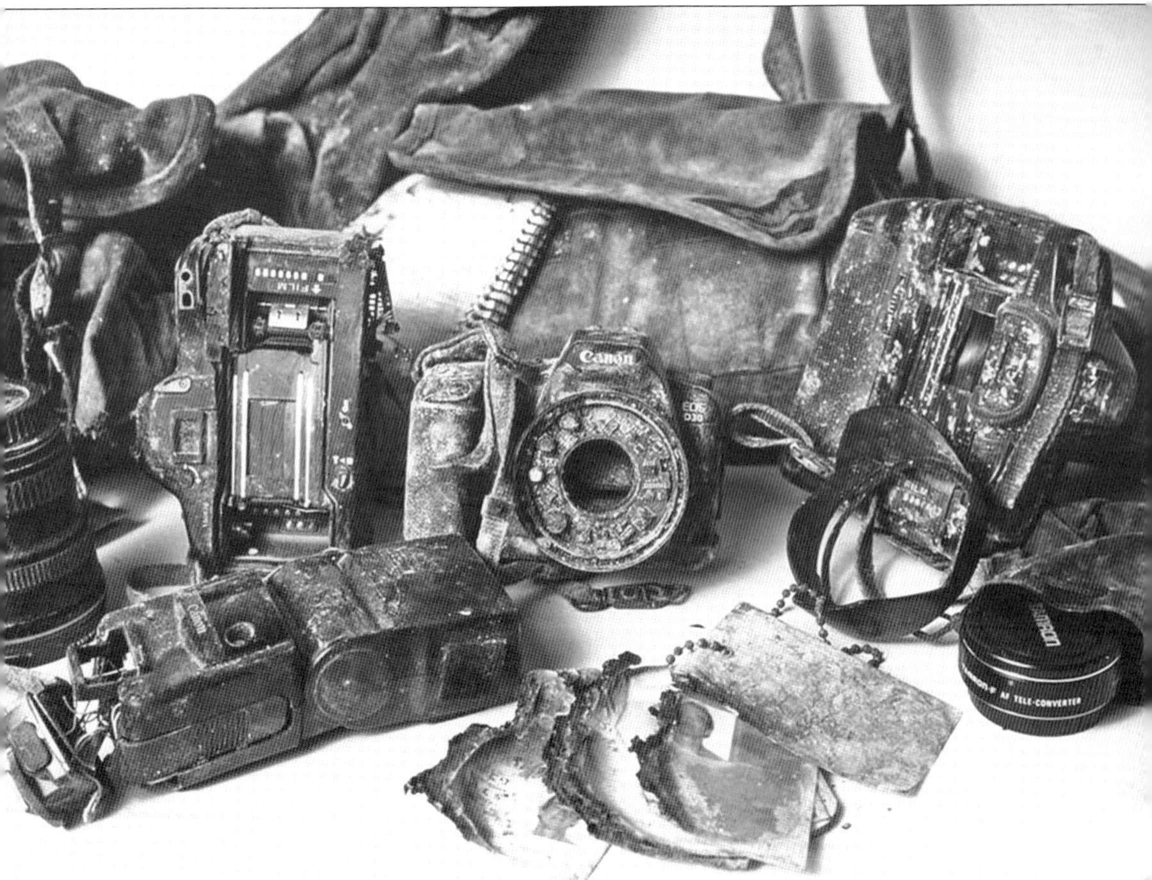

On the morning of September 11, 2001, Bill Biggart, a 54-year-old freelance photographer whose work had taken him to the Middle East, Northern Ireland, and all across America, found himself, laden with three cameras, rushing down a Manhattan street toward the burning World Trade Center. Shooting as he went, he arrived at the scene shortly before the collapse of the first tower. A short time later, Biggart perished in the collapse of the second tower. His body was found four days later, as was his equipment, from which colleague Chip East was able to recover over 150 of Biggart's final photographs. (Courtesy of Chip East.)

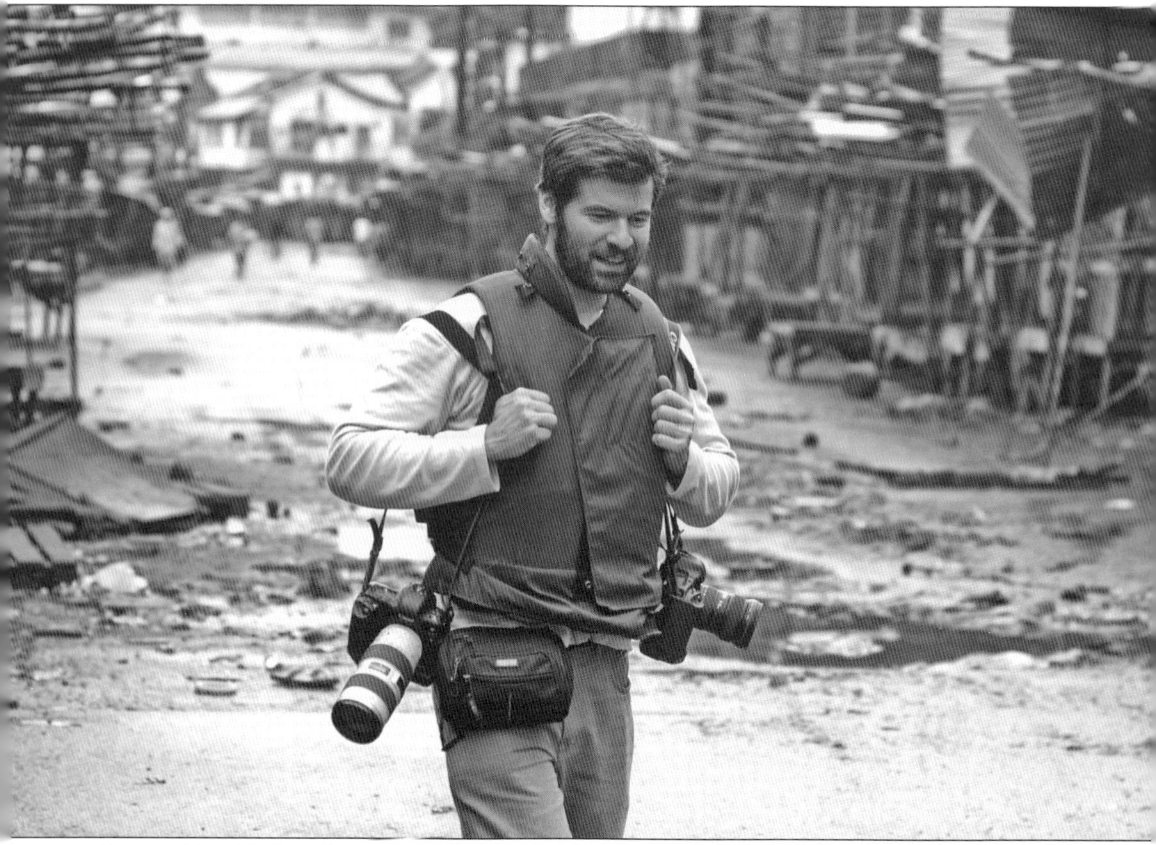

Born in New York and raised in North Carolina, Chris Hondros had returned to his native city after a stint at the *Fayetteville Observer* when he began covering international news in 1998. His diverse assignments for Getty Images took him to war zones in Kosovo, Afghanistan, Iraq, and Liberia; along the campaign trail with Sen. John Kerry; and to every type of local news story, from the United Nations to the streets of Brooklyn. In 2011, when Hondros and his fiancée were planning their August wedding, turmoil erupted in Libya, and there were pictures to be made. On April 21, Hondros and several other photographers were trailing rebels through the streets of Misrata when they came under mortar fire. Hondros was killed, along with Brooklyn-based freelancer Tim Hetherington. The Chris Hondros Fund was created in his memory to support and promote the work of photojournalists in conflict zones. (Courtesy of Nic Bothma.)

Four

Emblems of a Trade

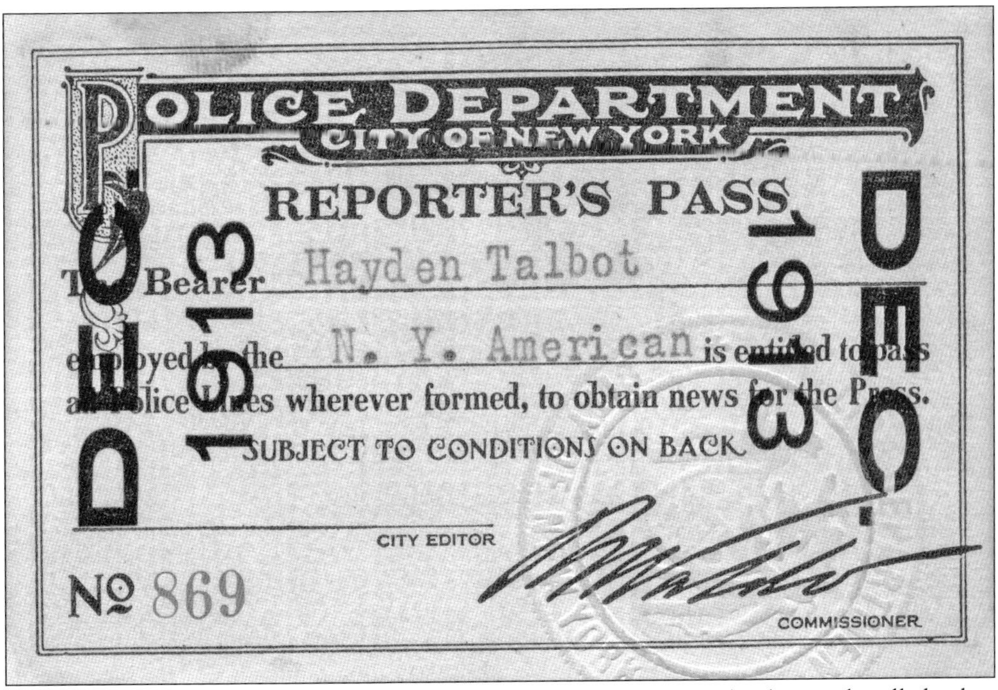

Since the early 1900s, the police department has issued press credentials, alternately called police cards, to members of the media. This 1913 card contained wording that would appear in one variation or another for over a century: "The Bearer . . . is entitled to pass all Police Lines wherever formed, to obtain news for the Press." Traditionally, the fire department distributed its own metal badges to authorized persons at the scenes of fires, but the police card would soon be modified to include this access, with the signature of the fire commissioner. (Author's collection.)

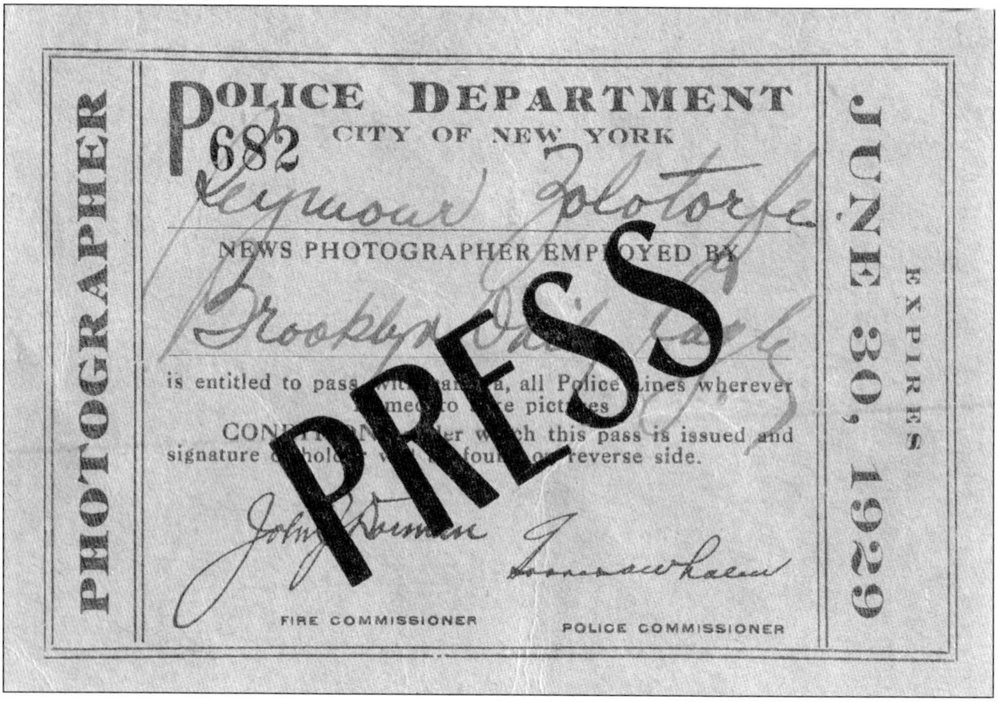

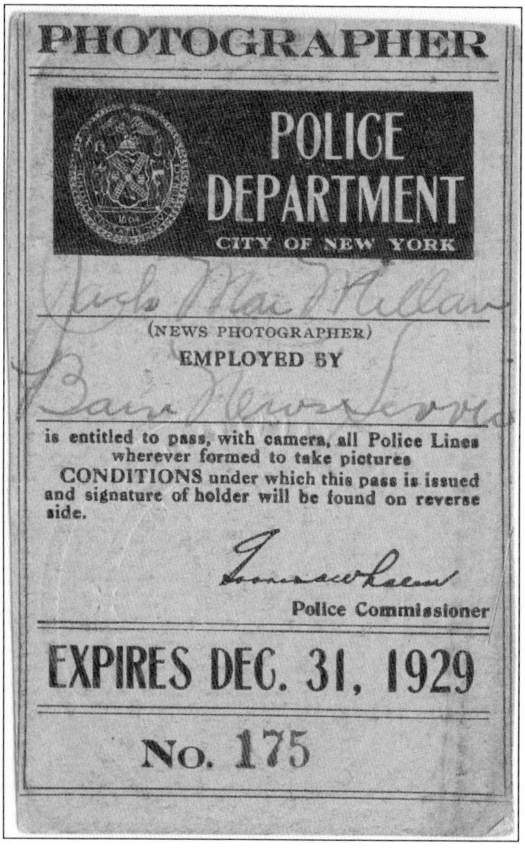

Evidently, for the first part of the 20th century, press cards did not distinguish between reporters and photographers; however, by the 1920s, a variant of the card had been issued especially for photographers. The influence of the News Photographers Association at this time was such that a member in arrears with dues, or otherwise in bad standing, could have his police card revoked. This card was issued to Seymour Zolotorofe, whose name has been misspelled. It was such a common occurrence that he simply became known to friends as "Zee."

The length of time for which press cards were issued varied widely over the years. Early on, they were issued monthly. By 1929, it had been extended to every six months. In the 1930s and 1940s, it was every three months. In the 1950s, it was annually. By the turn of the 21st century, it was every two years. Designs and colors would change often as well. This card, used in the latter half of 1929, marked a switch to a vertical format, meant to be displayed more prominently in the user's hatband.

By 1934, the amount of press cards in circulation was felt to have gotten out of hand; those with questionable affiliations or who did not regularly cover emergency scenes were widely deemed ineligible. Under the chairmanship of Mayor La Guardia's secretary, ex-newspaperman Les Stone, the Advisory Committee on Press Cards was organized, of which Press Photographers Association president Walter Ranzini was a part. Redesigned as an elongated police badge, the number of cards was curtailed, and their issuance was strictly regulated. (Author's collection.)

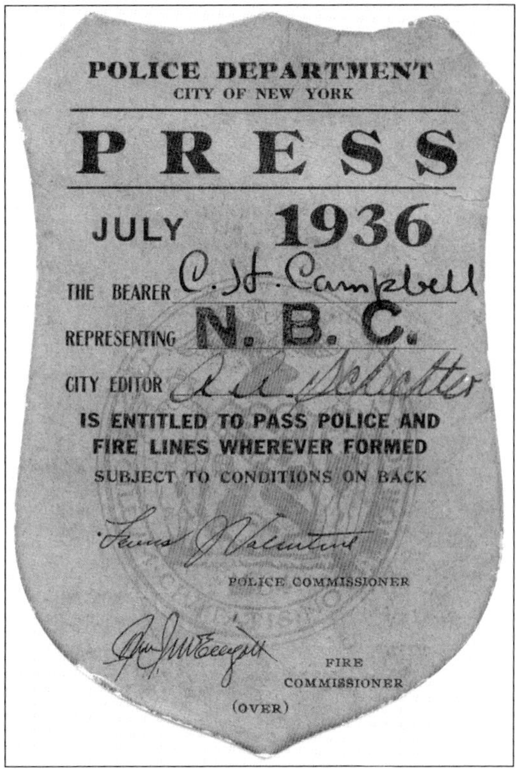

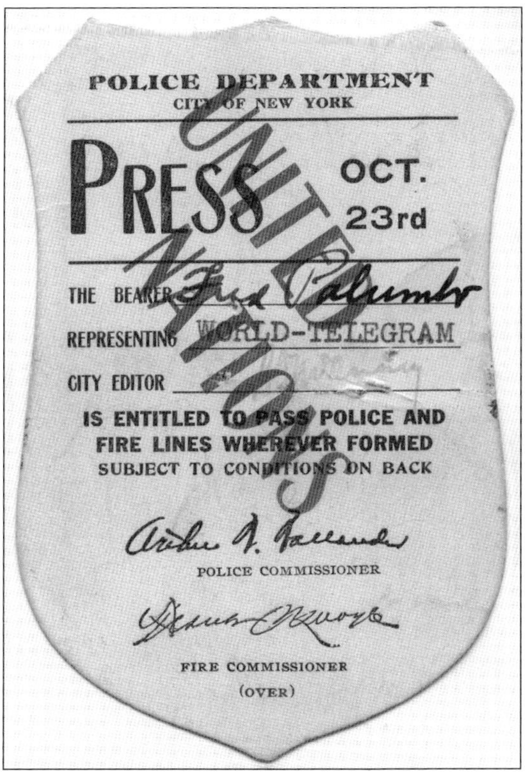

Major events taking place within the city often warranted their own temporary cards, particularly when visiting media would be present. Even the locals, such as *World-Telegram* photographer Fred Palumbo during the 1946 UN General Assembly, would have to carry the event's special credential. They were practically identical to the standard card, except they bore the imprint of the event and the dates of validity. (Author's collection.)

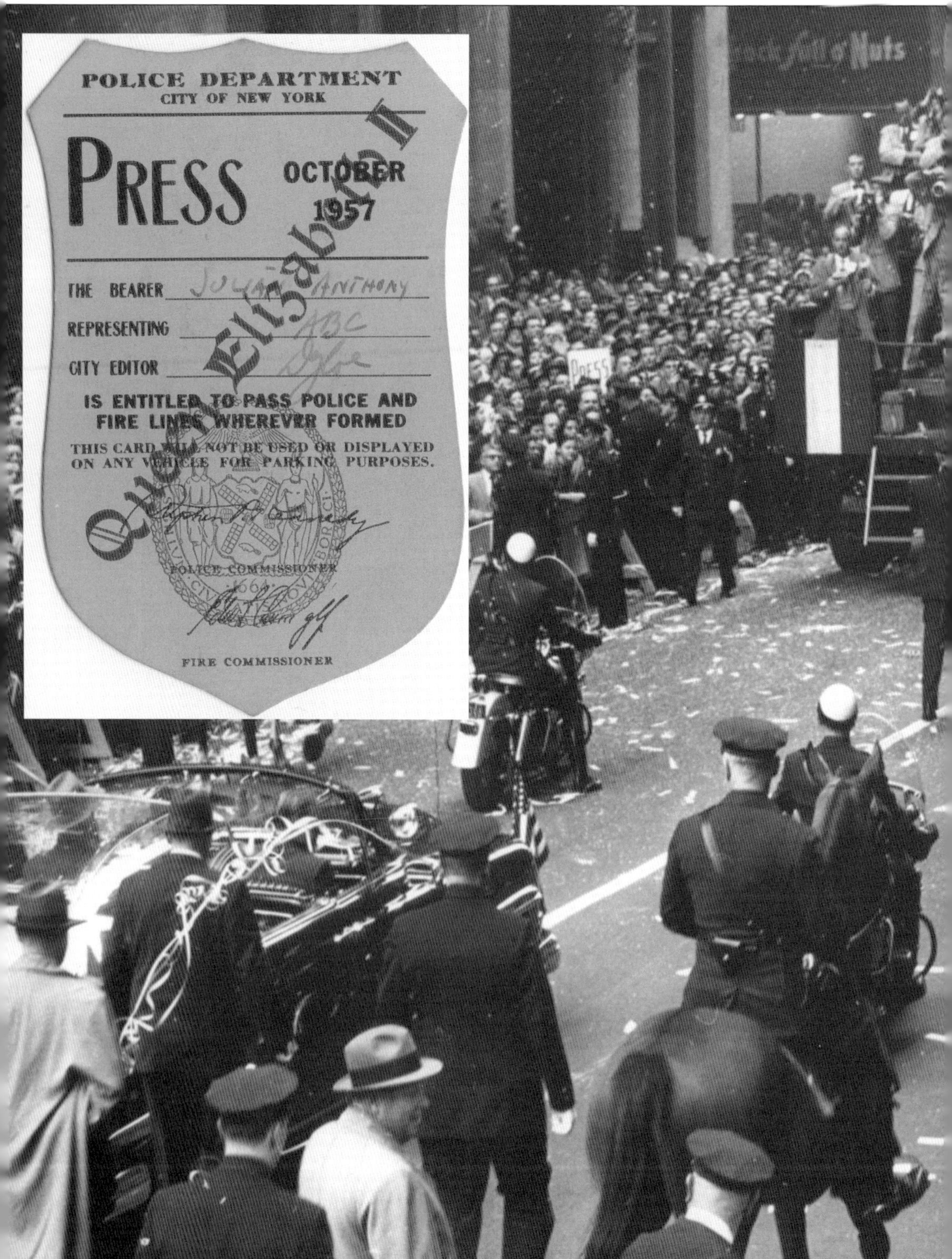
POLICE DEPARTMENT
CITY OF NEW YORK
PRESS
OCTOBER
1957
Queen Elizabeth II
THE BEARER
REPRESENTING
CITY EDITOR
IS ENTITLED TO PASS POLICE AND
FIRE LINES WHEREVER FORMED
THIS CARD WILL NOT BE USED OR DISPLAYED
ON ANY VEHICLE FOR PARKING PURPOSES.
POLICE COMMISSIONER
FIRE COMMISSIONER
PRESS

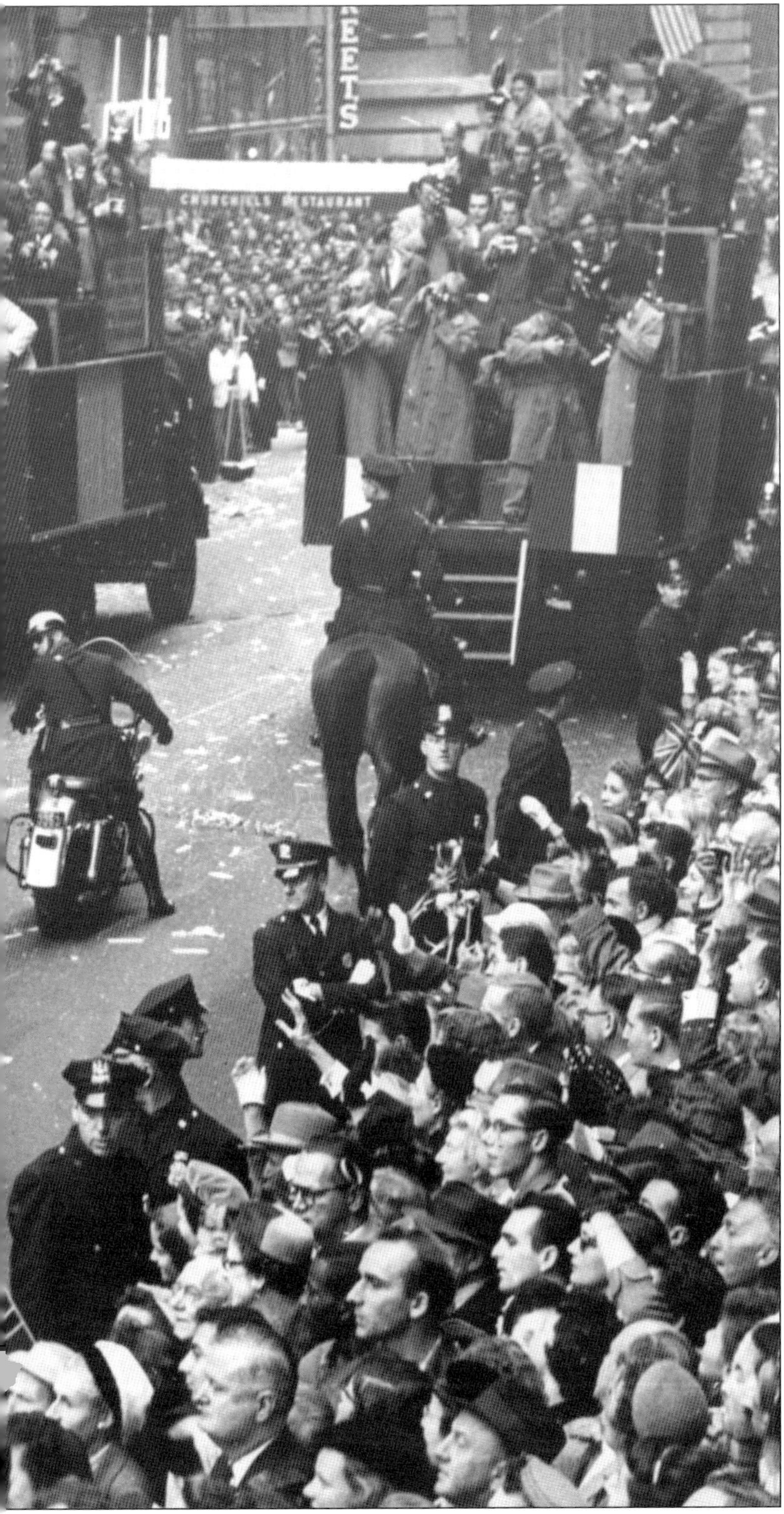

Few stories in New York attracted such international attention as the October 1957 visit of Queen Elizabeth II. Royal events included a huge ticker tape parade up Broadway, as seen here. The police issued special event cards in at least three colors—red, green, and blue—to identify the press at various locations. An Old English font was also used as a nod to the visiting monarch. (Author's collection.)

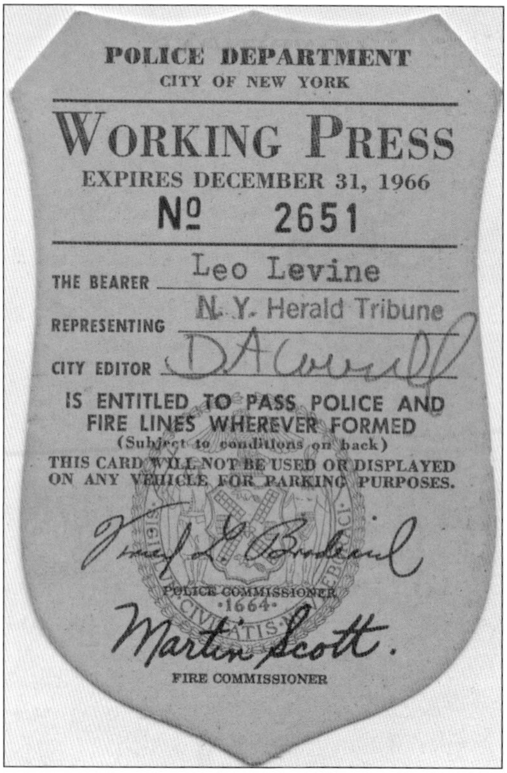

Throughout the 1950s and 1960s, the design of the card remained essentially unchanged, albeit now with the phrase "working press" spelled out across the top. In 1966, the nearly 3,000 cards in circulation were printed on a fluorescent avocado green paper to increase their visibility at nighttime scenes. As men's hats disappeared from the fashion scene, the cards, more often than not, were displayed on short chains looped through front buttonholes. (Author's collection.)

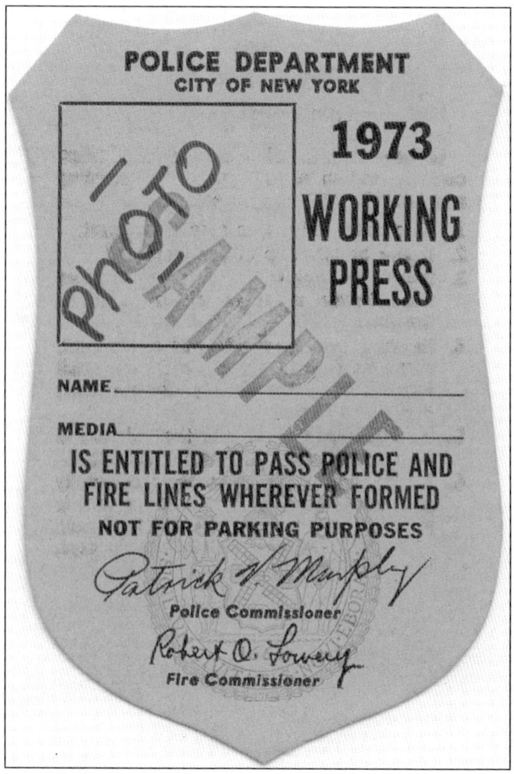

Since 1929, a list of physical traits on the reverse side of the press card identified its bearer. Starting with the 1972 series, however, identification photographs were required. This unissued sample from 1973 shows the basic format of the card as it would appear for the next 30 years. The last badge-shaped paper card expired in 2003, replaced with a series of digitally printed plastic cards.

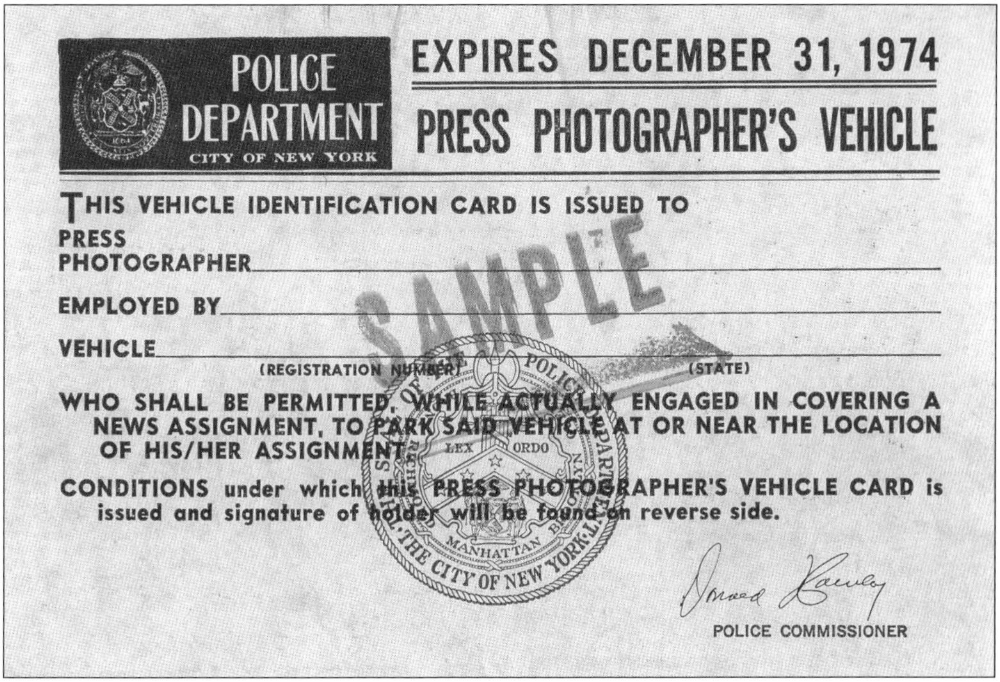

POLICE DEPARTMENT
CITY OF NEW YORK

EXPIRES DECEMBER 31, 1974

PRESS PHOTOGRAPHER'S VEHICLE

THIS VEHICLE IDENTIFICATION CARD IS ISSUED TO

PRESS PHOTOGRAPHER____________

EMPLOYED BY____________

VEHICLE____________
(REGISTRATION NUMBER) (STATE)

WHO SHALL BE PERMITTED, WHILE ACTUALLY ENGAGED IN COVERING A NEWS ASSIGNMENT, TO PARK SAID VEHICLE AT OR NEAR THE LOCATION OF HIS/HER ASSIGNMENT.

CONDITIONS under which this PRESS PHOTOGRAPHER'S VEHICLE CARD is issued and signature of holder will be found on reverse side.

SAMPLE

POLICE COMMISSIONER

With newspapers deploying fleets of radio cars to get photographers to emergency scenes, a committee of the Press Photographers Association convinced city hall to authorize police-issue vehicle identification cards in 1947. With the assurance that these would be "jealously guarded," cards such as this one from 1974 were issued until 2009.

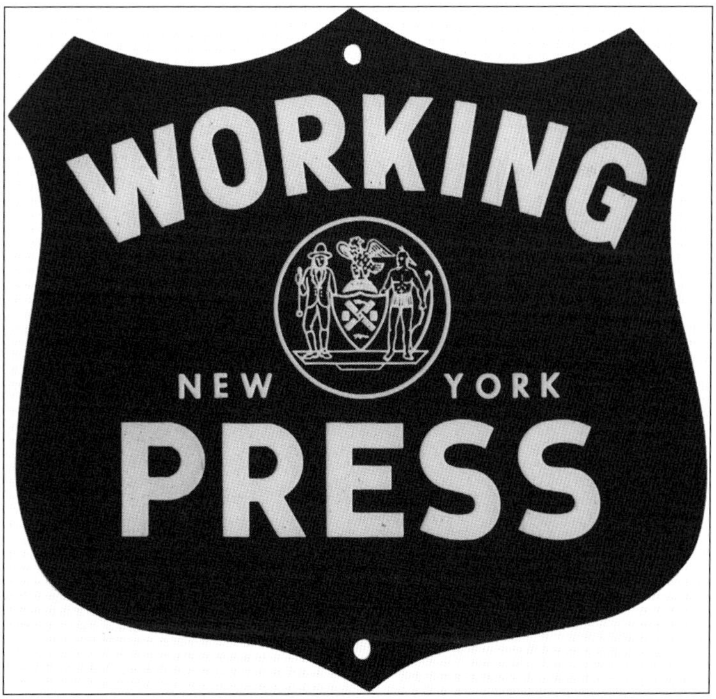

In 1950, the Press Photographers Association joined forces with the Newspaper Reporters Association (forerunner of the New York Press Club) to lobby for special vehicle registration for news media. In 1950, license plates bearing the initials "NYP," for New York Press, were first issued. Fourteen years later, many members of the press opted for enameled steel shields such as this one, which were mounted to the front of their cars for added visibility. (Author's collection.)

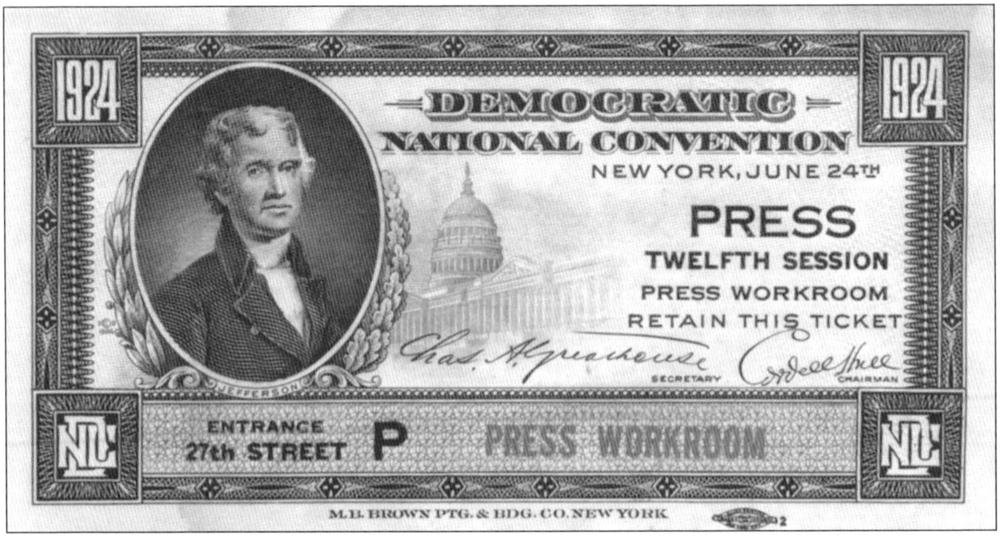

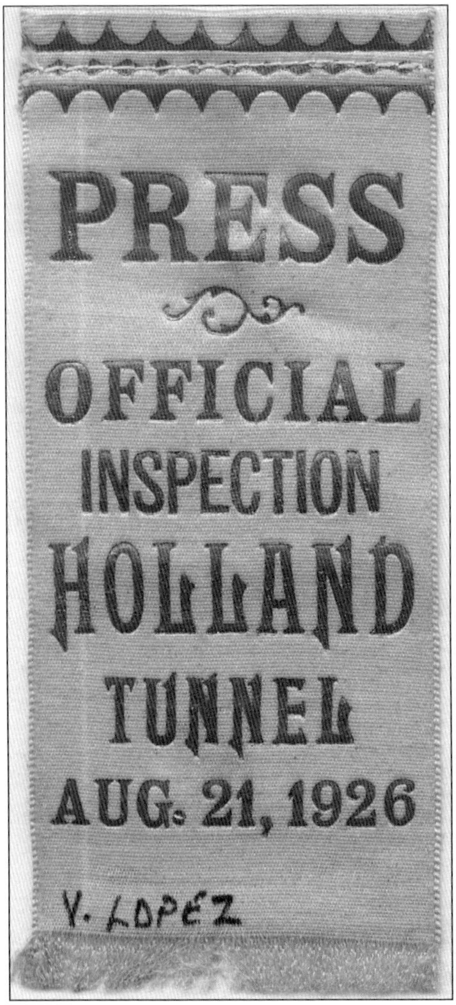

While the city's own press card was, as one columnist put it, "the magic talisman that opens grim doors," many events required their own credentials. For example, these currency-grade tickets with detachable stubs, produced by the M.B. Brown Printing & Binding Co., were distributed for access to the 1924 Democratic National Convention, held at Madison Square Garden.

In contrast to the police credentials, which were ostensibly turned in upon their expiration, some press identifiers doubled as souvenirs. Vincent Lopez retained this ribbon as a memento from the 1926 opening of the Holland Tunnel.

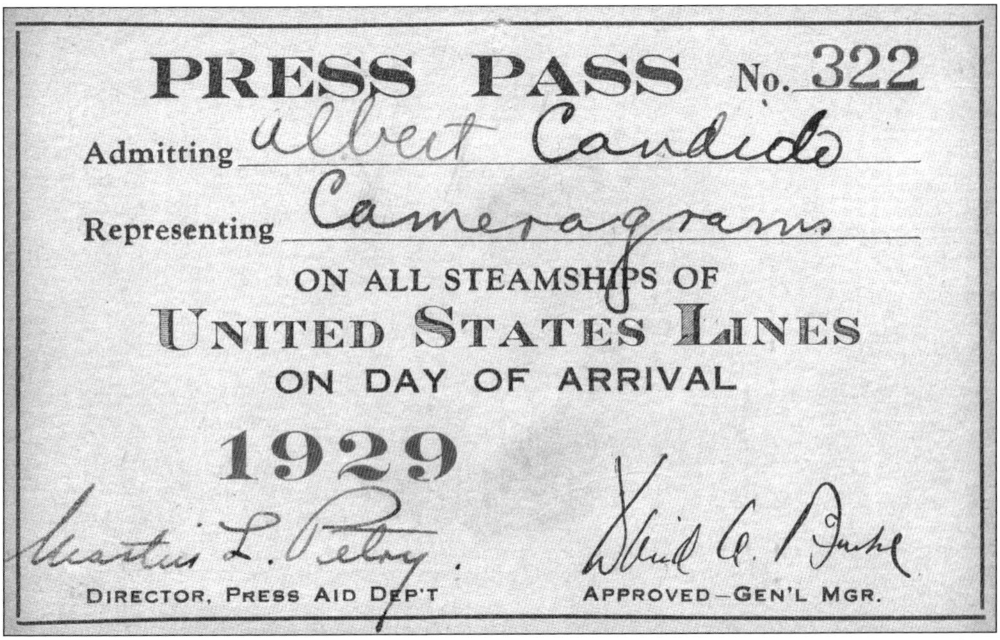

PRESS PASS No. 322

Admitting Albert Candido

Representing Cameragrams

ON ALL STEAMSHIPS OF

UNITED STATES LINES

ON DAY OF ARRIVAL

1929

DIRECTOR, PRESS AID DEP'T

APPROVED—GEN'L MGR.

Ship news was a staple of New York press coverage through much of the 20th century. A who's who of celebrities and their comings and goings was a regular appearance in the paper, and photographers would be ferried out to incoming cruise ships to document the notable passengers. Albert Candido used this card in 1929 to access the ships of the United States Lines, which would launch the record-breaking (and oft-photographed) SS *United States* in 1952.

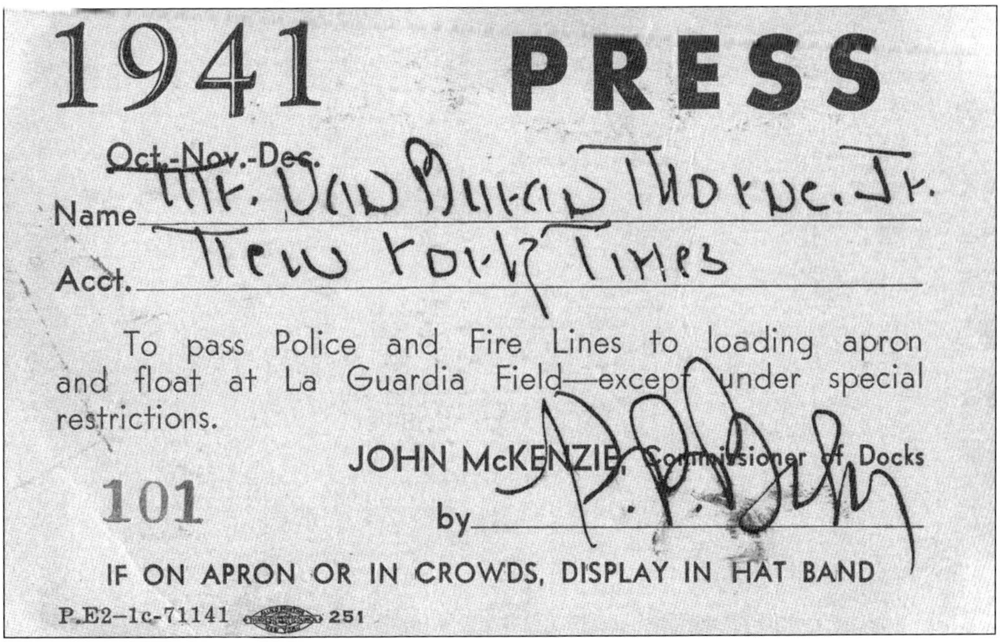

1941 PRESS

~~Oct.-Nov.-Dec.~~

Name Mr. Van Duran Thorne, Jr.

Acct. New York Times

To pass Police and Fire Lines to loading apron and float at La Guardia Field—except under special restrictions.

JOHN McKENZIE, Commissioner of Docks

101

by

IF ON APRON OR IN CROWDS, DISPLAY IN HAT BAND

P.E2–1c-71141 251

La Guardia Field (now LaGuardia Airport) required its own credential for photographers hoping to get a shot of someone boarding a plane or, at times, some sort of disaster. The Department of Plant and Structures required a similar card for photographers wishing to photograph the city's bridges. (Author's collection.)

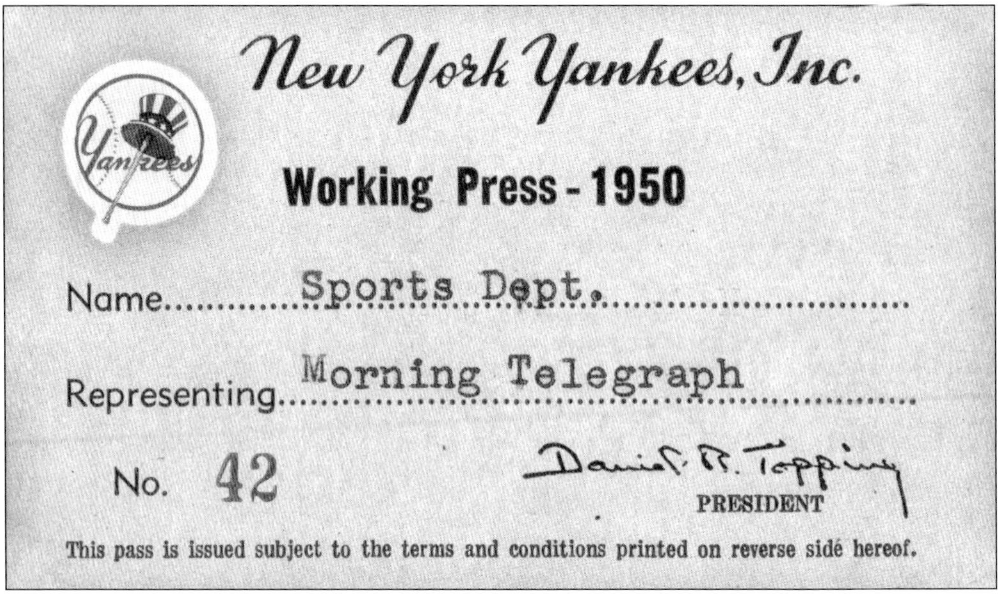

New York Yankees, Inc.

Working Press - 1950

Name.......Sports Dept.

Representing.......Morning Telegraph

No. 42

Daniel R. Topping
PRESIDENT

This pass is issued subject to the terms and conditions printed on reverse side hereof.

Here is a 1950 New York Yankees pass issued to the *Morning Telegraph*. Sports venues required a variety of passes and credentials for media, issued either for one game or, in the case of regularly assigned personnel, the duration of a season. Much like ticket holders, the press is reminded of the physical hazards of being close to the action, but with the additional reminder that seeking autographs is prohibited. (Author's collection.)

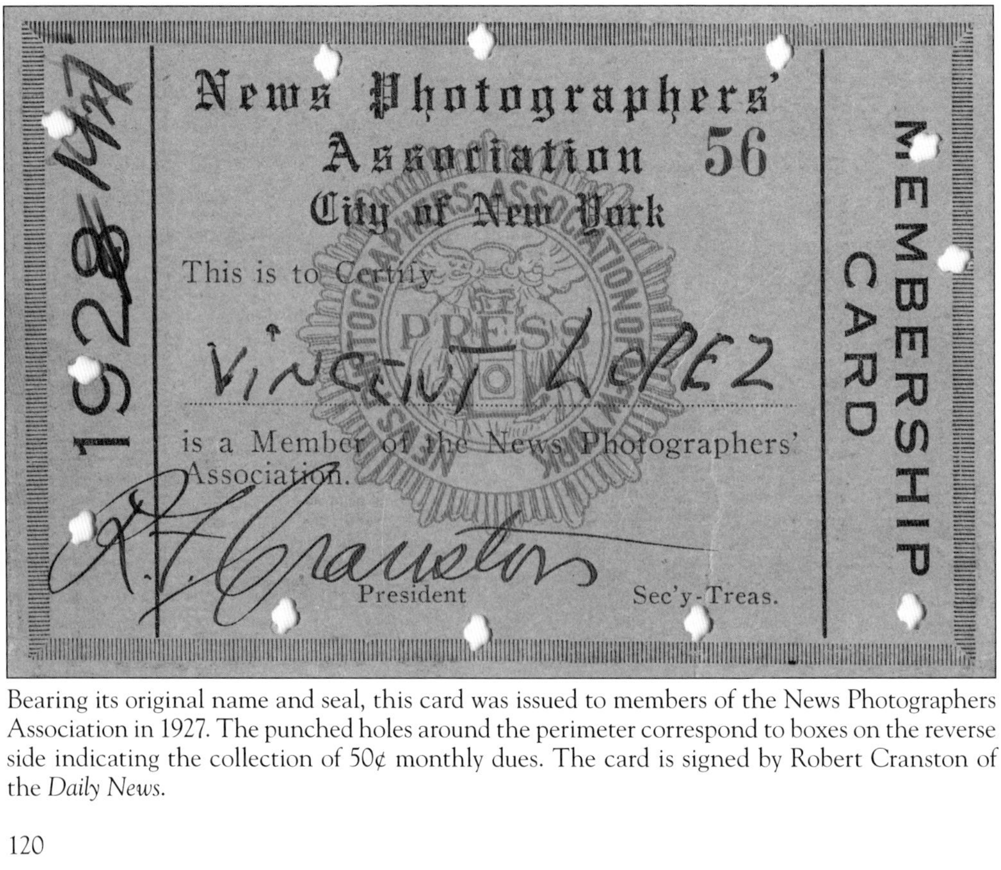

1928 1927

News Photographers' Association 56
City of New York

This is to Certify

Vincent Lopez

is a Member of the News Photographers' Association.

R. F. Cranston
President

Sec'y-Treas.

MEMBERSHIP CARD

Bearing its original name and seal, this card was issued to members of the News Photographers Association in 1927. The punched holes around the perimeter correspond to boxes on the reverse side indicating the collection of 50¢ monthly dues. The card is signed by Robert Cranston of the *Daily News*.

The Press Photographers Association issued this membership card with a space for a photograph on the reverse side 35 years before the official press credential required a headshot of the bearer. It is not clear why, but this card was not reissued after 1937.

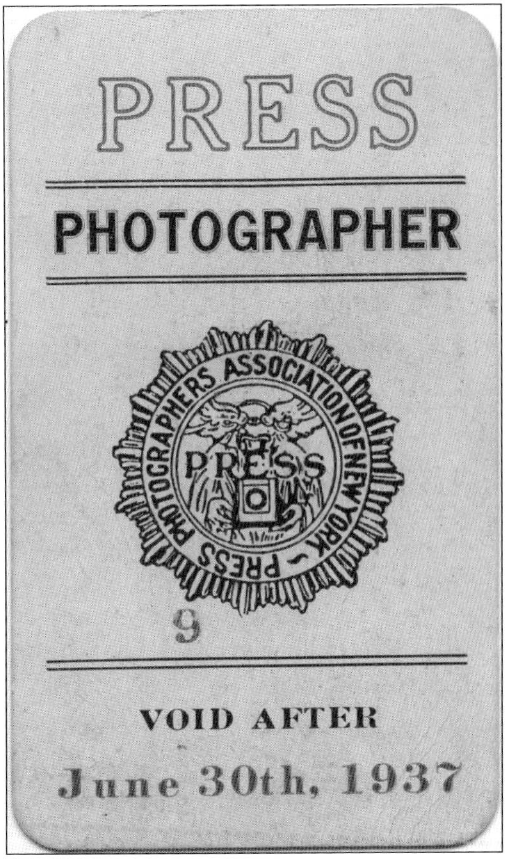

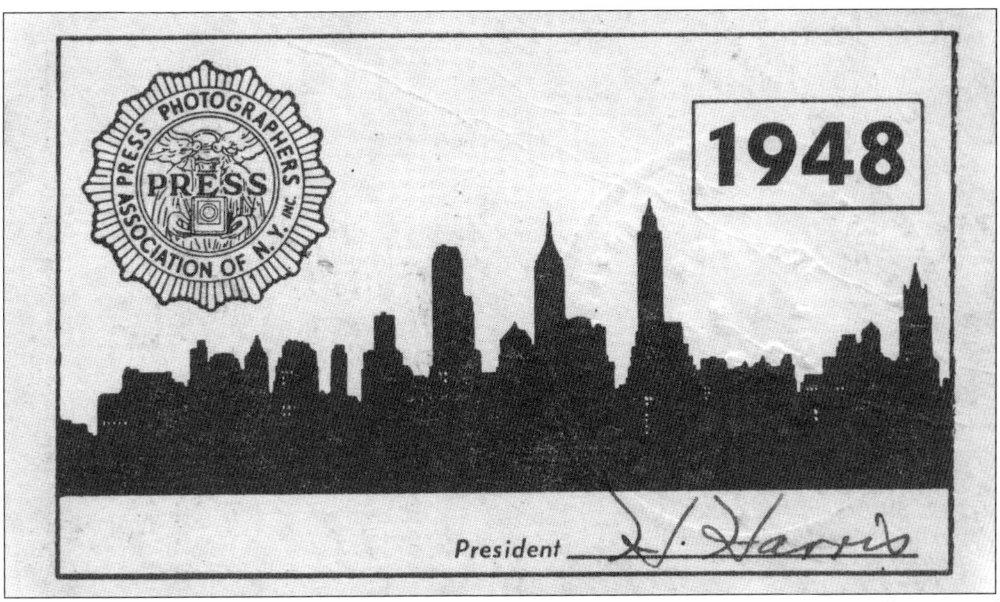

A 1948 membership card, signed by association president Harry Harris, features a silhouette of the New York City skyline, the group's emblem, and an embossed corporate seal. The reverse side is also countersigned by the treasurer. (Author's collection.)

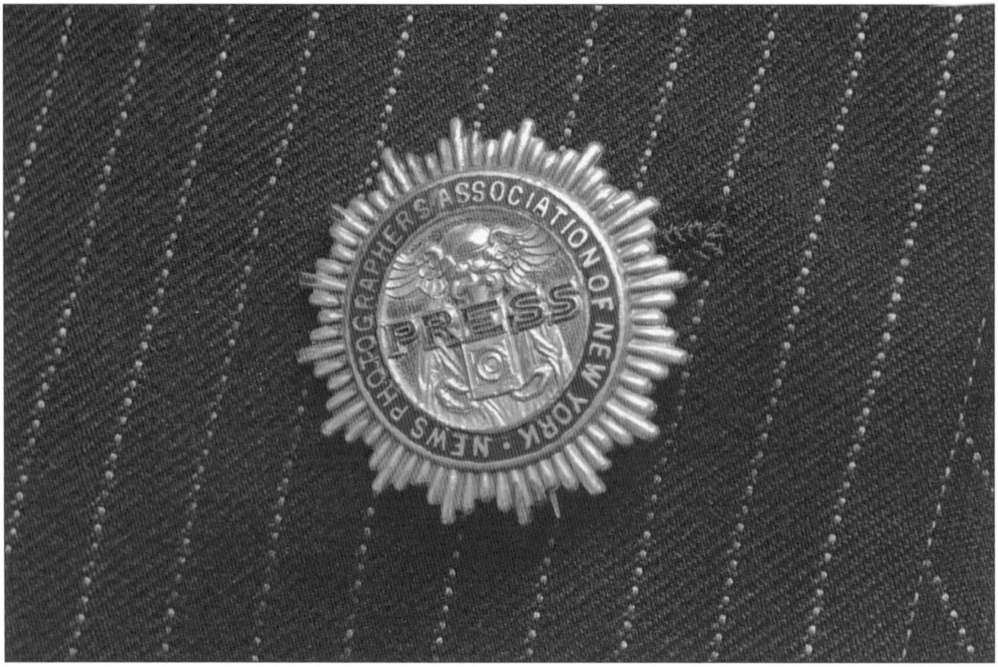

Over an inch in diameter, this was the first style of pin issued to members of the association. While somewhat unwieldy as an accessory when worn on the lapel, the pin had the unintended effect of official recognition in lieu of a press card for photographers crossing police lines. (Author's collection.)

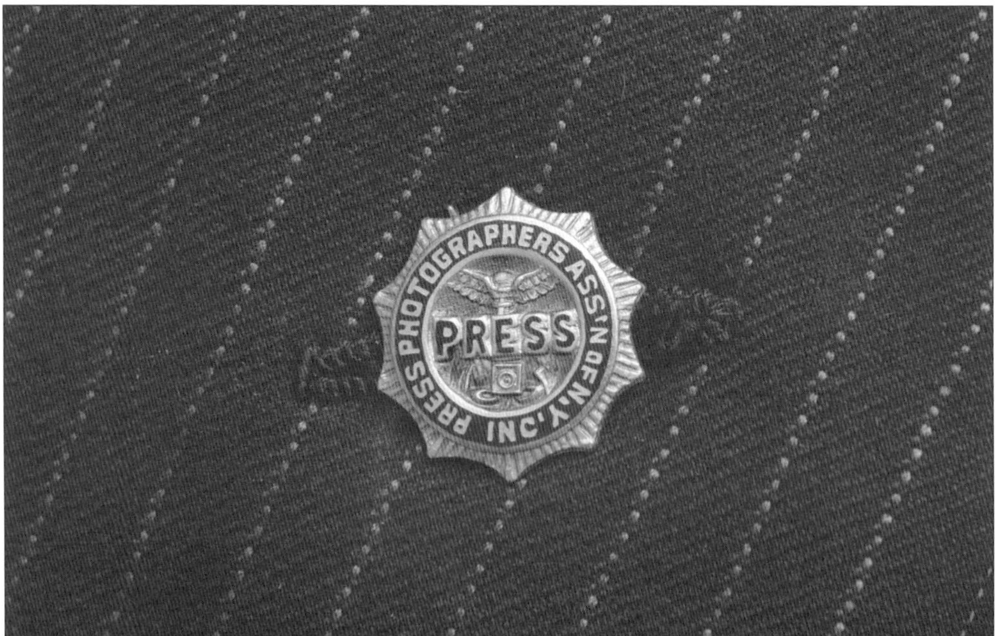

Bearing the new name of the association, a smaller, gold-plated pin was issued to members in January 1940. Regularly seen on the jackets of members in the field, these pins provided not only a symbol of fraternal pride but also utility by means of pinning on the press pass. (Author's collection.)

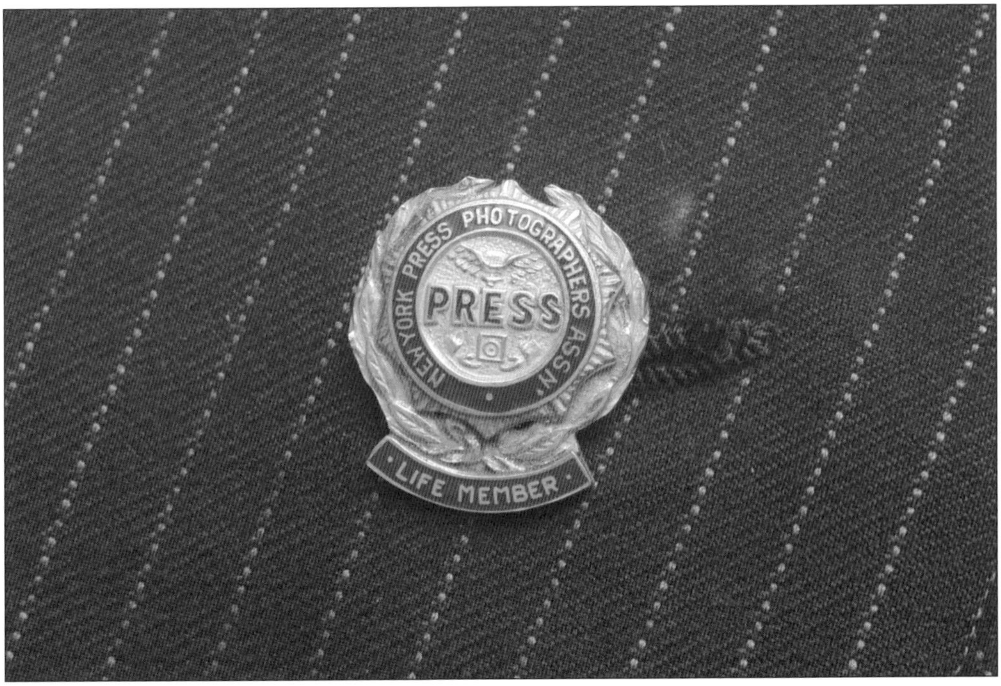

With its third and final designation as the New York Press Photographers Association, a special variant of the membership pin is shown with a laurel wreath and "Life Member" scroll. The first such honor was bestowed posthumously to Christian Detrick in 1951. A person must reach the age of 60 and belong to the association for 25 years before being considered a Life Member. (Author's collection.)

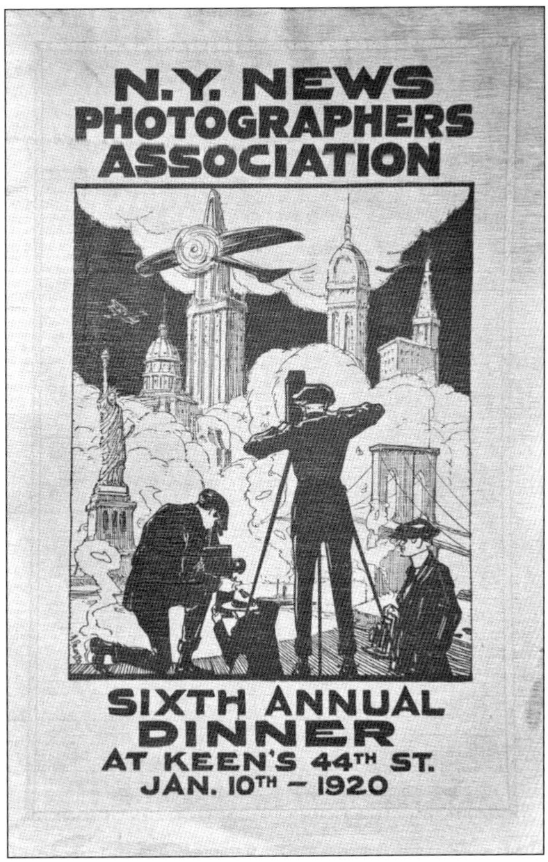

The cover of the association's 1920 dinner journal shows an interesting array of photographers, seemingly with the best seat in the house to cover all of New York City. What is interesting, however, is the centrally located newsreel cameraman, as 1920 was the year of a mass exodus of members during a disagreement over whether the movie men should be allowed into the group.

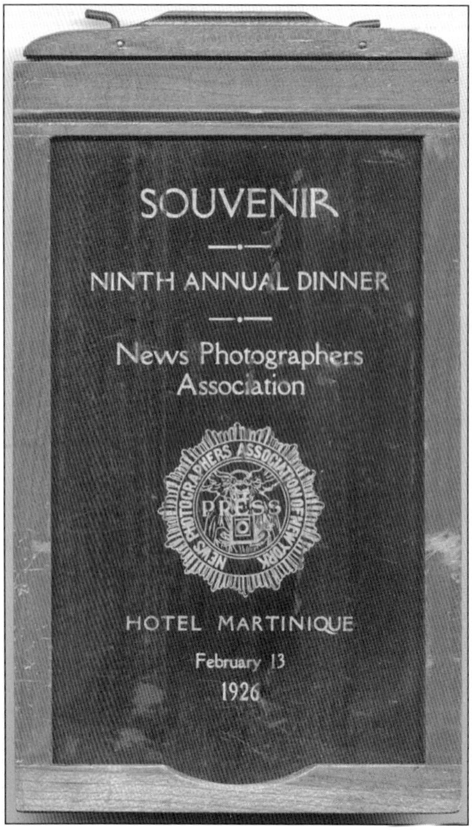

This souvenir from the 1926 annual dinner is made from a wooden camera plate holder. Removing the dark slide revealed not a photographic plate but the evening's menu. Because of the association's shaky beginnings, it took some time before 1915 was agreed upon as its official launch date, thus the 1926 dinner was considered the ninth annual gathering.

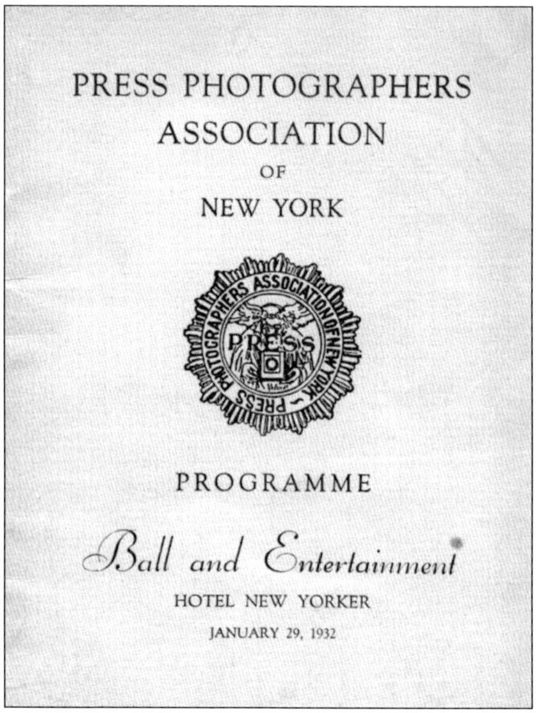

A program from 1932 speaks to the lavish nature of the Press Photographers' Ball, held at the Hotel New Yorker that year. Dancing in the Grand Ballroom went from 9:00 p.m. to 10:30 p.m., then continued throughout the night in a separate ballroom. At 10:45 p.m., the entertainment program began, hosted by Roxy Theatre impresario Samuel Rothafel. Sections of the ballroom and its balcony were accessible only with special tickets.

An elaborate postcard from 1935 advertises that year's Press Photographers' Ball, to be held at the Hotel Commodore on East Forty-second Street, next to Grand Central Station.

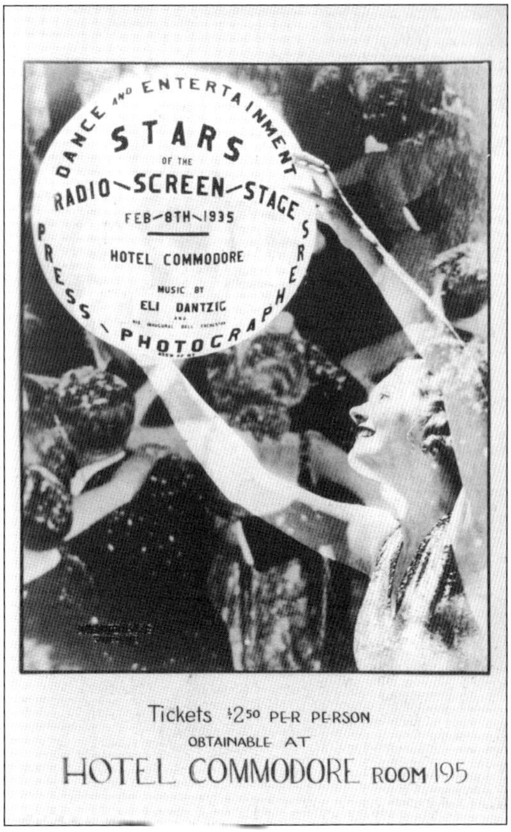

In 1938, it would cost an extra 25¢ to attend the Press Photographers' Ball. By then, columnists Ed Sullivan, Walter Winchell, and Damon Runyon had been brought on board as honorary members of the dance committee, and Buddy Clark, Gary Cooper, Guy Lombardo, and Henny Youngman were some of the headline acts who appeared. Col. Fulgencio Batista of Cuba was among the heads of state who placed congratulatory ads in the annual journal.

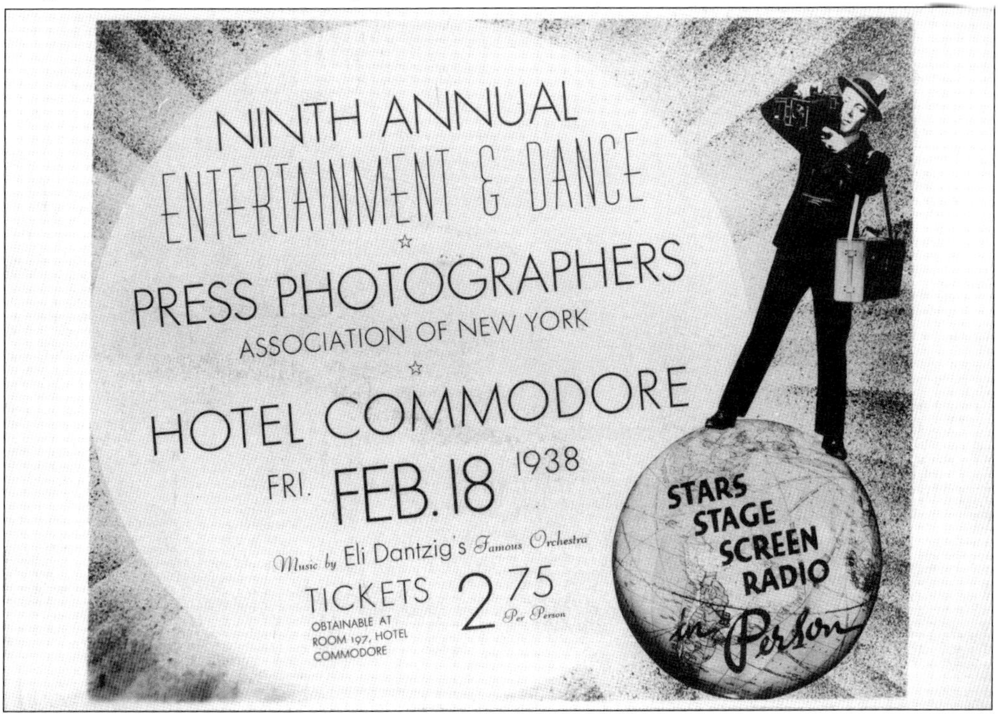

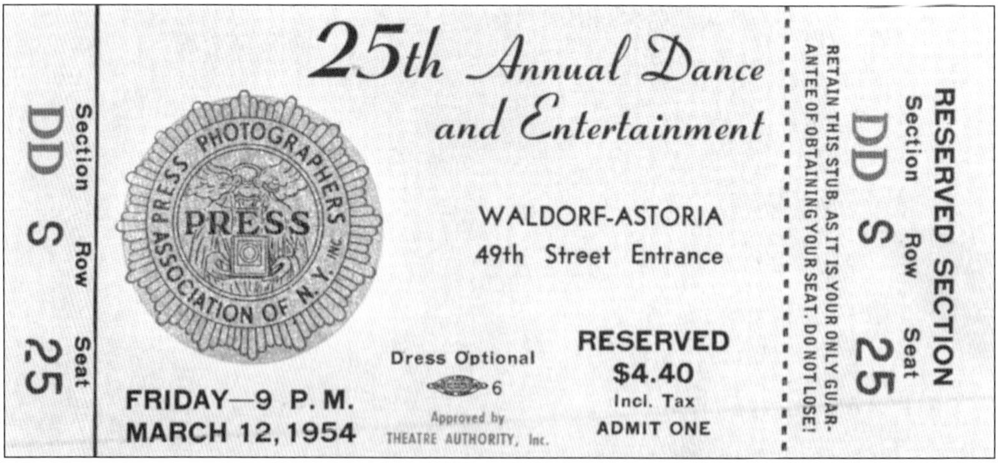

Here is a ticket from the 1954 annual dance, held at the Waldorf-Astoria that year. White Plains resident Jackie Hansen, 18, who barely survived an auto accident three years before, was chosen as that year's queen.

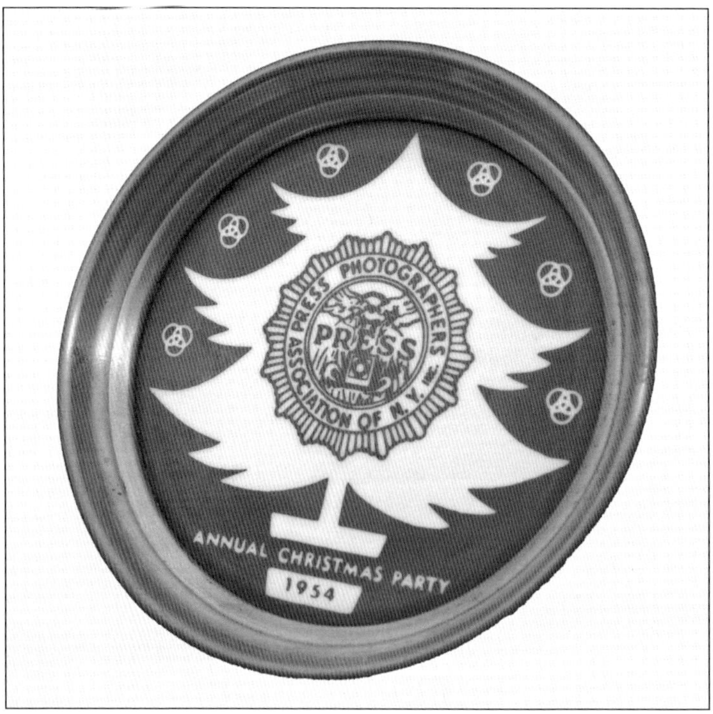

While some functions were meant to bring attention to the association with big-name stars, another tradition was the holiday party. Trinkets such as this ashtray, also bearing the logo of sponsor Ballantine Beer, were given out to members, but the true purpose of the gathering was to provide charity for others, not the photographers. Each participant brought a gift that was donated to the New York Foundling Hospital. The association still hosts a holiday toy drive every December. (Author's collection.)

About the NYPPA

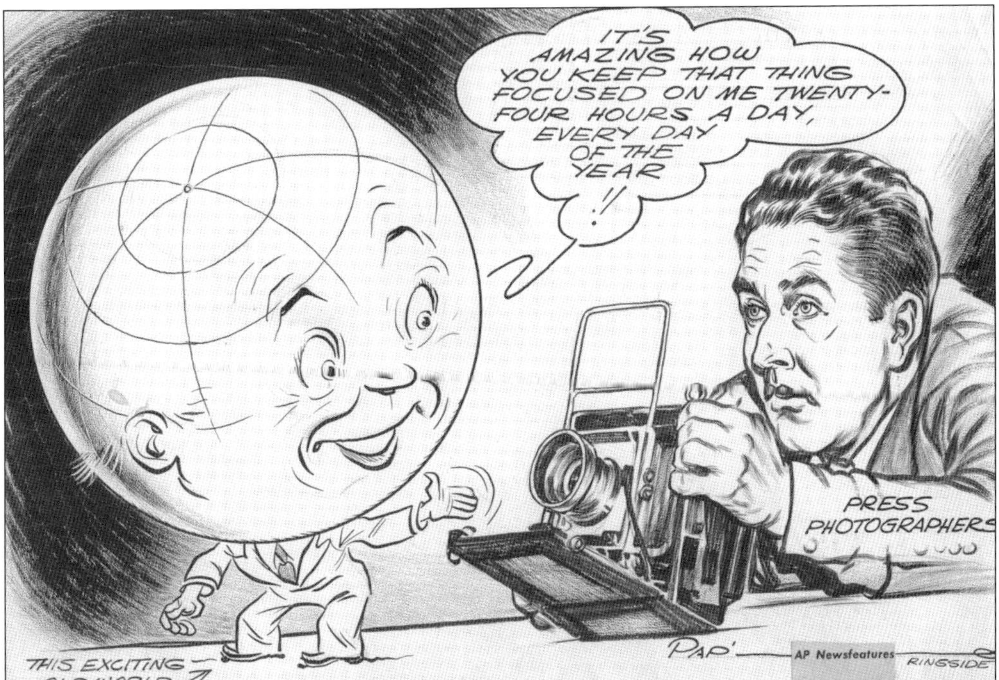

The New York Press Photographers Association, Inc., (NYPPA) exists to promote and protect the interests and welfare of the press still and video photographer, advance press photography through education of its members and the public, and create and promote among its members cooperation, fraternalism, the interchange of thought and opinion, and a high standard of conduct. It continues to sponsor an annual photograph contest, maintains liaisons with government agencies, and hosts meetings to discuss and encourage better business practices for its members. The NYPPA is a registered 501(c)(6) organization. For more information, visit NYPPA.org. (Cartoon by Tom "Pap" Paprocki.)

Discover Thousands of Local History Books Featuring Millions of Vintage Images

Arcadia Publishing, the leading local history publisher in the United States, is committed to making history accessible and meaningful through publishing books that celebrate and preserve the heritage of America's people and places.

Find more books like this at
www.arcadiapublishing.com

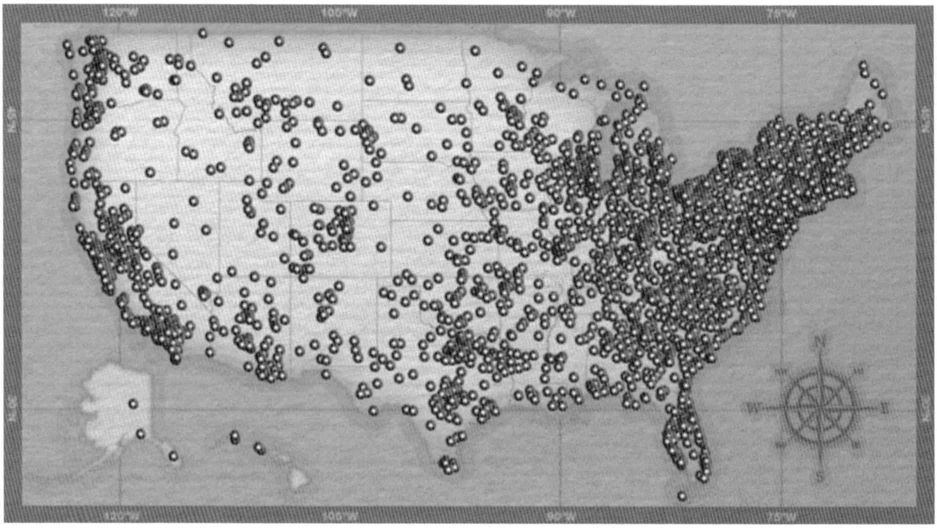

Search for your hometown history, your old stomping grounds, and even your favorite sports team.

Consistent with our mission to preserve history on a local level, this book was printed in South Carolina on American-made paper and manufactured entirely in the United States. Products carrying the accredited Forest Stewardship Council (FSC) label are printed on 100 percent FSC-certified paper.

MADE IN THE USA